THE 10TH (P.W.O.) ROY

AND

THE ESSEX YEOMANRY

DURING THE EUROPEAN WAR, 1914-1918

LIEUT-COLONEL F. H. D. C. WHITMORE,

C.M.G., D.S.O., T.D., D.L.

Commanding Essex Yeomanry, September 1915–April 1918.

Commanding 10th (P.W.O.) Royal Hussars, April 1918–April 1919.

The Naval & Military Press Ltd

published in association with

FIREPOWER
The Royal Artillery Museum
Woolwich

Published by
The Naval & Military Press Ltd
Unit 10 Ridgewood Industrial Park,
Uckfield, East Sussex,
TN22 5QE England
Tel: +44 (0) 1825 749494
Fax: +44 (0) 1825 765701
www.naval-military-press.com

in association with

FIREPOWER
The Royal Artillery Museum, Woolwich
www.firepower.org.uk

The Naval & Military Press

MILITARY HISTORY AT YOUR FINGERTIPS

… a unique and expanding series of reference works

Working in collaboration with the foremost regiments and institutions, as well as acknowledged experts in their field, N&MP have assembled a formidable array of titles including technologically advanced CD-ROMs and facsimile reprints of impossible-to-find rarities.

CONTENTS.

CONTENTS—*continued.*

LIST OF ILLUSTRATIONS.

LIST OF MAPS.

vi.

PREFACE.

The narratives contained in this Volume may perhaps be better described as local events connected with the fortunes of the two Regiments to which I have become so attached. Having accompanied the two Regiments, either jointly or severally, to every billet from the date of my landing in France in November 1914 until March 1919, also having taken part in every engagement in which these two Regiments have distinguished themselves during the same period, I feel that a record should be made, necessarily brief as it is, in order that incidents which united the Regiments together in close friendship during the world's greatest War may not be forgotten —and that generations to follow may learn that their fathers who served in either of the two Regiments concerned were comrades in arms.

The long lists of Casualties tell their own tale, but it must not be forgotten that it is those, who have either died or bled for their country, who have contributed so much to maintain the best traditions of their Regiments.

F.H.D.C.W.

FOREWORD.

I know that all X.R.H. and Essex Yeomen will welcome the publication of this work.

It is the unvarnished record of the battles and operations of the two Regiments; one of which is where I first learnt what soldiering was, and the other is the mounted unit of my County.

Colonel Whitmore, who has compiled it, served in both units. He was present throughout the operations, and to him is due that friendship between the Regiments which I feel sure will be fostered as long as the history of the late war is read.

Byng of Vimy
General

THE 10th (P.W.O.) ROYAL HUSSARS
AND
THE ESSEX YEOMANRY,
In The European War, 1914 - 1918.

IN order to appreciate the early stages of the part taken by the 10th Royal Hussars and the Essex Yeomanry in the Great European War of 1914-1918, it is necessary to follow briefly the movements of the Cavalry generally, prior to the arrival of the 6th and 7th Cavalry Brigades, and then to follow the fortunes of the 6th and 7th Cavalry Brigades prior to the formation of the 8th Cavalry Brigade ; which Brigade in its formation drew off 1 Regiment from each of the 6th and 7th Brigades, the Royal Horse Guards, and the 10th (P.W.O.) Royal Hussars. These 2 Regiments together with the Essex Yeomanry formed the 8th Cavalry Brigade, and in consequence the 6th, 7th and 8th Brigades together formed the 3rd Cavalry Division.

I.

THE RETREAT FROM MONS, 1914.

Immediately following the outbreak of war a force of Cavalry, consisting of one Division of four Brigades, and one Brigade separately organised, was landed in France and detrained at Maubeuge. These 5 Brigades marched north, observed the line Binche—Mons, and reconnoitred the line La Louvière—Soignies.

The Infantry took over from the Cavalry, and the Cavalry then concentrated on the left of the Infantry near Quiévrain. The German successful advance on Mons led to the retreat of the Allied forces, and it was at the Battle of Mons that had it not been for the timely assistance of the Cavalry, the precarious situation thereby occasioned would have been much accentuated. During the retreat, the Cavalry covered the rear and flank of the Army. The advance from the Marne to the Aisne followed the retreat, and at the battle of the Aisne the Cavalry protected the

2

right of the British, and at the same time filled up the gap between the British and the French.

Following the battle of the Aisne 10 days march brought the Cavalry into Flanders, where it covered the detrainment of the British forces at Aire and St. Omer.

On October 12th the British Cavalry Corps (1st and 2nd Divisions), under Major-General E. H. H. Allenby, C.B., advanced and captured Mont des Cats and neighbouring villages. The German cavalry, under General Von der Marwitz, were then forced to retire from Bailleul behind the Lys, between le Quesnoy and Warneton.

During these operations, the 2nd Cavalry Division advancing from the west joined hands with the 3rd Cavalry Division at Kemmel, this Division having moved south through Ypres.

From Kemmel the 3rd Cavalry Division counter-marched to the north, through Ypres, and eventually linked up on the left of the 2nd Cavalry Division on the Hollebeke railway.

At this period the 3rd Cavalry Division consisted of five Regiments only, as shown below, together with "K" Battery, R.H.A.

The 6th Cavalry Brigade commanded by
Brigadier-General E. Makins, C.B., D.S.O:
>   1st Royal Dragoons.
>   10th Royal Hussars.

The 7th Cavalry Brigade commanded by
Brigadier-General C. T. McM. Kavanagh, C.V.O.,
D.S.O. :
>   1st Life Guards.
>   2nd Life Guards.
>   Royal Horse Guards.

II.

FIRST BATTLE OF YPRES, 1914.

It was on the 7th October that the 6th and 7th Cavalry Brigades landed at Ostend and Zeebrugge, and during the night of 8th and 9th proceeded to Ypres, where they operated with the 7th Infantry Division. Information was received on October 13th that one Bavarian Cavalry Division was at Warneton, 20,000 all arms at Tournai, 20,000 at Hazebrouck, and heavy fighting was reported at Lille, and that the Germans were bombarding that town.

The 6th Cavalry Brigade was then ordered to occupy a protective line south-east of Ypres, Warneton to Gheluvelt, and on October 14th billeted at Wytschaete.

On October 16th the 6th Cavalry Brigade marched to Poelcappelle in support of the 7th Cavalry Brigade, and spent the night E. of Zonnebeke. On the 18th, the 6th Brigade billeted near Passchendaele. On October

19th the enemy received strong reinforcements and the Cavalry were forced to retire ; on the morning of the 20th, the 6th and 7th Brigades, together with the French, took up a line through Westroosebeke, but were forced to retire to Langemarck ; during the night the Germans made a night attack and the Brigade retired to Ypres. On October 21st, the 6th Brigade proceeded to Zandvoorde and took over the defensive line from the 4th Brigade of Guards. On this occasion 3 other ranks were killed, and Colonel R. W. R. Barnes, D.S.O., Major The Hon. C. B. O. Mitford, Captain G. C. Stewart, and 9 other ranks were wounded, all 10th Hussars.

On October 25th the 6th Brigade relieved the Household Cavalry Brigade in the trenches at Klein Zillebeke, and on the following day, October 26th, the 10th Royal Hussars lost Captain Sir Frank Rose, Bart., Lieut. C. R. Turnor, and 4 other ranks killed, and 8 wounded. On the 27th October the 6th Brigade was relieved by the 7th Brigade. Fighting took place on 30th and 31st around Hooge and E. of Zillebeke, during which period the 7th Cavalry Brigade, after a gallant resistance, was forced to vacate the Zandvoorde ridge, the Germans capturing Hollebeke, Wytschaete and Messines, many casualties being incurred in both Brigades. Col. Barnes and

6

Capt. W. A. Gibbs, X.R.H., were wounded, the former having been already once wounded less than a fortnight before.

On November 5th the 6th Brigade went into the trenches dismounted, at Heronthage Chateau, and on the following day the enemy heavily shelled the front line.

On Saturday, November 7th, the 6th Brigade was relieved by the Royal Fusiliers at 2 a.m., but at 11 a.m. received orders to move forward in support of the 4th Guards Brigade, and at 4 p.m. a position of readiness was taken up in Zillebeke.

On November 10th the 6th Brigade supported Lord Cavan's 4th Guards Brigade, and went into the trenches between Zillebeke and Klein Zillebeke.

It was on November 12th that Major the Hon. W. Cadogan, M.V.O., was hit in the groin and died almost immediately.

On November 15th the 6th Brigade moved up to support 4th Guards Brigade between Hooge and Zillebeke. Capt. the Hon. A. Annesley was killed in the afternoon of November 16th, by a sniper.

On November 17th the Germans delivered an attack, and the 10th Royal Hussars suffered many casualties, amongst whom were Capt. C. H. Peto, who was shot in the head, Lieut. R. F. Drake, and 10 other ranks being killed, also 9 wounded. The 6th Brigade was relieved by the 7th Brigade; the former returning to billets near Vlamertinghe. The 9th and 20th Corps of the French Army then took over the line from the Cavalry which was by now firmly established.

On November 20th and 21st the Brigades moved back into billets in the Vieux Berquin area. The 3rd Dragoon Guards, the North Somerset Yeomanry and the Leicestershire Yeomanry had by now landed in France and they took part in this first battle of Ypres, " C " and " K " Batteries, Royal Horse Artillery, already formed part of the Division, and as soon as the Essex Yeomanry arrived on November 28th, and " G " Battery in December, the 3rd Cavalry Division was complete.

The composition of the 3rd Cavalry Division commanded by Major-General the Honble. Sir Julian H. G. Byng, K.C.M.G., M.V.O., was now as follows :—

6th Cavalry Brigade. 1st Royal Dragoons.
3rd Dragoon Guards.
North Somerset Yeomanry
commanded by Brigadier-General D. Campbell, C.B.

FIRST BATTLE OF YPRES, 1914.

7th Cavalry Brigade.   1st Life Guards.

2nd Life Guards.

Leicestershire Yeomanry.

commanded by Brigadier-General C. T. McM. Kavanagh, C.V.O., D.S.O.

8th Cavalry Brigade. Royal Horse Guards.

10th (P.W.O.) Royal Hussars

Essex Yeomanry.

commanded by Brigadier-General C. Bulkeley Johnson, A.D.C.

III.

THE ESSEX YEOMANRY, 1914.

At the declaration of War, telegrams were despatched from Regimental Headquarters, Colchester, to all Officers bearing the one word, "Mobilise," and it was on Friday, August 7th, that the Regiment assembled at Ipswich, the concentration area of the Eastern Mounted Brigade, commanded by Brigadier-General H. Hodgson, C.V.O. The other two Regiments of the Brigade, the Norfolk Yeomanry, under Major Morse, and the Suffolk Yeomanry, under Lieut.-Colonel Jarvis, also the Essex Battery Royal Horse Artillery, under Major Lord Belhaven, were billeted at and about Ipswich. After a few days, for convenience and in order to be closer to the East coast, the Brigade moved to the Woodbridge area, and the Essex Yeomanry were billeted at Melton. Constant training and exercises in horsemanship, and use of arms, soon raised the efficiency of the Regiments. On November 10th the Brigade was inspected by His Majesty the King; and it was on the 12th November, 1914, that orders were received for the Essex Yeomanry to proceed overseas.

The Regiment entrained at Woodbridge on Sunday, November 29th, 1914, and embarked at Southampton on arrival, and after a rough passage, and travelling under the usual discomforts of a transport ship, arrived at Havre at mid-day November 30th; disembarked on Tuesday December 1st, and marched in a deluge of rain to the " Rest Camp," which was a veritable sea of mud, and it may be safely said that although the discomforts to follow were bad, at times to the extreme, it is difficult to be assured that they were any worse than the first night's experience at the " Rest Camp," Havre.

The Officers of the Regiment, however, will always remember with marked appreciation the kindness of Colonel Harry Cooper, C.M.G., Vice-Chairman of the Essex County Territorial Force Association, who was then employed at Havre, for entertaining them at dinner on their arrival overseas.

It was on December 3rd, at noon, that the Regiment entrained for St. Omer, and detrained in a heavy storm of rain and snow, and proceeded to Wardrecques, and it was here that the Regiment made its acquaintance with Brigadier-General C. Bulkeley Johnson, A.D.C., who commanded the 8th Cavalry Brigade.

On December 11th, 1914, the Regiment marched from Wardrecques, via Hazebrouck, to Grand Sec Bois, which was to be the billeting area of the Regiment. The 10th Royal Hussars and the Royal Horse Guards being close by, near the Forêt de Nieppe, the Brigade Headquarters being at Hazebrouck.

The first occasion which brought the Regiment into proximity with the enemy was on December 14th, when the 3rd Cavalry Division, under Major-General the Honble. Sir Julian Byng, K.C.M.G., M.V.O., formed a mobile Reserve near the Belgian Frontier at Locre, whilst an attack was being made on the enemy's trenches near Wytschaete. The Division, however, was not committed, and the Regiment went into billets that night at St. Jans Cappel, and on December 16th the Division returned to its former billets, the Regiment returning to Grand Sec Bois.

On January 27th, 1915, the Kaiser's Birthday, the Brigade "stood to" ready to move, and in the afternoon the Brigade was inspected, dismounted, by the Commander-in-Chief who was accompanied by the Prince of Wales.

On January 28th the Brigade moved into a new billeting area, the Essex Yeomanry being billeted

The Curé of Sec Bois at entrance to his house, which was destroyed
by the bombardment in the Spring of 1918.

Ruins of the Cloth Hall and Cathedral, Ypres.

at Mt. Croquet, the 10th Royal Hussars at Sercus, and the Royal Horse Guards at Lynde.

The Curé at Sec Bois was always a great friend to all Essex Yeomen, and on the evening before the Regiment left, he, in the course of a long speech, wished every success and good fortune to officers and other ranks, and expressed himself as being very sorry that the Regiment's stay in his village had come to an end.

IV.

ZILLEBEKE, 1915.

On February 3rd, 1915, the 3rd Cavalry Division left its billets in the Hazebrouck area in motor buses, proceeding via Hazebrouck, Steenvorde, Popperinghe, Vlamertinghe to Ypres, arriving at Ypres at about 9 p.m. Then marched to billets in Ypres reformatory school on the Ypres-Menin road. " A " Squadron Essex Yeomanry, under Major E. Hill, went straight into the trenches.

The Division went up for the purpose of taking over a section of the line East of Ypres from the French. The Division was composed of 2 Echelons, the 1st Echelon, under Brigadier-General C. T. McM. Kavanagh, C.B., C.V.O., D.S.O., consisting of the 7th Cavalry Brigade, the Royal Horse Guards and " A " Squadron Essex Yeomanry ; the 2nd Echelon, under Brigadier-General D. G. M. Campbell, C.B., consisting of the 6th Cavalry Brigade and the 10th

Royal Hussars, also the Essex Yeomanry less 1 Squadron.

The 10th Royal Hussars together with " B " and " C " Squadrons Essex Yeomanry went into the trenches on February 8th, leaving the billets at 11.30 p.m., marching to Zillebeke, where the kits were taken off the wagons and carried.

On taking over the trenches " A " Squadron 10th Hussars was next to the French on the left of the sector. On the right of " A " Squadron 10th Hussars was a squadron of the Essex Yeomanry and " B " Squadron 10th Hussars was on the right of the Essex Yeomanry, and " C " Squadron 10th Hussars was in support in dug-outs about 100 yards in rear. Taking over the trenches was complete by 4 a.m.

The distance between the German trenches and the line occupied by the Cavalry varied from about 12 to 15 yards on the left of the line, to about 80 yards on the right, and the trenches were very wet in places.

The close proximity of the trenches is illustrated by the fact that a German threw a match-box into the trench occupied by the Blues containing a note which stated : " We are a battalion of an Alsace regiment ; don't shoot us, and we won't shoot you. Vive la France, but Germany comes first." This note was picked up by Capt. G. Bowlby, Royal Horse Guards, who was afterwards killed during the 2nd battle of Ypres.

An incident during this period in the trenches was the introduction of a colossal periscope made by the Essex Yeomanry. This periscope was made out of a length of rain pipe taken from the Reformatory at Ypres, measuring about 20 feet in length, and about three inches diameter. This pipe, when covered with bark from the trees in the wood at Zillebeke, in which the trenches were situated, made a complete representation of the trees themselves, most of which had the tops blown off, leaving jagged ends varying from 15 to 30 feet from the ground.

Mirrors were inserted at each end of the pipe, similar to an ordinary periscope, the top-most mirror being concealed by broken pieces of bark and chips to represent the broken end of the tree. The first of these was erected during the night, and was a great success, and by turning it in any direction, it was possible to see much which was otherwise impossible to observe. This giant periscope remained in position for many weeks, and was taken over by the relieving troops.

The success of this achievement caused many more to be erected, with the result that before long the forest of periscopes became observed by the enemy, who directed their snipers on to them, with the result that they were shot down as soon as put into position. But the original stood the test and remained for the whole time undetected.

On February 8th the first casualties suffered by the Essex Yeomanry were caused during the occupation of this sector in the trenches. A fatigue party, whilst fetching rations, was badly shelled, which resulted in Pte. W. Roberts being killed, and 9 others wounded.

The 8th Cavalry Brigade remained, holding the line until February 12th and 14th, when the Regiments returned to their former billets in two parties in motor-buses.

V.

YPRES, 1915.

When the 3rd Cavalry Division arrived at Ypres on February 3rd, the damage already caused in the town, although of course very great, was not then to be compared with many towns in Belgium and France, at that date. There were very few inhabitants, but as soon as the Cavalry arrived and took over the line from the French, it was astonishing to note how the former inhabitants returned, opened up their shops, and did a very large business, especially in provisions, of which there seemed an almost inexhaustible supply. The large provision shop in the Square, commonly called " Harrod's Stores," must have done a very large business during that and the next month. It is true that the town was shelled periodically, but not sufficient to alarm any of the tradesmen, who were reaping a very good harvest from the British and French troops holding the line only a few miles away from the outskirts of the town.

The famous Cloth Hall was quite a ruin, as was the magnificent Cathedral, but they were not so destroyed that the splendour of their architecture and paintings of their frescoes could not be distinguished.

This artificial prosperity of the now famous town was not to last long, and those who were bold enough to return to their homes were doomed to make good their escape within 5 months, never to return to their homes again.

VI.

NEUVE CHAPELLE, 1915.

On March 10th, 1915, owing to the attack being made by the 1st Army at Neuve Chapelle, the 3rd Cavalry Division " stood to " in billets from 5 a.m. The Brigade turned out at 3 p.m., but eventually returned to billets again, arriving about 5 p.m.

On March 11th the Brigade moved off at 4.30 a.m., a very dark morning. The Divisional concentration place was at La Motte, and the Division remained in readiness until 4 p.m., and then went into billets near La Motte. The following two days the Regiments remained in the area " standing to," but returned to their former billets on the 13th.

It was soon after this that H.R.H. Prince Arthur of Connaught, who was attached to the Head Quarters of the 8th Cavalry Brigade, offered a Silver Cup for the winners of a Brigade Marathon race. This was won very easily by the Essex Yeomanry, and the

Cup is now in their possession. The winning Regiment was decided on the greatest number of men of one unit who were amongst the first 20 past the winning post. Corpl. Wilson, of the 10th Royal Hussars, was the individual winner of the race, and Lieut. S. J. Tufnell, Essex Yeomanry, a very good second. The next places were nearly all taken up by Essex Yeomen. The result of the scoring was as follows :—Essex Yeomanry 260 points, 10th Royal Hussars 180 points, Royal Horse Guards 100 points.

During the last week in March His Royal Highness the Prince of Wales, and Lieut.-Colonel S. L. Barry, D.S.O., came to the 10th Hussars and were attached for a week or more at Sercus.

The month of April was spent mostly in training, and lectures on trench warfare were given. The weather was now fine and much appreciated after the constant rain which fell during the winter months.

VII.

THE SECOND BATTLE OF YPRES, 1915.

At the end of April the first German gas attack was launched; this attack made a bad hole in the line North-East of Ypres; the inhabitants were forced to evacuate the whole of the Ypres Salient.

The lamentable spectacle of the forced retreat of the civilian population at the time when the 3rd Cavalry Division went up to co-operate with the 5th Corps, during the last week in April, can never be forgotten, the entire population moving west, taking with them as much of their belongings as they were able to carry, drag or drive. It was not an uncommon sight to see a bedridden old man, or woman, lying in a bed which had been hoisted on to the top of a farm cart already filled with furniture and belongings of all description.

The roads were indeed a sorry sight with farm waggons, carts, carriages, cattle, old men, women

22

with children, some in arms, some in perambulators, and every conceivable form of domestic life moving West, and on the other hand Troops, Cavalry, Artillery, Limbers and Supply lorries moving towards the battle area.

Even with the evacuation being carried out at the pace it was, many civilians became the victims of the incessant enemy artillery bombardment. In Vlamertinghe, a family was evacuating from an estaminet, and had cleared the whole premises into a field not far away; during the removal of the last load a shell burst over the cart and killed the whole family with the exception of one small boy, who had both his legs broken. But this is only one instance of the horrors of the time. Every village anywhere in or about the Ypres Salient witnessed terrible experiences for its population, and towards the end of the month not only Ypres itself was doomed, but every place within the Salient was bound to have the same fate. Shell after shell went straight into the ancient city of world-wide renown. The tower of the old Cathedral became visibly less day by day, the Cloth Hall had almost vanished, and when the 8th Cavalry Brigade marched through the old city during the night before the memorable 13th of May, the whole town was in flames and shelled continuously

23

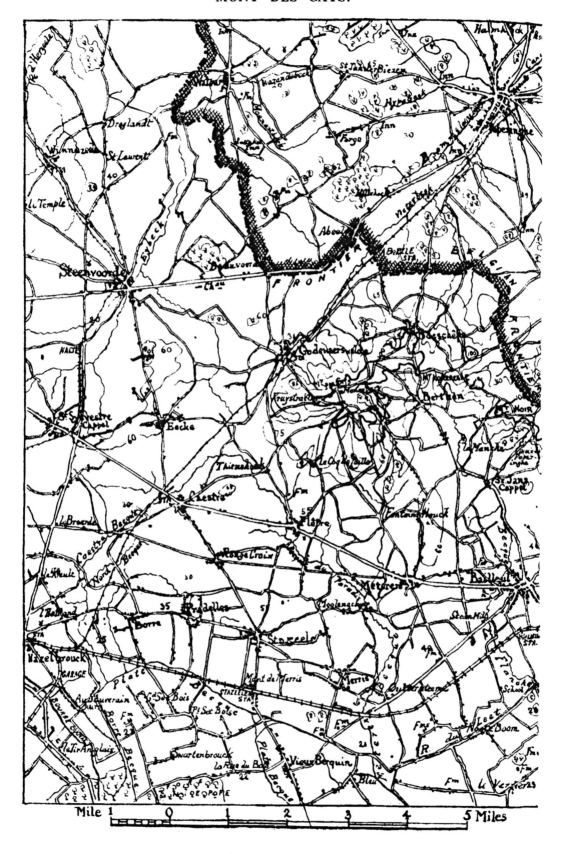

Mile 1   0   1   2   3   4   5 Miles

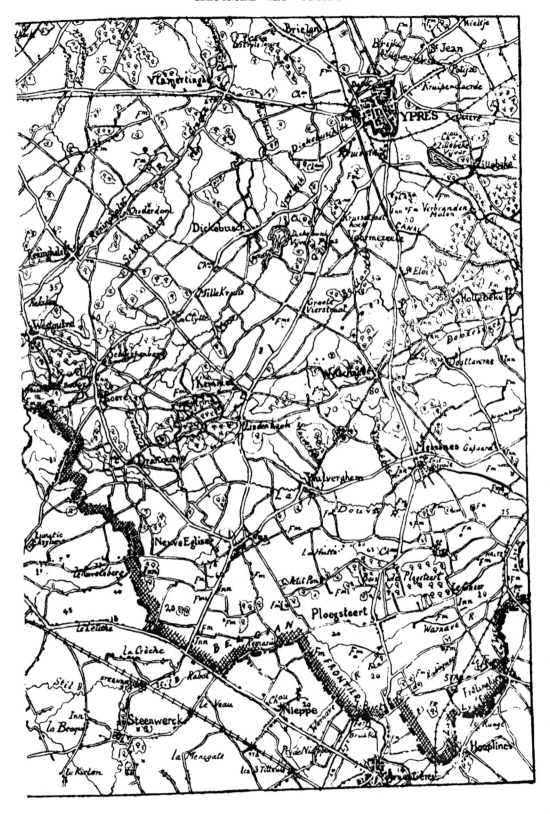

from end to end. The incessant bombardment, however, failed entirely in its purpose to prevent the advance of the British troops, or deny the bridge over the river. A continual stream of guns, ammunition and supplies passed through irrespective of the many casualties which were being caused. The determination, so characteristic of the British nation, seemed to be well established, that Ypres should be held in the 2nd battle of Ypres as it was in the 1st Battle of Ypres, and so it succeeded. The prominent part taken in its defence by the 8th Cavalry Brigade, commencing at the time of the German first gas attack until the attack on the Potijze-Zonnebeke road on the 13th May is briefly as follows :—

On April 23rd orders were received at 10.30 a.m. to turn out at once ; at 1 p.m. the Brigade marched via Hazebrouck and Caestre to Abeele Station, arriving there at 5.30 p.m. and bivouacked in the open. On the following day, April 24th, the Brigade moved at 10 a.m. via Boeschepe to a position of readiness South of Vlamertinghe ; arriving there about noon off-saddled, and every man was issued an additional 100 rounds ammunition, and billeted there for the night.

On April 25th the Brigade saddled up at 6 a.m., " stood to " and at 10.30 a.m. the Brigade off-saddled at point 35, $2\frac{1}{2}$ miles S.W. of Vlamertinghe. At

1 p.m. the Brigade moved to Peselhoek, North of Poperinghe, and remained there for about an hour, during which time Poperinghe was being heavily shelled. At about 6.30 p.m. the Brigade went into billets in the Steenvoorde area, the Essex Yeomanry being billeted at Winnezeele. April 26th, saddled up at 6 a.m. and moved to Brigade rendezvous at Droglandt, and off-saddled. At 11.15 a.m. saddled up and marched to Abeele, off-saddled, and remained there until 8.30 p.m. The Brigade then moved to a point 2 miles South of Poperinghe, where the horses of the whole Brigade were picketed.

The Commanding Officers, Adjutants, 10 Squadron Officers, and 304 N.C.O.'s and men, M. Gun detachments, and " A " Echelon wagons then proceeded to huts at Vlamertinghe, arriving there about 4.15 a.m., Major F. Whitmore going on in advance in a car, to prepare the billets for the Essex Yeomanry.

The following day, April 27th, at 5 p.m. the Camp and Town were heavily shelled, and some casualties occurred both in men and horses. The horses had to be let loose on account of the consistent shelling of the horse lines.

On April 28th the Camp was again shelled at 9.15 a.m., and several N.C.O.'s and men were wounded.

At 12.30 the whole Brigade marched back to their horses, saddled up, and moved off at 8.15 p.m. to Abeele, arriving there about 9.30 and billeted in that area.

The following four days were spent at Abeele "standing to" ready to move.

On May 3rd the Brigade moved to point 35, S.W. of Vlamertinghe, horses pegged down in the open and a dismounted party, consisting of 15 Officers, 300 other ranks per Regiment, marched out at 10 p.m. to a field on the Poperinghe-Ypres road, $1\frac{1}{2}$ miles E. of Vlamertinghe, arriving at 1.15 a.m., remaining there till 4.45 a.m. The rain came down in torrents all this time. The reason for this move was that a section of the front line in front of Ypres was being adjusted by the infantry, and it was necessary to hold a Brigade in reserve to meet eventualities. The Brigade marched back to the horses, arriving at 6.15 a.m., and on the following day, May 4th, billeted at and about Houtkerque.

On May 5th the Brigade marched to Brielen, arriving there at about 7.30 p.m. ; dismounted parties, consisting of 10 Officers and 170 other ranks per Regiment, marched to the Canal, $\frac{1}{4}$ mile North of Ypres, the whole dismounted party, under the command of Lieut.-Colonel E. Deacon, Essex Yeomanry, for the purpose of digging trenches for the 5th Corps near the Yser Canal. Digging commenced at 9.45 p.m. and finished at 1.30 a.m., during which time Ypres was heavily shelled, and a considerable portion of the town became enveloped in flames.

At 1.45 a.m. the dismounted party returned to their horses, and then marched back to billets, arriving about 5.30 a.m.

On May 7th the Brigade returned to its former billeting area about Sercus, the Essex Yeomanry returning to Mt. Croquet.

On May 9th the Brigade proceeded by motor-buses to Brielen, strength 80 men per Squadron. At Brielen the whole of the 3rd Cavalry Division was concentrated under Major-General C. J. Briggs, C.B., D.S.O. The huts in which the Division were billeted were intermittently shelled both by day and night.

During the night of May 10th, dismounted parties were sent to dig on the Ramparts at Ypres.

On May 11th a party left Brielen at 7 p.m. to take over trenches from the 8th Infantry Brigade (60th Rifles and Rifle Brigade), near Hooge Chateau, but this order was cancelled and the parties returned to huts at about 1.30 a.m.

On May 12th, after dark, the Essex Yeomanry, under Lieut.-Colonel E. Deacon, were ordered to dig a communication trench at Bellevarde, East of the Reservoir and railway, north of the Ypres-Menin road, close to the G.H.Q. line of trenches near Potijze, and the remainder of the Brigade went into the G.H.Q. line (support trenches) in reserve to the 7th Cavalry Brigade, the 6th Brigade being already in the trenches on the right of the 7th Brigade.

The trench to be dug was a long one, and the time to do it in was short, because daylight would not permit any work being done above the ground.

Very heavy machine gun and rifle fire were delivered during the night, which rendered the task still more difficult, and frequently the digging parties were forced to lie prone under a storm of rifle and machine gun bullets. The task was not completed when Lieut.-Colonel Deacon decided to withdraw 2 squadrons the first rays of daylight already beginning to make themselves apparent. Major Whitmore was accordingly left to endeavour to complete the task with B. Squadron, under Capt. E. A. Ruggles-Brise. The men worked their hardest, but daylight appeared, and the task had to be abandoned, casualties becoming frequent. At dawn, on May 13th, the Regiment marched to rejoin the remainder of the Brigade, and the preliminary stages of the German attack began.

Major F. Whitmore was wounded before arriving at the G.H.Q. line.

Very heavy shelling commenced at 4 a.m. The bombardment was at first directed on the front line on a breadth of about one mile, held by the 6th and 7th Cavalry Brigades and the 2nd Dragoon Guards. A dense cloud of smoke hung over the whole area; buildings and trenches alike were demolished beyond recognition. At about 6 a.m. the enemy brought his barrage over the line held by the 8th Cavalry Brigade, and by 7 a.m. the 1st and 2nd Life Guards were forced to retire through the lines held by the 8th Brigade. The Essex Yeomanry were in the support trench just West of the Potijze-Verlorenhoek road on the N.E. edge of Potijze Chateau garden. At about 9 a.m. a message was received through the telephone from the Front line saying " Front line absolutely intact," but all the same it was evident that a retirement was in progress.

At mid-day Colonel Deacon was informed that the Royal Horse Guards and 10th Royal Hussars had been moved forward; consequently the Essex Yeomanry were moved into the trenches on the East of the Potijze-Verlorenhoek road, which had been occupied by the Blues and the 10th Hussars.

THE SECOND BATTLE OF YPRES, 1915.

At about 1.30 p.m. Brigadier-General Bulkeley Johnson, A.D.C., who had established his Brigade Head Quarters in the Chateau Gardens, sent for Lieut.-Colonel Deacon, and as a result of that interview the Squadron leaders were informed by Colonel Deacon that a counter-attack was to be undertaken at 2.15 p.m., in order to regain the front line which had been occupied by the enemy. The Brigade for the purpose of the attack was disposed as follows :—Royal Horse Guards on the right, 10th Royal Hussars on the left, and the Essex Yeomanry in support. Colonel Deacon ordered C. Squadron, under Major Roddick, to act on the right; B. Squadron, under Captain E. A. Ruggles-Brise, on the left, and A. Squadron, under Captain J. O. Parker, in support. The Regiment was to move off in 10 minutes and take up a line on the right of the 10th Hussars. The 10th Hussars, it was thought, were in some trenches half way up the rising ground with their right near a White Farm, and their left on the road.

Colonel Deacon gave orders to Major Buxton to take two scouts with him, and report to Lieut.-Colonel E. R. A. Shearman commanding the 10th Hussars to the effect that the Essex were coming up on his right. Major Buxton came under heavy rifle fire from the direction of the White Farm, but

Ruins of Zonnebeke Church.

The trenches at Potijze, looking towards Verlorenhoek.

found Colonel Shearman near the road. Major Buxton delivered the message, and Colonel Shearman pointed out to Major Buxton the trenches which were to be his objective, and said " That is the trench that I am going to take. I shall do it with the greatest ease, there is no doubt about it whatever."

The Essex Yeomanry were by this time running up towards the right of the 10th Hussars, led by Major Roddick and Captain E. A. Ruggles-Brise; the men had bayonets fixed, and cheered as they ran for their objective. Major Roddick was killed almost instantly. Captain Ruggles-Brise continued gallantly at the head of his Squadron.

Lieut.-Colonel Shearman realising that it was not yet the time to deliver the attack, told Major Buxton to do his utmost to stop the advance of the Essex ; this he was able to do, and the Essex lay down on the right of the 10th Hussars. At this moment a group of Germans fled from the positions they were holding, and someone holloaed, " Tally ho ! Yonder they go." As a response to the view holloa the whole line, the Essex on the right and the 10th Hussars on the left, rose as one and rushed the hill. The going was deep, but no one halted until the trench was reached as were also a series of holes which the line degenerated into on the right. Very heavy casualties were suffered in both regiments. Lieut.-Colonel Shearman, 10th Hussars, was killed, also his Adjutant, Capt. Stewart ; Lieut.-Colonel Deacon, Essex Yeomanry, was missing, and Capt. Steele, his Adjutant, was wounded. The objective, however, was gained, and held under very trying conditions. A large amount of German equipment was found in the line, as was also coffee and sausages. Some prisoners were taken. The line now held was at once consolidated. Captain E. A. Ruggles-Brise and Lieut. R. A. Thomson, with very few men, put up a splendid resistance and held on to some ruins just on the right and in front of our line. Major Buxton, who was now in command of the Essex Yeomanry, despatched a man with a message to get into touch with the Royal Horse Guards on the right, but this messenger was instantly killed. Any movement on the part of anybody on the right of this line was impossible, and many were killed or wounded in attempting to take ground in any direction. A very heavy bombardment with great accuracy was, by this time, concentrated on to the line now held, and a large body of the enemy moved forward from the Verlorenhoek hill. A small dark red flag was placed in a trench by the enemy about 150 yards in advance of our line ; this was doubtless a signal for the enemies' artillery to ascertain the position of their front line. The rain fell heavily, and the mud was indescribable, rendering rifles unserviceable in a very short time; in fact, these had by now become almost completely ineffective. After about 2 hours a message came through from the 10th Hussars to the effect that they were retiring behind the crest and filing out of the left end of the trench. Capt. E. A. Ruggles-Brise and Lieut. R. A. Thomson were still gallantly holding on with their small group of men at and about the ruined cottages, and communication with them was impossible. Their only hope of falling back was to wait till after dark. Two of their officers were killed, Lieut. C. P. N. Reid and Lieut. A. G. Swire.

A general retirement behind the crest was then undertaken, to a position on the reverse slope of the hill, about 600 yards in rear of the advanced position. This line was held until about 6 p.m.

The general line taken up by the 2nd Dragoon Guards on the left of the 10th Hussars had been maintained throughout, and their assistance by thus maintaining their position contributed much towards the result of the day's fighting.

At about 6 p.m. orders were received for the Essex Yeomanry to concentrate at a house near the G.H.Q. line on the main road.

The 10th Hussars took up a support line and then the Essex Yeomanry moved into the G.H.Q. line. It was here that the Squadrons rallied under Major A. Buxton, now commanding the Regiment. Captain Ruggles-Brise, Lieut. R. A. Thomson and about 6 men returned, having remained the whole time holding on to the positions which they had captured. Wounded men also kept coming in under cover of the darkness. Many Officers and men were missing, many were known to be killed and wounded. No news, whatever, was forthcoming of Lieut.-Col. E. Deacon.

Lieuts. G. P. N. Reid, A. G. Swire, and G. S. Johnston were killed. Capt. A. Steele, Lieuts R. Edwards and P. Holt seriously wounded ; Lieut. V. Hine slightly wounded.

Lieuts. Edwards and Holt were brought in in a critical condition ; no trace of Colonel Deacon was ever found. His courage, cheerfulness, and unselfish character will always be remembered, and his valuable presence as Commanding Officer will always be mourned by his devoted followers. Major Roddick's cool, level-headed leadership of men was an example to follow, and the respect which he commanded by every man of his Squadron might well be the envy of every soldier. Lieuts. Reid, Swire and Johnston will ever be remembered as the real right sort to give confidence to their men—always cheerful, never idle.

The Regiment suffered no less in other ranks than it did in Officers. Many valuable lives of N.C.O.'s and men, if they had been spared, would indeed have been assets to the interest of their Regiment in the battles to follow.

In the special Order which was issued by the Brigadier-General commanding the 8th Cavalry Brigade, which was published immediately after the action, and which appears later, a special paragraph was inserted referring to the gallant stand made by Capt. E. A. Ruggles-Brise as follows :—

" The behaviour of the Squadron which maintained its position in the ruined houses although cut off, until after dark, and its subsequent withdrawal in good order was especially meritorious."

Regimental Orders by Major A. Buxton, dated 16/5/15, contained the following commendations :—

Major A. Roddick	For the pace and dash with which he led the attack.
Capt. E. A. Ruggles-Brise Lieut. R. A. Thomson Sergt. Howard L./Cpl. Wardell Pte. Lucy	For their gallantry in holding an advanced position in some ruined houses until dark and after they had been cut off.

37

Corpl. Frost
Pte. Schweir
Pte. Johnson
Pte. Dean
} For stretcher-bearing under heavy fire.

Pte. Abbott
Pte. Wear
} For bravery and coolness in action.

Pte. Holland
Pte. Bates
} For useful reconnaissance and coolness in action.

The following are also mentioned as having been noticed doing especially good work :—

Sergt. Hodge	L./Corpl. Seabrook
Sergt. Pritchard	L./Corpl. Rex
Sergt. Ledger	Pte. Middlecoat
Sergt. Walker	Pte. Smart
Corpl. Bird	Pte. Skinner
Corpl. Bosworth	Pte. Tompkins
L./Corpl. Turnell	Pte. Anning

The total casualties in the Essex Yeomanry were as follows :—

Officers—Killed	.. .. ..	4
Wounded	.. ..	5
Missing ..	.. ..	1
Other Ranks—Killed	.. .. ..	47
Wounded	.. ..	86
Missing ..	.. ..	18
	Total	161

THE SECOND BATTLE OF YPRES, 1915.

LIST OF CASUALTIES, ESSEX YEOMANRY,
13TH MAY, 1915.

KILLED.

Major	A. Roddick		747	Sgt.	Pearce, A.
Lieut.	G. S. Johnston		476	Cpl.	Bird, E. S.
Lieut.	G. P. N. Reid		1405	Pte.	Smith, H.
2/Lt.	A. G. Swire		1227	Pte.	Lagden, R.
1129	Pte.	Bell, F. E.	1269	Pte.	McTurk, H.
964	Cpl.	Allen, T.	735	Pte.	South, A. T.
1246	Pte.	Truefit, J.	32	Sgt.	Draper, J. W.
956	Pte.	Taylor, C.	26	Sgt.	Clark, T.
991	Pte.	Snell, B.	839	Pte.	Wild, A. J.
990	Pte.	Propert, E. P.	1401	Pte.	Jones, W. E.
674	Sgt.	Ledger, D.	1297	Pte.	Taylor, D.
1080	L./C.	Seabrook, F. M.	1314	Pte.	Christie, D. W.
1055	Pte.	Askew, O.	1092	Cpl.	Diggens, E.
1338	Pte.	Blencoe, B. W.	1388	Pte.	Day, W.
1225	Pte.	Deighton, F. J.	1149	Pte.	Pharaoh, E. J.
1135	Pte.	Gardiner, W. E.	1331	Pte.	Taylor, H.
989	Pte.	Petchey, J.	723	Cpl.	Deverell, G.
1275	Pte.	Ridgewell, R. C.	1632	Pte.	Mann, B.
1307	Pte.	Seabrook, E. J.	917	Pte.	Newman, S. E.
1117	Sgt.	Deakin, L. C.	1350	Pte.	Beggin, B. W.
1093	Sgt.	Newman, S.			

DIED OF WOUNDS.

53	Sgt.	Packer, R. C.	1277	Pte.	Rust, J. S.
820	Cpl.	Ridgwell, E.	1132	Pte.	Beeney, W.
621	L./C.	Croxon, A.	838	Pte.	Rayner, W.
1207	Pte.	Free, M. D.	1252	Pte.	Rowell, H.
1114	Pte.	Robins, C. A.	1271	Pte.	Swann, H.

WOUNDED AND MISSING.

Lieut.-Col. E. Deacon
1189 Pte. Nunn, W.
1703 Pte. Fairhead, S.
981 Pte. Mansfield, H. E.
977 Pte. Taylor, J. W.
710 Sgt. Butcher, L.
1026 Pte. Cattell, C. H.
927 Pte. Millar, H.
1576 Pte. Green, C. E.
1261 Pte. Barker, J.

MISSING.

686 Pte. Hill, L. A.
1048 Cpl. Appleton, E.
870 Pte. Prime, E. J.
1681 Pte. Taylor, J.
1128 Sgt. Brock, C. E.
1230 Pte. Hurst, D.
1651 Pte. Milbank, J.
953 Pte. Cottee, G.
1656 Pte. Wright, H.

WOUNDED.

Major F. H. D. C. Whitmore
1655 Pte. Finney, J. C.
Capt. A. R. Steele
1438 Pte. Dunmore, W. T.
Lieut. V. T. G. Hine
1005 Pte. Jenkyn, L. H.
Lieut. R. Edwards
650 Pte. Hallett, J. L.
2/Lt. H. P. Holt
1660 Pte. Conolly, W.
1730 Pte. Last, W.
975 Pte. Richards, H.
1697 Pte. Austin, G.
827 Pte. Curtis, C.
764 Pte. Smith, A.
1281 Sgt. Hoare, P.
1263 Pte. Newcombe, E. G.
1641 Pte. Caines, R.
1203 Cpl. Grant, K.
1079 Pte. Scrivener, G.
1670 Pte. Pennell, W. H.
1286 Pte. Townsend, R.
1181 Pte. Manning, P. D.
1282 Pte. Thompson, S.
1074 Pte. Goody, H. W.
767 Sgt. Walker, E.
1433 L./C. Baker, W.
1648 L./C. Chapman, W.
1043 Pte. Holland, R.
1032 Pte. Finch, E. H.
923 Pte. Harvey, P.
948 Pte. Bond, A. J.
1116 Pte. Ball, A.
1310 Pte. Sparrow, J.
1812 Cpl. Blyth, A.
461 Pte. Hazelton, E.
1191 Pte. Smith, L.
957 Pte. Revell, W. J.

THE SECOND BATTLE OF YPRES, 1915.

1123	Sgt.	Mann, H.
910	Pte.	Leeder, N.
590	Pte.	Cunningham, N. J.
1678	Pte.	Moss, E. G.
845	Pte.	Fox, G. W.
1676	Pte.	Hutton, H.
1228	Pte.	Harvey, T. W.
1259	Pte.	Pegrum, E.
761	Cpl.	Hart, W.
891	Pte.	Adams, G.
1665	Pte.	Dorrington, E.
862	Pte.	Butcher, W.
1562	Pte.	Joyce, W.
448	Sgt.	Pritchard, H.
1078	Pte.	Franks, J. K.
1192	Pte.	Errington, C.
1199	Pte.	Hall, R.
1652	Pte.	Waller, H.
1369	Pte.	Rivers, G.
1686	Pte.	Woods, F.
1167	Pte.	Mills, A. J.
853	Pte.	Green, J.
963	Pte.	Cunningham, H.
625	Cpl.	Glew, E.
1213	Pte.	Brazier, C.
461	Pte.	Hazelton, E.
429	Sgt.	Speakman, F.
639	Pte.	Wyatt, A. J.
490	Sgt.	Moody, J. H.
1121	Cpl.	Williams, G.
649	Pte.	Steward, D.
1151	Pte.	Brice, A. E.
715	Pte.	Bentley, W.
1379	Pte.	Curtis, C.
877	Pte.	Jordan, J.
912	Pte.	Sutton, O. T.
1194	Pte.	Minns, E.
1696	Pte.	Dyer, P.
1101	Cpl.	Brown, S.
1395	Pte.	Bewers, E.
1083	Pte.	Hughes, O.
640	L./C.	Wyatt, G.
866	Pte.	Banks, J. E.
1568	Pte.	Baynes, A.
868	Pte.	Robinson, R.
900	Pte.	Lang, H.
890	Pte.	Clare, R.
973	Pte.	Baker, R.
1453	Pte.	Bruce, C.
1027	Pte.	Sergeant, J. H.
904	Pte.	Veal, C.
1327	Pte.	Whent, H.
518	S.S.M.	Newman, H.

THE SECOND BATTLE OF YPRES, 1915.

NARRATIVE OF 10TH (P.W.O.) ROYAL HUSSARS,
COMMENCING 7 A.M., MAY 13TH. 1915.

When the 1st and 2nd Life Guards were forced to retire from the front line trenches near Verlorenhoek, Lieut.-Colonel E. R. A. Shearman, commanding 10th Royal Hussars, Major C. W. H. Crichton, and Capt. G. C. Stewart, Adjutant, worked hard to rally the men, and all the time shelling became more and more severe.

At 8 a.m. the order was given for the Regiment to leave all kit behind in the trenches; rifles, bandoliers, bayonets and spades only to be carried. The task of the Regiment was to dig in on the right of the 2nd Dragoon Guards (Queen's Bays). Whilst concentrated behind Potijze Chateau, Capt. M. de Tuyll and several other ranks were killed by shell fire. Advancing alongside the road the leading Squadron " A " came under very heavy Artillery and rifle fire. Half the Squadron, under Lieut. R. Gordon Canning, went forward to fill in a gap between the Queen's Bays and the 5th Dragoon Guards, and later on supported the counter-attack of the 8th Cavalry Brigade by rifle fire. The remaining $2\frac{1}{2}$ Squadrons and M. Guns then attempted to dig themselves in alongside of the road, and they remained there until 2 p.m. Lieut. J. M. Wardell was here wounded.

At 2 p.m. our guns opened a heavy fire on the enemy's trenches, and at 2.20 p.m. the Essex Yeomanry and Royal Horse Guards advanced up to the right of the 10th Royal Hussars.

At this moment the 10th Royal Hussars, led by Lieut.-Colonel Shearman, jumped up out of the dugouts and charged the attacking forces of the enemy. The Germans retired instantly, vacating their trenches. Both Lieut.-Colonel Shearman and Capt. Stewart were at this moment killed, and Major Gibbs was wounded. Major Crichton was severely wounded whilst directing the fire on the retiring enemy. He showed great gallantry, continuing to direct operations whilst lying in the open, until he handed over command to Major the Hon. C. B. O. Mitford.

A retirement was ordered at 4.30 p.m.

During this retirement casualties were very heavy. Major Mitford was killed, and Lieuts. G. Alexander, Lord Chesham and C. Humbert were all wounded.

The survivors of the counter-attack were rallied under Lieut. T. Bouch and Lieut. the Earl of Airlie in the dug-outs on the right of the Queen's Bays.

Lieut. R. Gordon Canning rejoined with his party and Lieut. R. G. Borthwick returned with his at 8.30 p.m. The strength of the Regiment was then reduced to 4 Officers and 98 other ranks. This party held the line protecting the right flank of the Queen's Bays, until relieved by the 9th Cavalry Brigade at 10.30 p.m. ; they then retired to the G.H.Q. line.

On the following day the remnants of the 8th Cavalry Brigade were amalgamated with the 6th Cavalry Brigade, and took up a line 300 yards in rear of the original firing line, remaining there until 8.30 p.m., when they were relieved by the Scots Greys, and the 8th Brigade returned to the huts at Vlamertinghe.

The bodies of Lieut.-Colonel Shearman and Capt. Stewart were brought back to Vlamertinghe and buried in the British Burial Cemetery at that place.

The total casualties in the 10th (P.W.O.) Royal Hussars were as follow :—

Officers—Killed ..	..	..	4
Wounded	..	..	6
Other Ranks—Killed ..	..	..	27
Wounded	..	..	101
			——
		Total	138

THE SECOND BATTLE OF YPRES, 1915.

LIST OF CASUALTIES, 10TH (P.W.O.) ROYAL HUSSARS,
13TH MAY, 1915.

KILLED.

Lieut.-Col. E. R. A. Shearman		3607	L./C.	Mason, T.
Major Hon. C. B. O. Mitford		5601	L./C.	Johnson, H.
Capt. G. C. Stewart		14789	L./C.	Masters, A.
Capt. M. A. de Tuyll		7998	L./C.	Smith, F.
		3205	Pte.	Fewster, W.
3941	S.S.M.	Keats, A.	7972	Pte.	Senior, B.
5610	Sgt.	Dicks, J.	1110	Pte.	McBryde, A.
4524	Sgt.	Keeley, A.	5119	Pte.	Cooper, J.
5413	Sgt.	Lurcott, E.	3472	Pte.	Chatton, C.
5238	Cpl.	Haddington, S.	4899	Pte.	Walker, A.
396	Cpl.	Bayston, A.	5469	Pte.	Fletcher, F.
5453	Cpl.	Chamberlain, T.	4310	Pte.	Hope, C.
18	Cpl.	Nepean, H	7671	Pte.	Sole, T.
4563	L./C.	Guyver, G.	14479	Pte.	Cobb, A.
5171	L./C.	Meads, H.	5042	Pte.	Cole, P.
5369	L./C.	Scales, H.	28439	Pte.	Kimmens, W.

WOUNDED.

Major C.W.H. Crichton, D.S.O.		25475	Pte.	Rowntree, W.
Major W. O. Gibbs		10552	Pte.	Meredith, H.
Lieut. J. C. Lord Chesham		4414	Pte.	Tee, A.
Lieut. G. Alexander		4376	Pte.	Metcalfe, T.
Lieut. J. M. Wardell		11296	Pte.	Page, H.
Lieut. C. Humbert		28521	Pte.	Fallon, E.
		2603	Pte.	Thompson, P.
5230	Sgt.	Hyland, G.	25376	Pte.	Austin
1484	Sgt.	Lloyd, R.	5199	Pte	Baines, G
8152	Sgt.	Hibbles, F.	1087	Pte.	Colville, W.
8756	Sgt.	Mitchell, A.	6807	Pte.	Roberts
5550	Sgt.	Stone, R.	10698	Pte.	Smith, H.

10791	L./Sgt.	Lock, F.
2280	Cpl.	Swadling, K.
2809	Cpl.	Eckers, S.
11294	Cpl.	Penfold,
4290	Cpl.	Broad, W.
537	Cpl.	Portway, C.
1500	Cpl.	Beech, W.
391	Cpl.	Parfrement, J.
8277	Cpl.	Price, A.
4698	Cpl.	Wilson, C.
4650	Cpl.	Snell, W.
61	Cpl.	Stevens, A.
2292	Cpl.	Brown, J.
2280	Cpl.	Warren, F.
7361	Cpl.	Hargreaves, P.
491	Tptr.	Jones, J.
7960	Pte.	Dickenson, A.
22563	Pte.	Sharp, H.
3353	Pte.	Barker, C.
14191	Pte.	Straight, R.
2823	Pte.	Allison, J.
6141	Pte.	Hobbins,
923	Pte.	Hayday, W.
12089	Pte.	Farrell, A.
4952	Pte.	Tansey, B.
10825	Pte.	Evans, E.
7706	Pte.	Frith, A.
6343	Pte.	Lockwood, A.
17114	Pte.	Pilkington, A.
20975	Pte.	Chapman, G.
7219	Pte.	Spice, J.
25262	Pte.	Smith, H.
20502	Pte.	Attwell, A.
6024	Pte.	Scott, E.
5037	Pte.	Whittaker, J.
25376	Pte.	Clay, J.
29042	Pte.	Glucksman
7952	Pte.	Holmes, J.
888	Pte.	Quatton, W.
253	Ptc.	Bentall, T.
25381	Pte.	Furness, W.
2809	Cpl.	Barker, F
7082	Pte.	Reading, M.
5285	Pte.	Gillard, W.
7459	Pte.	Spriggs, W.
2791	Pte.	Bellwood, F.
10857	Pte.	Lancaster, G.
7720	Pte.	Atkinson, A.
3034	Pte.	Burke, E.
3736	Pte.	Derrington, W.
5057	Pte.	Glazebrook, T.
12270	Pte.	Marples, A.
6289	Ptc.	Jennings, A.
9350	Pte.	Wallis, T.
6816	Pte.	Whatmore, S.
6434	Pte.	Barrett, A.
5016	Pte.	Wigley, J.
7194	Pte.	Wright, T.
2574	Pte.	Moreton, W.
4533	Pte.	Wilson, T.
17388	Pte.	Widdowson, J.
5218	Pte.	Kelly, J.
1818	Pte.	Holdsworth, R.
7656	Pte.	Wyett
12052	Pte.	Swift, T.
10694	Pte.	Noble, H.

46

THE SECOND BATTLE OF YPRES, 1915.

10412 Pte. Hicks, A.
954 Pte. Mayes, H.
10427 Pte. Pearcey, H.
1954 Pte. Arscott, D.

12676 Pte. Burnell, J.
8483 Pte. Fountain, P.
25764 Pte. Egerton, F.

DIED OF WOUNDS.

622 Sgt. Porter, F.
3610 Cpl. Joel, E.
882 Pte. Sykes, B.

1353 Pte. Fetrol, W.
1358 Pte. Rose, W.

MISSING, BELIEVED KILLED.

7128 L./C. Treasure
8423 Pte. Armstrong
4891 Pte. Hole, S.

8200 Pte. Draper, W.
2291 Pte. Battye, A.

WOUNDED AND MISSING.

5561 Sadd.-Cpl. Pollikett.

The casualties suffered by the Royal Horse Guards during this engagement were as follows :—

KILLED.

Capt. G. V. S. Bowlby
Capt. Hon. C. E. A. Philipps
Lieut. T. G. Davson

Lord Spencer Compton
Viscount Wendover
2nd Lieut. G. H. Pullen

WOUNDED.

Capt. A. W. Foster
Capt. M. J. Wemyss
Lt. Lord A. S. Leveson Gower

2nd Lieut. L. S. Ward Price
2nd Lieut. J. E. Murray Smith

Other Ranks—Killed 18
Wounded 78

47

The total number of casualties in the 3 Regiments of the 8th Cavalry Brigade amounted to the following :—

				OFFICERS	OTHER RANKS.
Royal Horse Guards	..	..	..	11	78
10th Royal Hussars	..	..	..	10	128
Essex Yeomanry	..	..	..	10	151
		Total		31	357

SPECIAL ORDER ISSUED BY THE BRIGADIER-GENERAL AFTER THE ACTION, MAY 13TH.

The Brigadier wishes to express his great admiration for the part played by each regiment in the attack made by the Brigade to regain the lost trenches, and his sympathy with the regiments for the loss of so many valuable lives in all ranks.

By driving the Germans out, who, during the retreat suffered great losses from our artillery, and by preventing them from consolidating their position in the trenches that they had captured, the Brigade undoubtedly saved the situation.

Had the Germans attained their object, the position of the whole of the 27th Infantry Division on the right would have been rendered very precarious.

As it was, the Germans retired so great a distance that we were enabled to establish an unbroken line during the night unmolested.

The following message was received from the G.O.C. 2nd Army :

> " Express my appreciation of the magnificent spirit shown by the troops to-day and the way they have stuck to their positions."

The following message was received from the C. in C. of the Allied forces :—

> " General Joffre expressed to the Lieutenant-General commanding the 5th Corps, his admiration and congratulations on the gallant stand they have made."

VIII.

BLARINGHEM AND MATRINGHEM, 1915.

After the 2nd Battle of Ypres the 8th Brigade remained at Vlamertinghe for about 7 days, and then returned to the Sercus area.

Towards the end of the month the 10th Royal Hussars went back into the trenches at Hooge, with the Royal Horse Guards and 2nd Life Guards, and the Essex Yeomanry, under Major Buxton, went into the Ramparts at Ypres in reserve, together with the Leicestershire Yeomanry. The 3rd Dragoon Guards, under Lieut.-Colonel A. Burt, joined them in the Ramparts, having suffered heavily at Hooge.

On June 5th the Brigade returned to former billeting area at Sercus.

Whilst in the Ramparts at Ypres, Major H. F. Wickham, King's Dragoon Guards, took over command of the Essex Yeomanry.

On June 18th the Brigade was inspected by the Commander-in-Chief, who, in an address, especially complimented the Brigade on its conduct in the engagement on May 13th.

The whole of the next 3 months were devoted to training in Cavalry work, also bombing, rifle practice and polo. From August 13th until September 4th digging parties were at work near Armentières.

On September 10th Lieut.-Col. H. F. Wickham took over command of the 10th Royal Hussars from Major the Honble. F. W. Stanley, and Major F. H. D. C. Whitmore took over command of the Essex Yeomanry from Lieut.-Col. H. F. Wickham.

The enthusiasm always shown by Lieut.-Col. Wickham in connection with the reorganising of the Essex Yeomanry after its severe losses in May, won for him a great reputation in the Regiment. He taught the Regiment a lot, and although the Essex Yeomanry did not go into action at all during the period in which he was in command, there was not a man in the Regiment who had not got the greatest confidence in his judgment.

The Brigade had by now moved into the Bomy Area, and the Essex Yeomanry were billeted at Matringhem.

BLARINGHEM AND MATRINGHEM, 1915.

It was the 2nd Sunday in September that Capt. the Rev. Jack Gibbs came as Chaplain to the Brigade, and he will always be remembered as one of the best, and one who was always willing to help anybody at any time.

On the occasion of a Brigade Night Scheme, Sept. 17th-18th, whilst the Squadrons of the Essex Yeomanry were marching back independently to their own billeting areas, a fox jumped up in a field, and the whole of " B " Squadron, under Major G. Gold, galloped the fox to a standstill, and Lieut. J. Swire was able to pick him up exhausted. He soon, however, recovered and went away contented.

IX.

BATTLE OF LOOS, 1915.

On September 21st the 8th Cavalry Brigade moved from its billeting area, near Bomy, at 12 noon, marched through Pernes and Marles les Mines, and reached Lapugnoy Station, 5 miles S.W. of Bethune at 9.30 p.m. Bivouacked in the Bois des Dames, " B " Echelon moved into Westrehem, near Therrouanne. The 3rd Cavalry Division (less the 7th Brigade) were placed under the orders of the G.O.C. 1st Army. 3 days rations were carried per man.

On September 25th the Brigade moved at 8.15 a.m., following the 6th Cavalry Brigade to Vaudricourt, the Head Quarters of the 5th Army Corps, commanded by General Rawlinson. Marched from there at 2 p.m., passing through Nœux-les-Mines, Noyelles-les-Vermelles, and halted between Fosse No. 3 de Bethune and Vermelles. Further progress was impossible until the Infantry had seized the Haute Deule Canal Crossings.

During the night the enemy recaptured their old line near Fosse 8 de Bethune.

On September 26th the Brigade " stood to " for the purpose of supporting the 7th Division.

At 2 p.m. the Brigade moved about 1,000 yards back, and bivouacked just S. of Noyelles-les-Vermelles.

At 6 p.m. the Brigade was turned out, dismounted, to dig and take over the old German line, pending the arrival of the Guards' Division. This Division, however, was already in the trenches before the Brigade was able to get there, and consequently the Brigade returned to former bivouac, arriving at 9 p.m.

The attack had so far succeeded, inasmuch as the village of Loos was already in our hands, and the enemy had suffered considerably in casualties and many prisoners had been taken.

At 1 a.m., on September 27th, orders were received for the Brigade to move on to Loos at once, the Essex Yeomanry, under Lt. Col. F. Whitmore, being detailed to act as Advance Guard to the Brigade, followed by the Royal Horse Guards, under Lt.-Col. Lord Tweedmouth, C.M.G., M.V.O., D.S.O., the 10th Royal Hussars, under Lt.-Col. Wickham, in support.

The road leading to Loos from Vermelles passes over the ridge which formed the front line of the German defences. The aspect of the battle-field in this sector, in the moonlight, was weird indeed, the debris of stubborn resistance, guns out of action, broken limbers, ammunition, many brave British Officers and gallant other ranks lying dead, in some cases still holding their maps or rifles in their hands.

The town of Loos was already in the hands of the 6th Cavalry Brigade, who had dug themselves in round the South and Eastern outskirts of the town, a London Territorial Brigade of Infantry, under Brigadier-General Thwaites, being on their right. The 3rd. Dragoon Guards, commanded by Lt.-Col. A. Burt, were holding the edge of the slag heap, which extended to the double Pylon. These two towers were being continuously shelled, as was the town itself and its civilian population. The Royal Horse Guards and Essex Yeomanry were ordered at once to take over the defences on the East of the town; the Essex Yeomanry taking over from the 3rd. Dragoon Guards. The slag heap itself formed part of the defence of the Essex Yeomanry. Guides were awaiting the arrival of the Brigade. It was necessary to complete the relief of the 6th. Brigade before daylight, time was running out and the first rays of light were already visible in the East. Lt.-Col. Whitmore disposed of the Essex Yeomanry and

55

machine guns as follows :—"C" Sqdn, under Capt. R. G. Proby, on the right, with its right against the quarry at S.E. exit of Loos, and its left against "B" Squadron, under Capt. E. A. Ruggles-Brise, M.C., at edge of slag heap. The left of "B" Squadron against the right of the Royal Horse Guards. The Machine Guns, under Lt. T. Preston, being distributed along the defences. "A" Squadron, under Major E. Hill, and Regimental Headquarters were established in the Garden City on the South-Eastern outskirts of Loos. The houses and cellars were put into a state of defence, walls loop-holed and manned with rifles.

Casualties occurred on the approach of daylight, the move being incomplete, it became necessary to expose troops to the view of the enemy in order to complete the relief.

The whole line and town were being heavily shelled and kept under continual machine gun fire throughout the day. Communication between the Squadrons and Headquarters, also between Headquarters and the Brigade was difficult during the whole day and the situation was very obscure. Water became unobtainable owing to the well being under direct observation of the enemy.

The town itself contained some 200 civilian inhabitants and a large quantity of wounded sol-

Ruins of the Church at Loos.

The remains of the Double Pylon at Loos.

diers, both British and German, and a very great number of dead.

In the haste of the German retreat from the town they had left large quantities of stores, kit and material of all kinds, and some prisoners were captured hiding in the cellars and demolished buildings.

During the afternoon the Guards' Division attacked Puis 14 and Hill 70 without success, and this Division lost very heavily in the attack. All the machine guns in the Brigade were brought into action to cover the attack. During this attack, the Germans shelled the town incessantly with every class of shell, including gas. The whole of the line occupied by the Essex Yeomanry was also bombarded. Capt. E. A. Ruggles-Brise, Lieuts. J. K. Swire and E. T. L. Pelly were wounded, also several other ranks.

The following day, September 28th, the pressure was somewhat relieved as a result of a successful attack by the Infantry, thereby gaining the high ground and wood which overlooked the garden city, also by the work put in during the night, establishing a means of communication by trench and telephone. At the same time a quantity of barbed wire was put out in front of the defences. The bombardment, however, continued very severe at times, inflicting many casualties in the Brigade, the dressing station itself being severely shelled and the Medical Staff being entirely put out of action.

There were many very gruesome sights in Loos. Children could be seen, in ignorance, playing in the road where lay many dead soldiers, both British and German.

In one house a party of Germans were still in a sitting position around a table all quite dead. Wounded Germans were discovered in cellars, having endured dreadful suffering from hideous wounds, in some cases with broken limbs, without either food or water.

The 10th. Royal Hussars remained in the town of Loos in support of the Royal Horse Guards and the Essex Yeomanry; they were used for the purpose of searching the cellars and houses for prisoners. Many were discovered, some still in communication with the enemy's forces by means of telephone. Many interesting stories are told regarding these search parties, some of the most humorous being contributed by Major E. H. Watkin Williams, who was in charge of one of these parties. His servant, Dawkins, whose one ambition in life seemed to be to kill a German and also a Turk, was given every opportunity of carrying out his life's desire as far as a German was concerned. Major Williams posted him as bayonet man in front of the cellar-searching party, and it was his duty to be first into each cellar. Dawkins being more accustomed to calling his master in the mornings than demanding the presence of an enemy who might well be armed to the teeth, would with difficulty restrain from politely knocking at the door, but would ask, with well chosen words, whether there was anybody in. This only happened until the real article was discovered. All subsequent cellar occupants were confronted by Dawkins with a loud " Come out you blighters."

The double Pylon, which was the great landmark at Loos, was supposed to have concealed in some portion of it a German General, and Capt. H. K. Bethell, then Brigade Major to the 8th Cavalry Brigade, is alleged to have encouraged Major Williams' search party to increase their scope of investigation by ascending what remained of the double Pylon, and impressed on Major Williams that his party might have the " unique opportunity " of capturing a German General. Major Williams took out his watch, and by careful timing ascertained that the Pylon was struck somewhere by a shell twice in every minute, and that it would with all probability take 2 minutes to get on the top and down again, going as fast as you could scale the remains of the stairway;

in other words, you could carry out the enterprise · with no fewer than four shells thrown at you during the time it would take you to seek for this unique opportunity. The story goes that Dawkins was quite satisfied with a German of junior rank than a General and was not " for it,"

During the night of September 28th the Brigade was relieved by the 1st. Infantry Division. The 9th. Liverpool took over the line from the Essex Yeomanry in torrents of rain. On arrival back with the horses at 3 a.m. orders were received to move to Gosnay; on arrival at that place the Brigade remained on half-an-hour's notice until October 1st, when at 2.30 p.m. the Brigade moved to Labeuvrière and from there on October 3rd to a new billeting area near Burbure, the Essex Yeomanry being billeted at Hurionville.

It was with the greatest regret that the Essex Yeomanry received the information that Lieut. Christopher C. Tower, who was A.D.C. 12th Division, had been killed near Vermelles on October 2nd. His body was buried in the Churchyard at Nœux-les-Mines.

Four months after this officer's death, whilst the Regiment was holding the line near Vermelles, his brother officers were able to place a wreath on his grave.

X.

EMBRY AND HUMBERT, 1915-16.

After the Battle of Loos the Brigade returned to its former billeting area near Fruges.

Major-General J. Vaughan, C.B., D.S.O., assumed Command of the 3rd Cavalry Division. The Essex Yeomanry moved from Matringhem to Embry, and this was the permanent billeting area of the Regiment until the Somme Offensive in the summer of 1916.

Early in January, however, a dismounted Batt-talion was formed in the Brigade, as was carried out in every Brigade in Cavalry Corps. The dismounted Division thus formed in Cavalry Corps took over the trench system near Vermelles, known as the Hohenzollern Redoubt.

Bethune at that time was very little damaged by shell fire and it became quite the centre of society during the period in which the Cavalry took over this section of the line. The Officer's Club was excellently managed, and there was an excellent oyster shop in the Square.

During the period in which the dismounted Battalion was in the line, continual training and riding school was carried out at Embry. Schemes were frequently carried out by the remainder of the men left in billets; also there were classes and lectures, map-reading also taking a prominent part in the weekly routine.

It was at Embry that Brigadier-General C. Bulkeley Johnson, when meeting a man of the Essex Yeomanry riding along the road, and wishing to ascertain whether this man could use his map, said, handing him his map :—" Now then, my man, show me exactly on this map where we are." The Yeoman looked at the General in astonishment, and said with a smile : " That ain't no good to the likes of me, General."

The 10th Hussars were billeted at Humbert and St. Michel and Major-Gen. J. Vaughan, who had just taken over command of the Division, meeting the S.S.M. of Major Watkin Williams' Squadron asked where his Squadron was billeted. The Squadron-Sergeant-Major answered promptly, " at a place called Saint Michel, Sir," but the French people calls it " Sir Meeshel."

EMBRY AND HUMBERT, 1915–16.

The billets at Humbert and Saint Michel may well be described as the worst and most insanitary that the Regiment has occupied for any length of time during the ampaign. But looking back on the many billets which the Regiment has lived in, nearly two hundred since landing in France, much enjoyment was to be found in these valleys, and the long time spent there was a means of making many friends, with the result that the civilian inhabitants of the villages of Humbert, Saint Michel, Saint Denoux and Embry will always be remembered with a kindly feeling by the 10th Hussars and the Essex Yeomanry.

XI.

HOHENZOLLERN REDOUBT, 1916.

On January 3rd, 1916, the Dismounted Battalion, consisting of 3 companies, one from each of the 3 Regiments of the Brigade, entrained at Maresquel.

This Dismounted Battalion formed part of the Dismounted Brigade commanded by Brig.-Gen. Bulkeley Johnson, A.D.C., and this Brigade formed part of the Division commanded by Major-Gen. Sir P. Chetwode, C.B., D.S.O.

The Dismounted Division took over the Vermelles Sector of the line from the 7th Division and was composed of dismounted parties from all the Cavalry Regiments in the Cavalry Corps.

The Head Quarters of the Battalion was composed as follows :—

Lt.-Col. Lord Tweedmouth, R.H.G.
  C.M.G., M.V.O., D.S.O.
Major W. O. Gibbs,   X.R.H.

Capt. A. C. Turnor	R.H.G. Adjutant
Lt. S. C. Deed	X.R.H. Bombing Officer
Capt. V. A. P. Stokes	X.R.H. Sig. Officer
Lt.-Q.M. E. Sayer	E.Y.
Med.-Officer Major Cowie, D.S.O.	R.H.G.

The Dismounted Companies each consisted of 8 Officers and 300 other ranks.

The Battalion detrained at 5 p.m., at Fouquereuil, marched to Bethune and billeted at the Ecole de Jeunes Filles, and the following day, January 4th, the Battalion marched by Companies to billets at Labourse. On January 5th there was a considerable amount of aerial activity.

On January 9th the Battalion paraded at 7 a.m. and marched up to relieve the 1st Battalion in Sector D.2. The X.R.H. Company to Kaiserin Trench and Hogs Back; the R.H.G. Company on the left in Sticky and Mud Trenches; the E.Y. Company in support in Railway Reserve Trench. Much activity on the part of the enemy continued during the night with rifle grenades and trench mortars.

On January 10th the enemy bombarded the R.H.G.'s in Northampton Trench and did considerable damage. Rifle grenades were again used. Enemy mining was suspected in front of Gap 10, held by the X.R.H. On January 11th it was believed that the enemy's mine, above mentioned, was complete. The front line was thereupon withdrawn to Westface. Hogs Back was from that time only patrolled and bombers were posted in readiness.

On January 13th the battalion was relieved by the 7th Dismounted Battalion; the 8th Battalion going in to support, Hd. Qrs. moved to Lancashire Trench South. The X.R.H. Company to billets in Sailly-Labourse. The R.H.G. Company to cellars in Vermelles and Lancashire Trench South. The E.Y. Company to cellars in Vermelles.

On January 14th the Battalion went into reserve in billets at Sailly-Labourse, being relieved by the 9th Battalion 1st Brigade.

On January 17th the Head Quarters were relieved by :

Lt.-Col. H. F. Wickham, X.R.H.
Major the Marquess of
     Londonderry, M.V.O.   R.H.G.
Capt. G. E. Gosling   X.R.H. Adjutant
Lt. F. Meyer   E.Y. Sig. Officer.
Capt. C. E. Harford, M.C.   R.H.G. Quartermstr.
Capt. Clarke   R.A.M.C. Med. Ofcr.

On January 21st the Battalion relieved the 2nd Battalion, 1st Brigade, taking over the same sector, D.2. X.R.H. on the right, E.Y. on the left, R.H.G. in reserve. The relief was completed by 10.15 a.m. There was considerable rifle grenade and trench mortar activity during the day.

On January 25th the Sector on the right D.1. was much troubled by enemy bombers, and in consequence the reserve bombers of the Battalion were sent to help the 6th Battalion. Corpl. Clarke, X.R.H., and L./Cpl. Cook, E.Y., both did very good work.

At 8 p.m., January 25th, the 8th Battalion was relieved by the 7th Battalion. Battalion Head Quarters and the Essex Yeomanry Company went to Lancashire Trench North. The X.R.H. Company went into billets at Sailly-Labourse, and the R.H.G. Company went to the cellars in Vermelles.

On January 26th enemy shelling on D.1. Sector increased to such extent that the 8th Battalion were warned to be ready to move up in support. All telephone wires were cut, and at 6 p.m. the Battalion Head Quarters and the Essex Yeomanry Company moved to Lancashire Trench South to replace the North Somerset Yeomanry Company, 6th Battalion, which had moved into closer support of 1st Royal Dragoons Coy. and 3rd Dragoon Guards Coy.

At 6.30 p.m. the R.H.G. Coy. moved to Gordon Alley; one platoon X.R.H. went to Central Keep, X.R.H. Company, less 1 platoon, joined Battalion Head Quarters in Lancashire Trench South. Those positions were maintained throughout the night.

On January 27th the 8th Battalion was relieved by the 1st Brigade and returned to billets in Sailly-Labourse.

On January 31st the Battalion Head Quarters were relieved by :—

Lt.-Col. F. Whitmore	E.Y.
Major G. Gold	E.Y.
Capt. the Marquess of Northampton	R.H.G. Sig. Officer
Capt. Knowles Jackson	E.Y. Adjutant
Lt. W. H. Druce	X.R.H. Quartermaster

February 1st was spent in clearing up billets. Lt.-Col. H. F. Wickham was recalled to relieve Lt.-Col. F. Whitmore who went into hospital at Bethune.

On February 2nd the Battalion took over D.2 Sector from the 1st Battalion. At 6.15 p.m. the Germans exploded a mine under Sap 10 in the Hog's Back.

The crater was occupied at once by a special party of R.H.G. bombers and X.R.H. diggers at 8.15 p.m.

Instructions were received from Brigade Head Quarters that one of our mines was going to be exploded in the Geman Line near Pigstail Crater. At 10.35 p.m. the Mining Officer decided to fire one mine at 11 p.m. and orders were issued to clear our front line in front of Westface and Kaiserin Trench, also the Saps 9, 9 (c) (b).

The mine, however, was not fired at that hour owing to an attempt being made to rescue a patrol of the R.H.G.'s who had been buried alive in the first explosion. This resulted in 2 casualties: 1 killed, 1 wounded.

The mine was fired at 12.5 a.m., with disastrous result o our own trenches.

Part of the Westface and Kaiserin Trenches were destroyed, the Saps 9, 9 (a) and (b) also Hog's Back round 6.15 crater were entirely filled in, also a piece of Northampton trench, burying 7 Essex Yeomen, of whom 1 was killed. The bomb stores in these places were buried.

The Battalion bombers, under Lieut. S. C. Deed, were at once moved up to re-occupy the old positions, but the way was blocked with debris. They, however, occupied the old trench in rear of Pigstail. The Germans commenced a heavy bombing attack on the Kaiserin Trench. Lt. Deed ran out of bombs owing

to the stores being buried, and had to retire to Westface nearer Savile Row. 2 Barricades were built
at the end of the destroyed trench and occupied by
bombers and 2 Maxim Guns, under Capt. V. J. Greenwood, X.R.H. Before dawn the Germans withdrew
and Westface and Kaiserin Trenches were cleared,
and the lip of 6.15 crater re-occupied.

On February 3rd digging and clearing continued all
day ; during the night the R.E. Officer was killed and
3 other ranks wounded.

On February 4th the Essex Yeomanry Company
relieved the X.R.H. Company, who went into Railway
Reserve Trench with 2 platoons in support in Northampton Trench.

On February 6th the 8th Battalion was relieved
by the 7th Battalion, the X.R.H. Company remaining
in reserve in Railway Reserve Trench, Head Quarters
to Lancashire Trench, and on February 8th the
Battalion was relieved by the 9th Battalion, the 8th
going into billets at Sailly.

On February 9th Lt.-Col. Whitmore returned
from Hospital and relieved Lt.-Col. Wickham.

On February 11th the Battalion returned by train
to Maresquel, arriving at 8.15 p.m.

XII.

EMBRY AND HUMBERT, 1916.

The Cavalry Dismounted Division was relieved by the 12th Division, having been in the line for 6 weeks.

During the period that the Dismounted Battalion was away in the line, continual training was carried out both as Cavalry and in trench warfare. The Hotchkiss Automatic rifle was introduced into the Cavalry, and much time was devoted to instruction in this new arm for Cavalry.

Training in box respirators had by now also become part of the routine for the improvement of the efficiency of the regiments.

The Anniversary of the 13th May was celebrated by a parade Memorial Service being held by the Essex Yeomanry.

Captain Gibbs, Brigade Chaplain, officiated, and a very impressive service was held. All names of

Officers and other ranks who fell on that memorable day were read out, whilst the Regiment rested on arms reversed.

It was during the Spring of 1916 that the whole of the Cavalry went for a short period of instruction and training on an area near St. Riquier, a large tract of country having been hired for the purpose, and very extensive training in Cavalry tactics was carried out. It was at Embry also that a military and string band was formed in the Essex Yeomanry and admirably trained by R.Q.M.S. Joscelyne; it was only after the serious casualties suffered by the Regiment at Monchy in April, 1917, in which engagement many of the band were killed, that it became impossible to keep it going.

XIII.

SOMME, 1916.

On June 24th the Brigade left the billeting area which it had occupied since November, 1915, and after three night marches arrived at Bonnay. The last march from St. Ouen to Bonnay was in a veritable deluge of rain and a very dark night. As the Regiment passed through Amiens the rain came down in torrents. The bivouac ground was a swamp, three parts under water, and it was a matter of great difficulty to find sufficient ground not under water to admit the men and horses of the Brigade.

The great Somme Offensive, which commenced with the huge mine being blown up at La Boisselle, followed by the capture of Fricourt and Mametz by the 13th Corps, developed into some of the hardest fought battles of the whole war. The 8th Corps was held up at Serre, and for a time two Infantry Battalions were cut off. Montauban was captured on July 2nd and many prisoners taken.

There never was, however, any opportunity for the employment of Cavalry. Day after day the Cavalry were " standing to " from half-an-hour to four hours' notice. With the exception of a few days when the Division was withdrawn to the Abbeville area, the Brigade spent the whole of July in the Swamp at Bonnay. It was here that " Orsett Hall " was painted on the house occupied by Regimental Head Quarters of the Essex Yeomanry and " Bocking Place " on the house opposite. A Cavalryman was heard to remark on reading the above names and looking at the Swamp which was covered with half dead, badly formed poplar trees. " I suppose they call that " blinking Epping Forest."

On July 4th the Division marched west, through Amiens, to the Abbeville area, the Essex Yeomanry being billeted at Bellifontaine and the 10th Royal Hussars at Liercourt.

On July 9th the Division returned to Bonnay, the 6th Cavalry Brigade halting at Corbie for one night on July 8th.

The Brigade left Bonnay on August 1st and marched by stages to the Erin, Blangy, Auchy les Hesdin area. The weather was beautiful and there were many trout to be caught in the river. The Essex Yeomanry were billeted at Blangy.

SOMME, 1916.

On August 12th a Divisional dismounted party was formed consisting of 2 Officers and 60 other ranks from all the Regiments in the Division. The whole under the command of Lt.-Col. Whitmore, with Major the Honble. E. Wyndham, D.S.O., 1st Life Guards, as 2nd in Command, Lt. Nangle, Royal Horse Guards, as Adjutant, and Lieut. Dulson, 3rd Dragoon Guards, as Quarter-Master. The Divisional party assembled at Bouzincourt for duty with the 2nd reserve Corps for the purpose of laying an underground cable from the Usna redoubt, near Albert, to Ovillers-la-Boisselle. The work was for the most part carried out in the early hours of the morning to avoid detection by enemy observation balloons. In spite, however, of such precautions being taken, the work parties were heavily shelled on more than one occasion. Bouzincourt itself was likewise heavily shelled, as was the village of Aveluy, which was afterwards occupied by the same work party.

On the return of this Divisional party to their respective regiments, the Division moved back to the Somme Area. After 5 night marches the Brigade arrived and billeted at La Neuville on September 16th and Vecquemont on the 18th. Again no opportunity occurred for the employment of the 3rd Cavalry Division.

XIV.

MARESQUEL AND AUBIN ST. VAAST, 1916.

On September 22nd the Brigade marched to the Maresquel area in 4 days' marches, the Essex Yeomanry being billeted in the Aubin St. Vaast area, with their Head Quarters at Plumoison.

Much time was spent and a lot of trouble taken in improving billets and stables in this area, and the Regimental Head Quarters at Plumoison was established in what was once very little else but a ruin; but by careful repairs, washing throughout, and with a liberal supply of whitewash, duresco and paint, quite an imposing Head Quarters presented itself and very comfortable it was.

On November 21st the 8th Cavalry Brigade Pioneer Battalion was formed. This Battalion was made up of 8 Officers and 260 other ranks per Regiment, and was created for the purpose of doing duty with the 5th Army. The Battalion was commanded by Lt.-Col. P. Hardwick, D.S.O., Commanding 10th Royal Hussars. He was relieved by Major the

Marquess of Londonderry. M.V.O., Royal Horse Guards, who was in turn relieved by Major A. Buxton, D.S.O., Essex Yeomanry.

The Battalion did much work in Acheux Wood and near Beaumont Hamel. It was here that Lt.-Quartermaster E. Sayer, Essex Yeomanry, narrowly escaped his death by a shell bursting within very few feet of his horse.

On December 21st the Pioneer Battalion returned to billets, detraining at Maresquel at 7.15 a.m.

The country around Aubin St. Vaast and Lambus lent itself very well for Regimental and Brigade Schemes. The village of St. Josse, standing out by itself, became renowned for its passive resistance, being a constant objective for attack and capture by all and every formation from a troop to a Brigade. St. Andre-au-Bois likewise became well known from the fact of its being conspicuous for its absence, except on the map, and thereby causing everlasting anxiety to parties sent out for the purpose of instruction in map reading.

The ready wit, and compositive powers of Sergt. Bulling, Essex Yeomanry, soon turned the renown of the above places into account, and the accompanying verses, which he sung to the tune of " Little Grey Home in the West," soon became as popular a turn

77

MARESQUEL AND AUBIN ST. VAAST, 1916.

in Captain Jack Gibbs' evening concerts, as Pte. Dirkin's, 10th Royal Hussars, humorous representations of George Robey.

I.

When the golden sun sinks in the west,
And you think that your day's work is o'er,
A cyclist comes round, with an order he's found
That the Squadron will turn out at four.
It's bound to be pouring with rain,
And so dark that you can't see your hoss,
When you get on parade, the announcement is made
That the scheme is to capture' St. Josse.

II.

There are hay nets that have to go on,
There are wallets, with brush on the near,
Your neck chains as well, you must burnish like——well
And your mess tin strap point to the rear. ·
Two shackles and pegs you must take,
Your great coat be rolled up quite tight,
And I've told you before that we shan't win this war
If your surcingle buckles aren't bright.

III.

We start off to make our first bound,
It's a way that we've oft been before,
We get to Lambus, then our map readers cuss
'Cos they can't find St. Andre-au-Bois.
We pick up the " Tenth " and the " Blues,"
The rain it is still falling fast,
Then the General says " Damn " ! ! !
I shall stop where I am,
You can go back to Aubin St. Vaast.

XV.

MERLIMONT AND FRESSIN, 1916-17.

On December 22nd the Brigade moved into new
billets by the sea. The 10th Royal Hussars at Merlimont, Royal Horse Guards at Rang-du-Fliers, the
Essex Yeomanry at St. Josse. During the period
that the Brigade was in this area, Gap Schemes were
exercised in detail, and regimental drill was carried
out on the sands at Merlimont Plage. The weather,
part of the time, was cold in the extreme. The memorable occasion when Major-Gen. J. Vaughan, C.B.,
D.S.O., inspected the Essex Yeomanry on the sands
was, without a doubt, one of the coldest days during
the whole War, the sea itself being frozen all along the
shore.

On February 1st the Brigade moved into the
Fressin area, and on April 5th Lt.-Col. P. Hardwick,
D.S.O., was appointed Lt.-Col. of the 10th Royal
Hussars, having commanded the Regiment since
June 1st, 1916.

Major A. Buxton, D.S.O., describes the period spent at Fressin as the best time he has had during the War. His Squadron bagged during February and March 9 pigs, killing 6 with the rifle and 3 with the sword. The 3 with the sword were killed by Lt. G. Wear, L./Cpl. Rowell and Pte. Hill, all of " C " Squadron. Lt. Geoffrey Wear stood a good chance of losing his own life at the hands of the boar with which he was engaged before being able to finally destroy him; they finished together on the ground in a hand to hand fight, in an overgrown ditch.

It is safe to say that Major Buxton, with his Squadron, were able to bag more pigs than any other Squadron in the Cavalry Corps. It is equally true to say that all the sporting adventures of this Squadron, carried out under his able leadership, were designed to train his men in making the best use of resources and initiative in the presence of any eventuality, and the following two descriptions of such occasions will amply illustrate this novel and interesting method of training men to use both eye and brain quickly, and make decisions without hesitation, a qualification which cannot be too highly valued in the character of a Cavalry Soldier.

Major Buxton's Squadron was practising shooting at iron plates across a valley west of Wambercourt, the iron plates being placed in position at the foot of a steep bank. About 50 men were on parade. Sergt. Baynes and Corpl. Pennal were standing about 200 yards away on either flank to warn any civilians crossing behind the targets. The first Squad of ten rifles had already fired and the iron plates had just been re-erected into their places, when Sergeant Baynes commenced whistling quietly. Major Buxton, thinking that some civilians were passing, delayed putting the next squad into position. The whistling continued softly, and Sergeant Baynes pointed with his hand. At that moment over the top of the bank behind the targets came 5 pigs—an old sow and her 4 young, all more than half grown. They came straight towards the firing point.

Major Buxton signalled " lie down." Lieut. Weatherby gave " load," an unnecessary order, inasmuch as instinct had already charged magazines ! The pigs were now galloping down the bank, actually knocking down 2 targets on the way. The last pig was hit at once, and Major Buxton told Corpl. Smith, who was lying next to him, to finish him off ; this he did with his first shot. The rest of the pigs galloped towards the firing party. The biggest one was killed at once, shot through the heart.

The 3 survivors disappeared into a sunk lane, but came into sight again about 60 yards away ; another pig was instantly killed, the remaining two turned half right, and their lives were saved by the advent of a person appearing in the line of fire, and " cease fire " being ordered on that account.

The 3 wild pig thus obtained were a welcome addition to the Squadron larder, and the morning's exercise in fixed and moving targets was at the same time well justified.

Major Buxton describes the next event as the natural outcome of an order given by his Commanding Officer, which was to the effect that Squadrons were to practice " instant decisions." He adds that there was a Squadron standing order that one eye in all ranks must always be open for pig.

His narrative is as follows :—

" I was by the Wambercourt-Lebiez road on the Lebiez side of the dip where the road passes a narrow strip of wood running from the Bois de Fressin and the Bois de Lebiez.

Three troops were manœuvring on the high ground on the Lebiez side of the dip.

" I was going across from them to the Stortford troop, which was dismounted at the edge of the strip of wood, when Corporal Pennal galloped across from the high ground to me, and told me that he had just seen 5 pig cross along the crest on the Wambercourt side of the wood going parallel with it towards the Bois de Fressin. There was not a moment to spare, because they only had a mile to go before reaching the Bois de Fressin where they would be in safety. I shouted to Lieut. Chaplin to mount the Stortford troop under Lieut. Wear, and to gallop the troop down the strip towards the Bois de Fressin and by doing so to head the pig back on to the plateau between the strip and the Bois de Sart. I waved to the 3 troops to rally on me, and we followed the Stortford troop down the strip at a distance of about 300 yards. Someone viewed the pig in the open, the 3 troops crashed out into the open, a hundred yards short of the Bois de Fressin. On the top of the hill was Lieut. Chaplin disappearing over the sky line, holding up his cap, screaming his soul out. As he and the Stortford troop came out of the strip, they had headed the pig in the very nick of time and turned them into the plain.

" At the head of the 3 troops I galloped up to the top of the hill, the men extending as we went ; as we reached the top there were the pig wondering what to do in the middle of the plain. We drew swords and went straight for them, Packponies, Hotchkiss and all. Lieut. R. C. Weatherby came out with his Dunmow troop from the strip last, not quite knowing what was up but guessing the best, seeing the hunt, bearing right handed shot up the side of the strip and cut right in at the head of the chase.

" The pig divided as we got close to them, 2 turning for the Bois de Sart pursued by Lieut. Wear, Capt. J. O. Parker and 2 or 3 others. These 2 pigs just saved their lives in the wood. The remaining 3 bore back, pursued by the rest of us towards the strip, near the edge of which was a single strand of barbed wire, under which 2 of them slipped and escaped. The other continued and Lance-Corporal Rowell, galloping clear of his troop, struck him about 10 yards from the edge of the strip. All 3—man, horse and pig—rolled over together. Corporal Rowell was first up and finished the pig on foot with his sword. Nobody took any interest in the horse which got up about 10 minutes later unhurt.

" In the afternoon I took Monsieur le Maire to the scene of operations and settled the damage to wheat, including his own and everybody else's, at 5 francs and a ham."

The cold was intense during the whole period the Brigade was in this area, snow lying on the ground nearly the whole of the time. This severe weather continued well into April, as will always be remembered by those who took part in the Arras Offensive, when it became necessary to lie out in the snow with no protection whatsoever.

In fact, as the Brigade marched out on April 7th intermittent heavy snow storms continued throughout the day.

In addition to the training and Field Exercises which were carried out during the winter, 1916-17, a 3rd Cavalry Division tactical school of instruction was opened at Merlimont, with Major H. A. Tomkinson, D.S.O., 1st Royal Dragoons, as Commandant.

The instruction was made especially interesting and the result was not only very beneficial to the Cavalry as a whole, but most satisfactory to the two Regiments under review, as the following tables will show.

Four Officers from each regiment in the Division attended each course, and an examination was held at the termination of each period.

MERLIMONT AND FRESSIN, 1916–17.

RESULT OF EXAMINATION OF THE 3 COURSES OF INSTRUCTION.

MERLIMONT, 1916-17.

1ST COURSE, NOVEMBER, 1916.

SUBJECTS.			NAME.	REGIMENT.
Cavalry Tactics	..	1st	Lt. Earl of Airlie	.. X.R.H.
		2nd	Lt. R. Henderson	.. 1st R.D.
		3rd	Capt. V. Stokes	.. X.R.H.
Training as	..	1st {	Capt. R. G. Proby	.. E.Y.
Leaders	..		Lt. R. Henderson	.. 1st R.D.
		2nd	Lt. Earl of Airlie	.. X.R.H.
		3rd	Lt. R. A. Thomson	.. E.Y.
Training as	..	1st	Lt. E. Clarke	.. L.Y.
Instructors	..	2nd	Lt. T. Robson	.. 1st L.G.
		3rd	Lt. Earl of Airlie	.. X.R.H.
Horsemanship	..	1st	Lt. W. Murland	.. X.R.H.
and Veterinary	..	2nd	Lt. Earl of Airlie	.. X.R.H.
		3rd	Lt. R. A. Thomson	.. E.Y.

Result on total number of marks obtained per Regiment during this course was as follows :—

1st	10th Royal Hussars ..	..	..	2011 marks
2nd	Essex Yeomanry ..	..	..	1958 marks
3rd	1st Royal Dragoons ..	..	..	1919 marks

2ND COURSE, DECEMBER, 1916.

SUBJECTS.			NAME.	REGIMENT.
Cavalry Tactics	..	1st	Lt. W. P. Browne	.. 1st R.D.
		2nd	Lt. H. M. P. Hewett	.. 1st R.D.
		3rd	Lt. Viscount Ednam	.. X.R.H.

MERLIMONT AND FRESSIN, 1916–17.

SUBJECTS.			NAME.	REGIMENT.
Training as	..	1st	Capt. Lord Somers	.. 1st L.G.
Leaders	..	2nd	Lt. H. M. P. Hewett	.. 1st R.D.
		3rd	Lt. J. C. Murray	.. 1st L.G.
Training as	..	1st	Lt. Viscount Ednam	.. X.R.H.
Instructors		2nd {	Lt. T. O'Callaghan	.. 1st R.D.
			Lt. C. H. Newton	.. 3rd D.G.
		3rd	Lt. W. P. Browne	.. 1st R.D.
Horsemanship	..	1st	Lt. H. M. P. Hewett	.. 1st R.D.
and Veterinary	..	2nd	Lt. Viscount Ednam	.. X.R.H.
		3rd	Capt. J. O. Parker	.. E.Y.

Result on total number of marks obtained per Regiment during this course was as follows :—

1st	10th Royal Hussars	..	..	.. 2298	marks
2nd	Essex Yeomanry	..	..	.. 2236	marks
3rd	1st Royal Dragoons	..	..	.. 2159	marks

3RD COURSE, FEBRUARY, 1917.

SUBJECTS.			NAME.	REGIMENT.
Cavalry Tactics	..	1st	Lt. R. B. Helme	.. 1st R.D.
		2nd	Lt. F. R. Gaskell	.. X.R.H.
		3rd	Lt. J. C. Chaplin	.. E.Y.
Training as	..	1st	Lt. M. W. A. P. Graham	.. 2nd L.G.
Leaders	..	2nd	Lt. K. G. Jenkins	.. N.S.Y.
		3rd	Lt. R. B. Helme	.. 1st R.D.
Training as	..	1st	Lt. J. K. Swire	.. E.Y.
Instructors	..	2nd	Lt. M. W. A. P. Graham	.. 2nd L.G.
	..	3rd	Lt. K. G. Jenkins	.. N.S.Y.
Horsemanship	..	1st	Lt. M. W. A. P. Graham	.. 2nd L.G.
and Veterinary	..	2nd	Lt. J. K. Swire	.. E.Y.
		3rd	Lt. O. Mowatt	.. X.R.H.

MERLIMONT AND FRESSIN, 1916—17.

Result on total number of marks obtained per Regiment during this course was as follows :—

1st	1st Royal Dragoons	..	..	..	2197 marks
2nd	10th Royal Hussars	..	..	..	2152 marks
3rd	North Somerset Yeomanry		..	..	2126 marks

NOTE.—In this course 2 of the Officers of the E.Y. went to hospital sick, consequently half the total number of marks only could be recorded to them.

It is only fair to say that the half which was recorded, 1150 marks, far exceeded the half total of any other Regiment in the course.

XVI.

THE BATTLE OF MONCHY LE PREUX, 1917.

On April 7th the Brigade marched from the Fressin area to Frévent, where they bivouacked at the East end of the town.

On April 8th the march was continued to Gouy en Artois, where the 3rd Cavalry Division was concentrated.

At 11 a.m., on April 9th, the Division moved out at a moment's notice towards Arras, and halted at the Western entrance to the Town on the racecourse and there watered and fed. Early in the afternoon orders were received by the 8th Cavalry Brigade to move forward. The Brigade was preceded by " B " Squadron, 10th Royal Hussars, under Capt. R. Gordon Canning, and " C " Squadron, Essex Yeomanry, under Major A. Buxton, D.S.O. These two Squadrons marched to the N.W. of Tilloy les

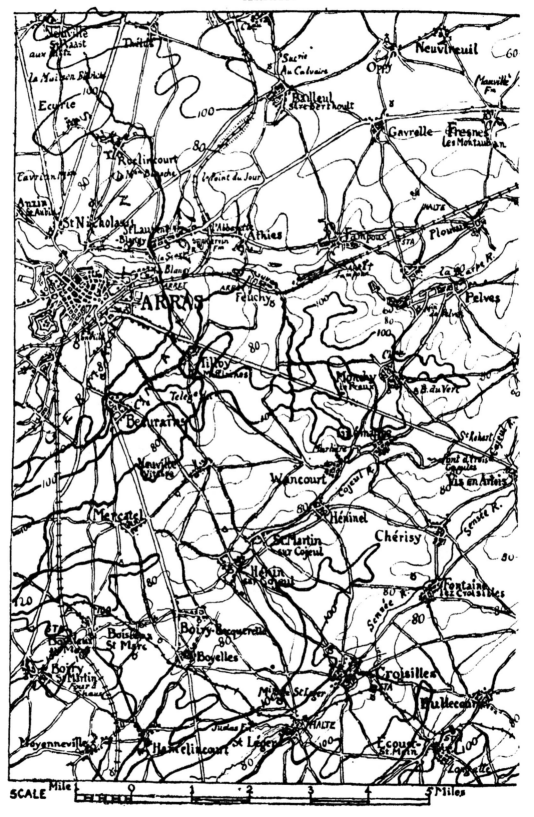

SCALE

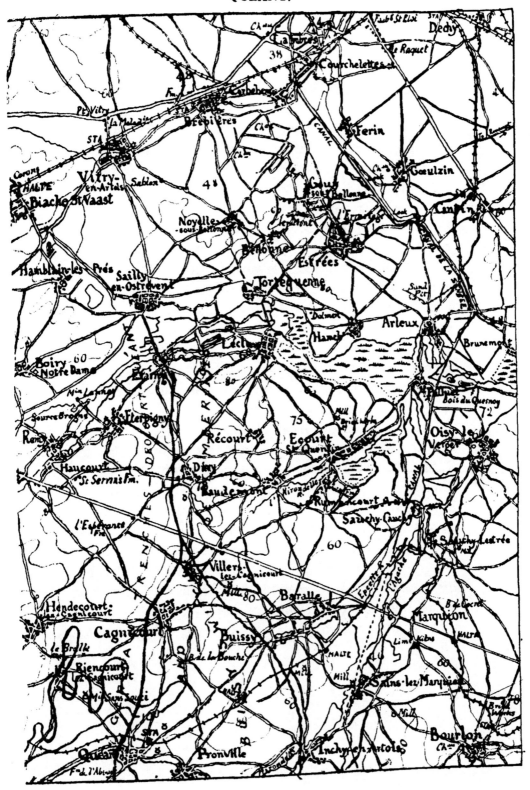

Mofflaines. The remainder of the Brigade halted at the Eastern outskirts of Arras on the cavalry track leading parallel to and N. of the Arras-Cambrai road.

Orange Hill was still occupied by the Germans, and further reconnaisance on the part of the leading Squadrons of the Brigade was rendered impossible on this account.

The Brigade moved forward to the N.W. of Tilloy and after watering in the river south of Athies, bivouacked for the night N. of Tilloy. There were frequent snowstorms during the evening and night.

At 1.30 a.m. on the night of 9-10th April the Brigade received orders to return to the racecourse, Arras, before light. Water, forage and rations were able to be obtained at this place.

At 11 a.m., on April 10th, the Brigade moved forward from the racecourse to a position N. of Tilloy les Mofflaines, Captain Gordon Cannings' Squadron, 10th Royal Hussars and Major Buxton's Squadron, Essex Yeomanry, reconnoitring towards Pelves on the south of the river Scarpe. Patrols sent out by these Squadrons reported that the slopes and spurs North of Monchy le Preux were still held by the enemy, who brought their Machine Guns into action against these patrols, Captain Gordon Canning's patrol suffering many casualties, whilst Lieut.

G. Wear, of the Essex Yeomanry, became cut off by the enemy and had to rejoin his unit under cover of the darkness. Lieut. R. C. Weatherby, Essex Yeomanry, was also sent out with a patrol and reports were all similar, and but for the fact of a very severe and blinding snowstorm which covered the retirement of those patrols, the casualties would have been greater. Major A. Buxton, D.S.O., was wounded by shell during the afternoon, Lieut. J. C. Chaplin taking command of his squadron.

The night of April 1)th was passed at Feuchy Chapel and a continuous and heavy shelling with high explosive caused many casualties amongst men and horses, the 10th Royal Hussars alone losing about 10 men and 50 horses. The Royal Horse Guards and the Essex Yeomanry were more fortunate. The Brigade " stood to " at 5.30 a.m. on the morning of April 11th.

At 8 a.m. Lieut.-Colonel Whitmore, D.S.O., commanding Essex Yeomanry, received orders " to advance." His Regiment would be followed immediately by the 10th Royal Hussars and the Royal Horse Guards would act in reserve.

The Brigade was required to carry out the role already prepared for the purpose of seizing and holding the high ground, villages and woods on the eastern spurs facing the river Scarpe about 4,000 yards E. and N.E. of Monchy.

These objectives were to be seized in the event of information being received (1) that the village of Monchy was in the hands of our Infantry, and (2) that the sunk road leading N.E. from Monchy to Pelves was in our occupation.

Information as to No. 1, and that the infantry were advancing in an easterly direction, had already been received by Brigadier-General C. Bulkeley Johnson, A.D.C., Commanding 8th Cavalry Brigade.

Lieut.-Colonel Whitmore asked for half an hour in which to confer with Brigadier-General Harman, D.S.O., Commanding the 6th Cavalry Brigade, Lieut.-Colonel Burt, Commanding 3rd Dragoon Guards, whose Regiment would be acting on the right and with Lieut.-Colonel Hardwick, D.S.O., [Commanding 10th Royal Hussars, whose Regiment would be acting on the left.

At 8.30 a.m. an advanced Squadron of the Essex Yeomanry, followed by an advanced Squadron of the 10th Royal Hussars, under the command of Lieut. Chaplin and Capt. Gordon Canning respectively, each with one section of Machine Guns, advanced over the Southern end of Orange Hill, meeting with severe barrage between that point and the enclosures on the N.W. of Monchy and at the same time meeting with Machine Gun fire, which apparently came from the North of the Scarpe canal. On this account both leading Squadrons changed their direction in a S. Easterly course and entered Monchy le Preux at the N. Western entrance. At this moment the remainder of the two leading Regiments of the Brigade (10th Royal Hussars and Essex Yeomanry) were crossing the Southern portion of Orange Hill, where they were met with a heavy artillery barrage and suffered some casualties, including Major E. Hill and 2/Lieut. S. White, both of the Essex Yeomanry.

At the N. Western entrance of the village only shell fire was met with, but many casualties occurred on account of the buildings and the hard roads offering greater resistance to the high explosive shell. The two advanced Squadrons then proceeded as follows :—Essex Yeomanry via central road leading to the Square and thence by the sunken road leading N.E. towards Pelves, the 10th Royal Hussars following the Essex Yeomanry to the centre of Monchy, thence turning due N. until they reached the outskirts of the village. On emerging from the village, both these Squadrons were held up by Machine Gun fire.

By this time the remainder of the two Regiments were already in the village and the whole force of the

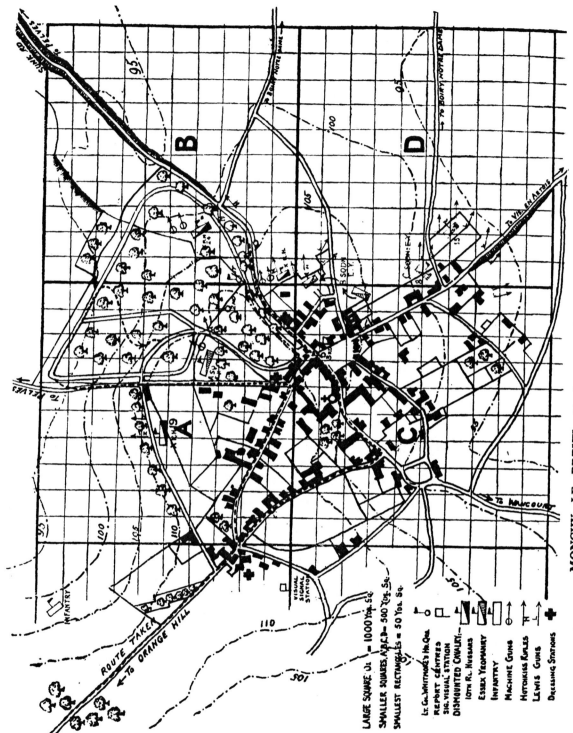

MONCHY LE PREUX.—Showing route taken by the 10th Royal Hussars and Essex Yeomanry on entering, also the dispositions made for the defence of the village.

German Artillery seemed to be concentrated upon it, causing many casualties to Officers, men and horses.

Machine Guns and Hotchkiss Automatic Rifles were brought up at once from both Regiments, and distributed in positions surrounding the South-East, East and North of the village, covering all entrances and slopes, and making two strong points, one in the Chateau garden and one at the North-Eastern exit of the village. At this time Colonel Hardwick, D.S.O., commanding 10th Royal Hussars, with one Squadron 10th Royal Hussars, endeavoured to make his way round the northern flank, but again met with severe Machine Gun fire on the Northern outskirts of the village, and was forced to turn in a South-Easterly direction through the wood. While doing so he was wounded. Capt. Greenwood, Adjutant, 10th Royal Hussars, was wounded immediately afterwards.

It was by now quite apparent that our Infantry, who had attacked the stronghold with such conspicuous gallantry and determination, were not holding the village, although the scattered remnants of the 111th and 112th Infantry Brigades were occupying isolated places in and W. of the chateau. These were collected, and they, together with the 10th Royal Hussars and Essex Yeomanry, the whole being under the command of Lieut.-Colonel Whitmore, D.S.O., consolidated the positions gained on the Northern and Eastern outskirts of Monchy.

The defence of Monchy was now maintained by solid determination on the part of the survivors of the 10th Royal Hussars, the Essex Yeomanry, Machine Gun Squadrons and Infantry. The casualties had already reduced the garrison to considerably less than half its original strength, and communication with the Brigade Headquarters was very difficult, owing to the severity of the barrage which isolated the town of Monchy from the reserves. At 11.10 a.m. Colonel Whitmore sent his 4th message which stated as follows :—" Have sent several messages conveying all information of E.Y. and X.R.H. What remains of those regiments are holding on to North-East, East and Southern exits of the village. Require both M.G.'s and Ammunition. Am afraid we have had many casualties. Counter attack expected. Colonel Hardwick and several officers wounded. Reinforcements required as reserve. Majority horses casualties."

This message was followed by another at 11.45 a.m. as follows :—" We are badly in need of reinforcements and Machine Guns, artillery barrage from 0.2. a. 1.9. to 0.2. central would be useful."

THE BATTLE OF MONCHY LE PREUX, 1917.

Lieut. R. Holland, Essex Yeomanry, did excellent service in the matter of getting through with information to the reserves, with the result that soon after 1 p.m. a message came through, saying that a Squadron Royal Horse Guards was coming up to support the Essex Yeomanry.

In the meantime, Lieut. the Hon. George Dawson-Damer, 10th Royal Hussars, had been killed and Lieut. Osmond Mowatt, mortally wounded. Information also came in that Lieut. The Earl of Airlie, Lieut. William Murland, Lieut. the Hon. Charles Winn and Lieut. Dermot Gough, all of the 10th Royal Hussars, had been wounded. The dressing stations were full, and overflowing, and no praise can be too great for the two Medical Officers, Captain Stork and Captain Wood, who attended to the ever-increasing number of cases which were being brought in.

Lieut. Jack Lingeman, the Intelligence Officer to the Essex Yeomanry, was dreadfully wounded whilst trying to get to the Headquarters with information. This brilliant young officer died in hospital. Further casualties in Officers of the Essex Yeomanry reduced the fighting strength to a minimum. Lieuts. W. Ritchie, Geoffrey Wear and R. C. Weatherby were all severely wounded, and Lieut. A. Winter Rose, although hit in the arm, remained at duty.

H2

Many senior non-commissioned officers in both Regiments had already been either killed or wounded. Squadron-Sergeant-Major Langdon, 10th Royal Hussars, Squadron-Sergeant-Major Howard, D.C.M., Essex Yeomanry, Sergt. Harding, 10th Royal Hussars, Sergt. May, Essex Yeomanry and Sergt. Grant, Essex Yeomanry, were killed, and S.S.M. Rawson, Sergt. Bradley, Sergt. Simkins, Sergt. Goodwin, Sergt. Harwood and Sergt. Robinson, all 10th Royal Hussars, were wounded. Also Regimental-Sergt.-Major C. Farrell, Squadron-Sergt.-Major McKellar, Squadron-Sergt.-Major Tyler, Sergt.-Trumpeter Osborne, Sergt. Siddons, Sergt. Ridgewell, Sergt. Hodge, and Sergt. Bugg, all Essex Yeomanry, were wounded.

At about noon enemy shell and machine gun fire increased to such an extent that it appeared to indicate a probable counter attack, and many of our machine guns and automatic rifles were put out of action. The employment of abandoned Lewis Guns, two of which were found, became necessary.

Great difficulty was experienced in removing the led horses when it had become apparent that a further advance was impossible. This difficulty was due in the first place to casualties already caused which blocked the roads, and secondly, to the fact that so large a number of horses of so many units

The Arras -Cambrai Road, looking West.

were seeking the same shelter outside the village, thus attracting the fire of the enemy's artillery.

On one occasion the enemy massed in the small copses, 1000 yards N.E. of the village. communication was difficult and artillery support hard to obtain, but no serious attempt at counter attack followed.

Throughout the day shelling was heavy, which rendered the work of consolidating the position difficult. This difficulty was further accentuated by the heavy state of the ground and by the fact that a large number of the tool packs had been destroyed.

Men of the 111th and 112th Infantry Brigades were detailed for the purpose of conveying the wounded to the two dressing stations which had been established, one at the Chateau by the Medical Officer of the 10th Royal Hussars, Capt. Wood, and the other at the N.W. exit of the village by the Medical Officer of the Essex Yeomanry, Captain Stork. Most of the Officers of both the 10th Royal Hussars and the Essex Yeomanry had by now been wounded, and information had been received to the effect that Brigadier-General C. Bulkeley Johnson, A.D.C., Commanding 8th Cavalry Brigade, had been killed.

Communication had been established with the 3rd Dragoon Guards on the right early in the day, but the left flank remained somewhat exposed, and it was only by the employment of men of the 111th Infantry Brigade that the gap on the left of our line was closed, and communication with the 63rd Brigade established. Lord Tweedmouth, now commanding the Brigade, sent Major the Earl of Pembroke's Squadron of Royal Horse Guards to support the defence, but this Squadron was not able to get into Monchy, Captain H. H. Wilson, D.S.O., being killed, Lieut. J. L. P. Back and 2nd Lieut. R. W. Wilson were both wounded, also many men and horses of this Squadron being killed or wounded. Captain Lord Gerard, Royal Horse Guards, was wounded in no fewer than 14 places, having one arm and one leg broken.

By 5 p.m. the village was in a fair state of defence, but there were no local reserves or supports available. Casualties continued throughout the evening both to Officers and other ranks, including Major Gold, Essex Yeomanry, Capt. Gosling, 10th Royal Hussars and Capt. Gilbey, Essex Yeomanry.

The greatest difficulty was experienced throughout the day in communicating with the Brigade, by any other means than by dispatch riders, who did admirable service throughout. The signalling equipment of both regiments was destroyed.

There were constant visits over the lines from enemy aeroplanes during the day, which were left to their own devices unmolested, except by ourselves. Enemy aeroplanes swooped down and shot at the led horses with their machine guns.

At dusk patrols were sent out from the two regiments, which established the fact that the enemy were digging themselves in about 300 yards from the North-Eastern outskirts of the village, and in sectional trenches on the forward crest of Hill 100, about 800 yards due East from the village.

At about midnight the 37th Infantry Brigade took over most of the defences of Monchy, but the remainder could not be relieved until the following day, owing to the insufficiency of troops. Lieut.-Colonel Whitmore, D.S.O., handed over the defences of Monchy to Lieut.-Colonel Dawson, D.S.O., commanding West Kent Regiment, about midnight, April 11th-12th, leaving Captain Palmes, 10th Royal Hussars, in charge of those detachments of the 8th Cavalry Brigade who were unable to be relieved.

The Essex Yeomanry, or indeed the 8th Cavalry Brigade, have every reason to be proud of Lance-Corporal Harold Mugford, who received the Victoria Cross for his gallant behaviour in action at Monchy. Although both his legs were broken, he remained with his Machine Gun in action, refusing to go to the dressing station.

Lance-Corpl. Harold Mugford joined the Yeomanry some years before the outbreak of War, and joined the Machine Gun Section. When the Machine Gun Corps was established, all those who were in the Regimental Machine Gun Section became part of the new Machine Gun units, and so Lance-Corporal Mugford became attached to the 8th Machine Gun Squadron.

It is impossible to exaggerate the splendid work done by the men of the Royal Horse Guards, the 10th Royal Hussars and Essex Yeomanry, who formed part of this Machine Gun Squadron. Many lost their lives and many were wounded in this gallant defence of Monchy le Preux. Their contribution to the tradition of their old Regiments will always be remembered.

On April 12th, after the main portion of the 8th Cavalry Brigade had been relieved, Captain Palmes, 10th Royal Hussars, with the detachments of the 10th Hussars, and Essex Yeomanry which had been left behind, held the Sector from the Eastern Monchy-Pelves road exclusive to the Western Monchy-Pelves road exclusive. The line and village were constantly shelled and hostile reinforcements were continually observed, but no further attacks were delivered.

In the evening, at about 5.30, Lieut.-Colonel Dawson, D.S.O., Commanding the West Kents, in-

Monchy le Preux.

The Monchy—Pelves Road, looking towards Ruins of Monchy.
The tree by the side of the road is about the position of Lt.-Colonel Whitmore's
first Headquarters during the battle.

formed Captain Palmes that our Infantry were about to make an attack on the enemy. This attack was a success, and the line was much improved on the North of Monchy. This enabled Captain Palmes to withdraw his force, which marched back to Arras, and thence by bus to Gouy-en-Artois, where the remainder of the Brigade had already assembled. The comparative comfort of these billets, which, in reality, were very bad indeed, and crowded to the extreme, gave much needed rest to what remained of the 8th Cavalry Brigade. The extreme cold, and the bivouac in the snow, during those memorable days and nights in the second week in April, will always remain fixed in the memories of all those who took part in the event.

The difficulties in obtaining water for both the men and horses added greatly to the strain and privations of all concerned. The garrison in Monchy had to collect snow and melt it in order to make tea, and it was a common sight to see the horses licking the snow off each others' backs in order to quench their thirst.

By the time the 8th Cavalry Brigade were withdrawn from Monchy-le-Preux, there was very little of the place left standing, although on entering it on the morning of April 11th, it was practically intact. The village stood on a hill and was a landmark for all the country around. It had the appearance of a wealthy village, which no doubt would be due to the fact of its close proximity to Arras.

By noon on that eventful day a continual storm of shells was pounded in with such severity that it had the appearance, to those who were outside, of a veritable furnace, and it was a wonder to them that it could be possible for any one to be alive in this heap of ruins.

The main street of Monchy was indeed a terrible sight, and the horrors are not being exaggerated when it is described as being littered with dead men and horses. In one place the horses were lying so thick that it was necessary to climb over them in order to pass along the street. The wounded horses were in a dreadful condition, and Lieut. J. Swire, of the Essex Yeomanry, was detailed to the horrible, but necessary, duty of destroying them.

After the Battle of Monchy, the 3rd Cavalry Division remained at Gouy-en-Artois for two or three days. The 8th Cavalry Brigade had been reduced to less than half the strength of which they had marched from that place only a few days before. Many valuable lives had been lost during the battle, including that of their Leader, Brigadier-General C.

Bulkeley Johnson, A.D.C. No General has ever
commanded the perfect admiration of all his command more than did this gallant Leader. He was
as determined as he was brave, and his magnificent
presence was a credit to the British Army.

His body was brought back to the village of
Gouy-en-Artois, and buried in the British Cemetery,
as was also at the same time the body of Lieut. the
Hon. G. S. Dawson-Damer, 10th Royal Hussars.
The Trumpeters of the 10th Royal Hussars sounded
the last post. With his death so ended a chapter
of the 8th Cavalry Brigade. Captain E. J. Hardy,
Scots Greys, his Brigade-Major, was a character
in himself, as was his Staff-Captain, Major Freddy
Stapleton Bretherton, whose perfectly harmonious,
well fitting, and spotless appearance was only to be
exceeded by his courtly good nature.

It is safe to say that the Brigade Staff of the old
8th Cavalry Brigade will never be forgotten, and the
memory of General Bulkeley Johnson will always be
cherished.

The casualties suffered by the 10th (P.W.O.) Royal
Hussars during the engagement were as follows :—

	KILLED.	WOUNDED.	MISSING.	TOTAL.
Officers	2	7		9
Other Ranks	25	150	5	180

THE BATTLE OF MONCHY LE PREUX, 1917.

Names of Officers and other ranks killed and wounded are as follows :—

DIED OF WOUNDS.

2/Lt. Hon. George Seymour Dawson-Damer.
Lt. Osmond Mowatt.

WOUNDED.

Lt.-Col. Philip Hardwick, D.S.O.
Capt. and Adjt. Victor John Greenwood, M.C.
Capt. George Edward Gosling.
Lieut. David Lyulph Gore Wolseley Ogilvy, Earl of Airlie, M.C.
Lieut. William Sydney Murland.
Lieut. Hon. Charles John Frederick Winn.
Lieut. Dermot Humphrey Gough.

KILLED.

4358	S.S.M.	Langdon	4490	Sgt.	Harding
5542	Cpl.	S. S. Norman	4940	Cpl.	Knight
1935	Cpl.	Marchant	243	L./Cpl.	Smith
7310	L./Cpl.	Mayes	25466	S.S.	Courtman
5342	Pte.	Green	14545	Pte.	Titchener
11087	L./Cpl.	Sanderson	19786	L./Cpl.	Fairbairn
12300	Pte.	Grey	28768	Pte.	Holliday
11559	Pte.	Twiddy	12220	Pte.	Chase
4544	Pte.	Jackson	3511	Pte.	Jarvis
19617	Pte.	Long	25929	Pte.	Parry
5596	Pte.	Salmon	1417	Pte.	Waterhouse
11866	Pte.	Willis			

DIED OF WOUNDS.

603	Sgt.	Bradley	591	Sgt.	Simpkins

MISSING, BELIEVED KILLED.

28999	Pte.	Sutton	28522	S.S.	Phillipson

THE BATTLE OF MONCHY LE PREUX, 1917.

WOUNDED.

4004	S.S.M.	Rawson
4821	Sgt.	Goodwin
3183	Sgt.	Harwood
7953	Cpl.	Hannell
8533	Cpl.	White
15161	L./Cpl.	Woods
20628	S.S.	Tregay
3635	Pte.	Burgess
28993	Pte.	Dunn
31203	Pte.	Deaves
7706	Pte.	Frith
1728	Pte.	Gaffney
10844	Pte.	Grainger
748	Pte.	Hammond
2227	Pte.	Ibbotson
840	Pte.	Long
6285	Pte.	Richards
6500	Pte.	Ray
6721	Pte.	Vaughan
19251	Pte.	Grocutt
7253	Pte.	Bradbury
1958	Pte.	Preston
2420	Pte.	Simpson
2735	Pte.	Johnson
30303	Pte.	Wilkinson
258	Sgt.	Roys
262	L./Cpl.	Breadmore
421	L./Cpl.	Norton
1726	S.S.	Coyle
20188	Pte.	Cattle
10557	Pte.	Cooney
31313	Pte.	Foster
21881	Pte.	Gent
4272	S.S.F.	Manser
4531	Sgt.	Robinson
2560	Cpl.	Fowler
961	Cpl.	Taylor
204	L./Cpl.	Moores
6434	L./Cpl.	Barrett
31397	S.S.	Coleman
5570	Pte.	Crombie
15282	Pte.	Dowson
4942	Pte.	Dillon
15250	Pte.	Fulton
12960	Pte.	Garrold
15227	Pte.	Holmes
20007	Pte.	Hodgson
28604	Pte.	Johnson
679	Pte.	Marshall
19256	Pte.	Shelton
14486	Pte.	Roache
1428	Pte.	Glencross
5418	Pte.	Wakefield
19748	Pte.	Arrowsmith
879	Pte.	Reilly
8498	Pte.	Wilkins
17792	Pte.	Lakin
983	Sgt.	Oliver
5540	Sgt.	Davies
17130	L /Cpl.	Tomkinson
6491	Tptr.	Green
8184	Pte.	Bird
25376	Pte	Clay
25221	Pte.	Fallon
1987	Pte.	Gauton
40	Pte.	Gladwell

THE BATTLE OF MONCHY LE PREUX, 1917.

28493	Pte.	Mills	11881	Pte.	Montgomery
4542	Pte.	North	2626	Pte.	Pallister
6204	Pte.	Rowson	6846	Pte.	Smith
25555	Pte.	Smith	12414	Pte.	Swainston
31297	Pte.	Stansfield	5603	Pte.	Thomas
2312	Pte.	Wraye	3996	Pte.	Wraye
17616	Pte.	Barras	15276	Pte.	Garfat
15230	Pte.	Gallagher	4945	Cpl.	Webb
11655	Pte.	Dawson	6655	Pte.	Moriarty
5487	Sgt.	Bullen	391	Cpl.	Parfrement
25542	L./Cpl.	English	14476	Pte.	Andrews
28892	Pte.	Ashton	28880	Pte.	Brown
4993	Pte.	Bush	28899	Pte.	Clements
12783	Pte.	Comber	7118	Pte.	Crumbie
544	Pte	Dine	28986	Pte.	Dixon
31238	Pte.	Elders	22086	Pte.	Ennion
25780	Pte.	Everitt	12136	Pte.	Franks
25198	Pte.	Garrod	6558	Pte.	Green
28456	Pte.	Hallam	7457	Pte.	Hart
31399	Pte.	Harwood	19635	Pte.	Hemblys
12341	Pte.	Hocking	948	Pte.	McCormac
31248	Pte.	Parkin	464	L./Cpl.	Redgrave
4695	Pte.	Sabin	1646	Pte.	Scott
1427	Pte.	Skipper	4623	Pte.	Smith
4755	Pte.	Smith	8193	Pte.	Smith
25364	Pte.	Weedon	19616	L./Cpl.	Welch
7102	Pte.	Whitbread	31188	Pte.	Willey
4997	Pte.	Williams	20920	Pte.	Woodward
31192	Pte.	Rowley	9925	Pte.	Stockwell
10828	Pte.	Turner	947	Pte.	Whitehead
19752	Pte.	Warfield	7750	Pte.	Barlow
7120	Pte.	Grundy	5592	Sgt.	Alderson
6687	Cpl.	Pearson			

THE BATTLE OF MONCHY LE PREUX, 1917.

WOUNDED AT DUTY.

2823	L./Cpl.	Allison	28641	L./Cpl.	King
15182	Pte.	Ayres	2924	Pte.	Malston
2879	Pte.	Wigham	31148	Pte.	Cartwright
5905	L./Cpl.	Baxter	17550	Pte.	Hume
128	Sgt.	Futcher	5016	L./Cpl.	Wigley
1954	Pte.	Arscott	6459	Pte.	Dorward
12159	Pte.	Dunn	12946	Pte.	Cherry
6788	L./Cpl.	Scarisbrick	3609	Pte.	Knight
1777	L./Cpl.	Mathieson	1489	Pte.	Day
12825	Pte.	Flack	4128	L./Cpl.	Rogers
144	Pte.	Purdon			

WOUNDED AND MISSING.

7729	L./Cpl.	Larkin	28901	Pte.	Hansome
31082	Pte.	Waddington			

WOUNDED—SHELL SHOCK.

25304	Pte.	Furniss	31034	Pte.	Robertson

The casualties suffered by the Essex Yeomanry during the engagement were as follows :—

	KILLED.	WOUNDED.	MISSING.	TOTAL.
Officers	1	12	—	13
Other Ranks ..	18	94	10	122

Names of Officers and Other Ranks killed and wounded are as follows :—

DIED OF WOUNDS.

2/Lieut. Jack F. Lingeman.

THE BATTLE OF MONCHY LE PREUX, 1917.

WOUNDED.

Lt.-Colonel Francis H. D. C. Whitmore, D.S.O.
Major Anthony Buxton, D.S.O.
Major Guy Gold
Major Eustace Hill
Capt. Charles Newman Gilbey
Lieut. John Kidston Swire
2/Lieut. William Richie
2/Lieut. Algernon Winter Rose
2/Lieut. Geoffrey Wear
2/Lieut. R. C. Weatherby
2/Lieut. Stanley White

KILLED.

80247	Sgt.	Grant, R. S.	80007	S.S.M.	Howard, W. C.
80403	Cpl.	Bareham, W. G.	80632	Pte.	Bright, H.
80567	Pte.	Digby, H.	81072	Pte.	Bunting, F. E.
80708	Pte.	Smith, J.	80524	Pte.	Rollinson, E. E.
81173	Pte.	Smith, F.	80652	Pte.	Gosling, C. F.
80963	Pte.	Wright, T. A.	80600	Pte.	Guiver, S. V.
80630	Pte.	Young, E.	80286	Pte.	Thomson, S. T.
81074	Pte.	Cracknell, H. E.	80167	Pte.	Hobrough, F. C.
80431	Pte.	Charlesworth, T. E.	80415	Pte.	Holland, E. A.

WOUNDED.

3217	R.S.M.	Farrell, C.	81280	Cpl.	Chappell, W.
80015	Sgt.-Tr.	Osborne, G.	80185	L./Cpl.	Warren, F. E.
80508	Pte.	Stone, B. J.	80951	L./Cpl.	Bennett, H. R.
80682	L./Cpl.	Packard, C. D.	81136	Pte.	Benson, G. E. S.
80123	Pte.	Thorn, H.	81221	L./Cpl.	Brown, A. J.
80327	Cpl.	Midgley, C. G. H.	80614	L./Cpl.	Woods, H. S.
81141	Pte.	Baker, F.	80951	Pte.	Andrews, G.
80536	L./Cpl.	Waller, H.	80618	Pte.	Carter, W. C.
80382	Cpl.	Brunwin, F.	80747	Pte.	Davis, G.

THE BATTLE OF MONCHY LE PREUX, 1917.

80473	Pte.	Burch, A. G.
80367	Pte.	Cardy, W. S.
80659	Pte.	Chopping, J. H.
81176	Pte.	Waspe, B. S.
80116	Sgt.	Siddons, G.
80693	S./S.	Deacon, N. C.
80674	Pte.	Appleby, W.
80696	Pte.	Partridge, F.
80047	S.S.M.	McKellar, W. W.
80321	Cpl.	Gladwell, E.
80895	Pte.	Etherdon, G.
80944	Pte.	Hume, E. W.
80613	Pte.	Steward, C.
80172	Sgt.	Ridgewell, W.
80329	Sgt.	Smith A. E.
80711	Cpl.	Payne, G. W.
80058	S.S.Cpl.	Woodford, W. F.
80271	L./Cpl.	Rowell, A. C.
80087	L./Cpl.	Green, P. J.
80100	Pte.	Adams, G. J.
81025	Pte.	Augur, A.
80531	Pte.	Bradford, W.
80273	Pte.	Britton, J. J.
80054	Pte.	Caton, O. J.
81193	Pte.	Decks, H. D.
81164	Pte.	Dellow, M. G.
80666	Pte.	Millard, S.
80959	Pte.	Page, F. J. C.
80426	Pte.	Rogers, T.
80299	Pte.	Rivers, A. J.
80904	L /Cpl.	Wakefield, E. T
80588	Pte.	Hodge, W.
80324	Pte.	Wood, D.
80121	Sgt.	Bugg, O. W.
80282	Pte.	Goodwin, L.
80660	Pte.	Goodinson, M.
80151	Pte.	Hatley, J.
81088	Pte.	Harvey, S. D.
81138	Pte.	Jackaman, S. J.
81196	Pte.	Jopson, A.
80145	Pte.	Moorse, T. H.
80177	Pte.	Peckham, A.
81960	Pte.	Riddell, W. R.
80477	Pte.	Searles, P.
81021	Pte.	Travers, H.
80214	Pte.	Wilson, F. W.
80465	Pte.	Warren, H.
80060	S.S.M.	Tyler, A. S.
80470	Sgt.	Hodge, G. S.
81066	Pte.	Searle, F.
81085	Pte.	Smith, A. C.
80624	Pte.	Webb, H.
81210	Cpl.	Bowd, G.
80259	Pte.	Harvey, T. D.
81012	Pte.	Gregory, L. H.
81183	Pte.	Corrall, A. C.
80285	Pte.	Peacock. S. E.
81151	Pte.	Taylor, S. R.
81162	Pte.	Bamber, W. J.
80902	Pte.	French, E. W.
80257	Cpl.	Tompkins, A. O.
80628	Pte.	Cullum, W. W.
81078	Pte.	Tolhurst, W. G.
81211	Pte.	Deeks, S. W.
80817	Pte.	Covill, W. H.
80115	L./Cpl.	Stock, W.
81170	Pte.	Radford, T.
80726	Pte.	Martin, P.

THE BATTLE OF MONCHY LE PREUX, 1917.

80056	F./Sgt.	Meredith, T.	80036	Pte.	Sutton, F.
80270	Cpl.	Rowell, G. E.	80873	Pte.	Warren, W.
81010	Pte.	Barrett, W. H.	80168	L./Cpl.	Wright, A.
81007	Pte.	Crees, C.	80433	Pte.	Barker, H.

MISSING, BELIEVED KILLED.

80240	Pte.	Matthams, D. T.	80785	Tptr.	Stowell, A. H.
80631	Pte.	Smith, B.	80444	Pte.	Bassett, G.
81194	Pte.	Steward, C. W.	80363	Sgt.	May, E.
80982	Pte.	Baines, W. H.	80668	Pte.	Bayman, F.

MISSING.

81023	Pte.	Gooch, J. T.	80704	Pte.	Tomkins, E.

XVII.

BOIS JEAN AND AUBIN ST. VAAST, 1917.

Lieut.-Colonel A. Seymour, D.S.O., Royal Scots Greys, who had till then been in command of the Northamptonshire Yeomanry, was given command of the 8th Cavalry Brigade, with the rank of Temporary Brigadier-General.

On April 15th Major-General J. Vaughan, C.B., D.S.O., addressed the regiments of the Brigade and conveyed the thanks of the Commander-in-Chief for the gallant resistance which the 8th Cavalry Brigade had maintained on the 11th April.

On April 18th the Brigade moved West, and after 2 days' march the Regiments were in comfortable billets in the Beaurainville area, the 10th Hussars at Aubin St. Vaast and the Essex Yeomanry at Bois Jean. All their privations and troubles were soon overcome, assisted by good billets, and the advent of perfect weather which followed.

Most of the time for some weeks after was spent in refitting and reinforcing with men and horses. It was necessary to practically re-arm the Regiments, the destruction having been so intense. Information was received with great regret by the Essex Yeomanry that Lieut. J. Lingeman, the Intelligence Officer of the Regiment, had died from wounds in Hospital at Boulogne.

The Corps Commander visited the Regiments of the Brigade whilst in this area, and presented medals to those Officers and other ranks who had distinguished themselves in the field, and who in consequence received immediate rewards for gallantry.

XVIII.

COURCELLES, 1917.

On May 13th the Brigade commenced its 6 days' march to the devastated area East of Peronne, halting for 2 nights at Hamel, near Corbie. At that time both Hamel and Corbie were fully inhabited, and they were comparatively far from the fighting line. It was the last thing that anyone thought of that, within one year this area would be in the hands of the enemy, or that the now famous Bois-de-Vaire, which was then glorious with all the beauties of Spring, and in which Major Buxton found the nest of the Golden Oriole, was to be amongst the many beautiful woods which are now only recognisable as a torn up and absolutely destroyed heap of fallen timber and debris.

The march through the devasted area was of immense interest, the Village of Biaches, which was so gallantly held, and lost, and seized, and lost again by the French, could only be described as a heap of destruction. Just above the village and overlooking Peronne and the famous Mount St. Quentin, are the ruins of the renowned Malmaison Farm, which offered so gallant a resistance and proved such an important position in the final capture of Peronne from the Germans.

Peronne itself was, of course, destroyed almost beyond recognition, and the whole place can best be described as hopeless devastation.

By the end of the 3rd week in May the whole of the 3rd Cavalry Division, in fact the whole of Cavalry Corps, were in the Valley which lies the whole length of the distance from Peronne to Villers Faucon. The 8th Brigade arrived at Courcelles on May 19th. The period spent in this Valley may well be said to have been enjoyed by all—the weather was good on the whole, although there were some severe thunderstorms.

There were ample opportunities here for cavalry training, also bathing, and some polo. Much hay was cut and made, Lieut. Harold Newman, Essex Yeomanry, having charge of the hay-making for the Brigade. This he carried out with great patience, and by his good judgment and organisation some 150 tons of good hay were stacked in the area.

The 4th of June was, of course, celebrated by the old Etonians of the Brigade. A Banquet was held' in the ruined Chateau of Courcelles; this was admirably prepared by Capt. A. Winter Rose, M.C., who, although not an Old Etonian, was called in for the purpose of organising the preparation of the impromptu feast on account of his extraordinary capability in this respect. It was unfortunate that some Old Etonians were unable to be present, but this was accounted for by the fact of a dismounted party being already in the line East of Epehy and consequently they were away doing duty with this party.

However, the evening was spent as most Old Etonian Dinners are spent, and in the unavoidable absence of Brigadier-General A. Seymour, D.S.O., who was himself dining at an Old Etonian dinner organised by his own Regiment, the Scots Greys, Lieut.-Colonel Whitmore, D.S.O., presided at the memorable dinner in his place, and the usual toasts were drunk amid enthusiasm until the early hours of the morning.

The following is the list of those attending the dinner :—

Capt. E. A. Fielden, Hd. Qrs., 8th Cav. Bde., X.R.H.
Lt. M. Herbert, Hd. Qrs., 8th Cav. Bde., R.H.G.
Lt. F. C. Meyer, Hd. Qrs., 8th Cav. Bde., E.Y.

Lt.-Col. F. H. D. C. Whitmore, D.S.O., Essex Yeomanry.

Major E. A. Ruggles-Brise, M.C., Essex Yeomanry.

Major The Earl of Pembroke and Montgomery, Royal Horse Guards.

Capt. Lord Alistair Leveson Gower, M.C., Royal Horse Guards.

Capt. P. Combe, Royal Horse Guards.

Lt. C. M. Greaves, Royal Horse Guards.

Lt. O. E. Greaves, Royal Horse Guards.

Lt. E. Henderson, Royal Horse Guards.

Lt. Gollen, Royal Horse Guards.

Capt. R. Gordon Canning, M.C., 10th Royal Hussars.

Capt. V. P. Stokes, 10th Royal Hussars.

Lt. Viscount Ednam, M.C., 10th Royal Hussars.

Lt. The Hon. G. Glyn, 10th Royal Hussars.

Lt. Lord W. Montague-Douglas-Scott, 10th Royal Hussars.

Lt. S. A. Ralli, 10th Royal Hussars.

Capt. T. Preston, 8th M.G. Squadron.

Guests :

Capt. The Rev. J. Gibbs.

Capt. A. Winter Rose, M.C.

Adjt. Interpreter Le Nouvel.

XIX.

"THE BIRD CAGE," 1917.

On June 2nd, 1917, dismounted parties from each Regiment of the Brigade which was then bivouacked at Courcelles, consisting of 3 Officers and 160 other ranks, the whole being commanded by Lt.-Col. Lord Tweedmouth, C.M.G., M.V.O., D.S.O., proceeded to Epehy and took over from the 6th Cavalry Brigade that section of the line East of Peronne, known as D.1. Sector. This Sector overlooked Vendhuille and Ossus Wood.

On June 9th the Head Quarters of the Dismounted party was taken over by Lt.-Col. Gibbs, commanding the 10th Royal Hussars, with Lt. Viscount Ednam, M.C., as Adjutant, and on June 15th the Head Quarters were relieved by Lt.-Col. Whitmore, D.S.O., commanding the Essex Yeomanry, with Capt. Winter Rose, M.C., as Adjutant.

Major the Earl of Pembroke, M.V.O., commanded the detachmment of the Royal Horse Guards,

Capt. Stokes commanded the 10th Royal Hussars, and Major E. A. Ruggles-Brise, M.C., commanded the Essex Yeomanry.

Considerable work was carried out in the trench system, and also that portion of an advanced position, known as " The Bird Cage." The latter was transformed into a strong Garrison. A long communication trench was also dug, which connected up the post known as G. Post with the Quarry, the Quarry being the supporting Garrison for the " Bird Cage."

Ossus Wood lay in a valley to the left of the " Bird Cage," and was occupied by the enemy, whereas further up the valley lay Catalet Copse, which was occupied by us and formed the left of D.1. sector. The post at this Copse held the valley, and was strengthened by the 8th Machine Gun Squadron, under Capt. Preston.

The German front line of defence was only about 400 yards in front of the front trench of the " Bird Cage."

Aeroplane reconnaissance proved that a Sap was being dug from the German front trench towards the " Bird Cage."

Night reconnaissance showed that this Sap was well wired, and work was being carried out in order to extend it, every night.

It was therefore decided to make a raid on this Sap, with the intention of :

    (1)   Preventing further progress.

    (2)   Obtaining identifications.

Lt.-Col. F. Whitmore, D.S.O., was instructed to organise a raid for this purpose, and this was carried out during the night of June 17th.

For the purpose of the raid the following parties were detailed :—

    (a)   Raiding party Essex Yeomanry, consisting of Lt. Holland and 10 other ranks.

    (b)   Bombing party Essex Yeomanry, consisting of Lt. Hore and 5 other ranks.

    (c)   Right covering party Royal Horse Guards, consisting of Lt. Sale and 15 other ranks.

    (d)   Left covering party 10th Royal Hussars, consisting of Lt. Lord William Scott and 15 other ranks.

    (e)   Stokes trench mortars, 2, under Lt. A. Lowther, 10th Royal Hussars.

The plans for the raid were as follow :—

All parties to be in position at Zero hour ; Lt. Holland's party was then to move forward and cut the wire in front of the German Sap head. If he was detected whilst carrying this out, he would complete the task under cover of a heavy barrage, which would be put down under orders from Lt.-Col. Whitmore through the telephone. A heavy bombardment would follow; this bombardment would shell all the main German approaches surrounding the Sap. The Field Guns were then to lengthen their range for 10 minutes, whereas the heavy guns would continue their bombardment. The 10 minutes thus allowed would admit sufficient time for the raiders under Lt. Holland and bombers under Lt. Hore to carry out their task and return to the " Bird Cage," and also the covering parties, under Lt. Sale and Lt. Lord William Scott, would have time to withdraw. On completion of the 10 minutes, all the guns available, Field and Heavy, also trench mortars, would carry out a close bombardment over the German trench system, and the raiders and covering troops would withdraw as quickly as possible, to avoid the approach of the enemy counter artillery barrage in answer to their S.O.S.

The result was that the Sap was gained, but the enemy had taken up a position outside. Many casualties were caused by Lt. Hore's bombing party, but the time allowed did not admit bringing back any identification. The losses to the enemy were estimated at 15 killed and wounded.

" THE BIRD CAGE," 1917.

In reply to the enemy S.O.S., a heavy bombardment followed, but no great damage was done, the only casualties being 2 Officers wounded, Lt. The Honble. G. Glyn and Lt. A. Lowther, both of the 10th Royal Hussars, and no other ranks.

There were all sorts of stories told about this time, of traps which had been left by the enemy in the form of German helmets being connected with explosive bombs, so that anyone moving the helmet would set the apparatus in motion, and in consequence the house in which the trap was set would be blown up. There were indeed several instances of such ingenious contrivances operating with disastrous results in this area from which the Germans had retreated only 2 months previous. There were also delayed action mines under houses which were likely to be occupied by the staff of incoming Divisions and Brigades, and it was said that there was an instance of this having occurred, whereby a General and the whole of his staff were blown up whilst holding a conference, some time during the first month of our occupation of this area.

The result of well founded legends and also true incidents, led to great precautions being taken when any article of German interest was found lying about, with the result that for months such tempting trophies as a pair of German field glasses, would be left on a table untouched, and perhaps even the room would be put out of bounds to troops. These were by no means unnecessary precautions to take, for there were many instances which led to disaster.

Many amusing stories are also told of incidents when such precautions have turned out to have been groundless.

Major the Earl of Pembroke, Royal Horse Guards, is fond of a story which is best told in his own words, regarding the existence of a roller which had been avoided by everybody for weeks on account of suspicion as to its being connected by wire to the cross roads at Catelet Copse, the idea being that if it was moved at all it would be moved down hill, and in doing so it would pass over a circular disc, which was declared to be a detonator, and consequently a mine would go up at Catelet Copse. It was perfectly true that a wire was in existence, one end of which did happen to enter the ground. The events which led to the destruction of the theory Lord Pembroke describes as follows:

"Well do I remember that momentous event in June, 1917.

"For months that 100 yards of road leading up to Little Priel Farm had been avoided like a plague spot.

Ration parties and others made wide detours, watching the deadly roller with breathless anxiety; people, whose duties forced them to go within 100 yards of it, spoke in whispers, and walked delicately like Agag.

"It was on one lovely afternoon in June that the Colonel of the Essex Yeomanry and the 2nd in Command of the Blues, after an excellent lunch, proceeded to visit certain posts in the Sector. As they reached the cross-roads at the bottom of the hill, half way up which lay atsride the road this deadly contrivance for blowing up the British Army, they stopped.

"'Let's go and look at that adjective roller,' said the Colonel. 'Right-O' replied the other, and to the horror of all onlookers, they side by side boldly walked up to it. They walked round it once or twice, and then proceeded to inspect the detonator. This was quite plain to the eye just a few yards below, so that the roller, if moved, must necessarily go right over it.

"'I don't believe a word of it,' said the Colonel, and producing his pocket knife, proceeded to scrape the earth away from around the cap, so as to see if it was connected.

"The 2nd in Command having grown pale at this fearsome deed of daring and the effects of the lunch having worn off, had half a mind to beat all previous records to the bottom of the hill. However, he conquered this momentary feeling of fear, and as the Colonel dug deeper and deeper, and the whole world did not dissolve into a cloud of smoke and debris, he became as brave as a lion.

"One final dig by the penknife and the detonator moved from its place and revealed 'nothing.' It was the lid of a cocoa tin!

"Now the daring of these two elderly Officers knew no bounds; they rushed at the roller, tore away the wooden props and proceeded in the heat of the afternoon to push the infernal thing down the hill. It got going and rolled rapidly down half-way and then subsided into a ditch.

"Nothing happened, and thanks to the heroism of these two Officers, yet another road to Berlin was open to the Allied Armies in the field."

The Head Quarters of the Royal Horse Guards detachment was in a shallow dug-out in what was called G. Post. In a corner of the ceiling of this dug-out, which was only just above one's head, a swallow had built her nest and she became, as did her husband, so tame, that they did not mind the occupants of the dug-out in the very least, but they would never allow themselves to be handled. The lady swallow answered to the name of Gertrude, and as each egg was hatched, an entry was made in the Regimental

War Diary, and so Gertrude's fame will be handed down to posterity as a real companion to those who lived in the dug-out in G. Post.

Again Lord Pembroke's description of Gertrude's infidelity is almost pathetic. He writes:—

"Yes! poor little Gertrude was a pretty story in some ways ; but do you not remember her infidelity ?

"I was sitting in the dug-out in G. Post talking to Gertrude and her spouse, when she told him she was hungry and off he flew to get food. In an incredibly short time he returned, as I thought, but without food, and Gertrude seemed very excited and they both talked hard to each other. Bingo Greaves, who was there, said 'Hullo! that is not the rightful owner.' I was naturally very shocked, and suggested he might be her brother, but the arrival of the husband in a few minutes, and the scene that followed, told a different tale. Alas! swallow nature seems as frail as human.

"However the matter was patched up, and one fine morning the inhabitants of G. Post were increased by one, and the last report I received on leaving the Sector was 'Mother and child doing well.'"

On the night of June 20th the Sub-section was taken over by the 7th Brigade, Lt.-Col. Herbert Combe,

D.S.O., commanding the Leicestershire Yeomanry, was in command of the party, with Major Tom Gurney, D.S.O., 2nd Life Guards, as his 2nd in command. Just as the relief was complete the enemy made a raid on the " Bird Cage," in retaliation for the raid which had been carried out against them a few nights before. The Leicestershire Yeomanry bore the force of the attack and inflicted very heavy losses to the Germans. Many of the enemy were killed whilst getting over the wire entanglement, and many were killed by their own artillery bombardment. A German Officer was killed on entering the trench, 3 prisoners were taken, 2 were severely wounded and died. The result of this attack was a failure to the enemy, who suffered very heavy casualties, and identification was obtained by us.

The Leicestershire Yeomanry suffered some casualties. Lt. P. M. Toulmin was killed, also 7 other ranks and 15 wounded. Lt. Toulmin was a very brave and determined officer and his death caused a great loss to his Regiment.

It was owing to the fact that identification was obtained on this occasion that another raid on our part, which was already being organised, was able to be cancelled, the object of the raid having been obtained.

XX.

THIENNES, MOLINGHEM & BERGUETTE, 1917.

The Brigade remained in the Courcelles area until July 2nd, when it moved to Camblain Châtelain, marching 5 days, passing through and billeting at, Suzanne, Mericourt, Authieule, Rebreuviette and, after halting there for 10 days, a new billeting area was occupied at Thiennes and Tannay, with the Royal Horse Guards against the Canal. It was during the time that the Brigade occupied this area that Armentières was heavily shelled with gas shells, and many of the inhabitants were either killed or dreadfully burnt. It was also during this period that the town of Aire was shelled by German long range guns, huge holes being made in the ground by the side of the road near Aire. The Horse Show Season had commenced, and by the time the Brigade went into fresh billets in the Molinghem-Ham-Berguette area, very few Brigades or Regiments had not organised a Horse Show. The Cavalry Corps Horse Show was the chief feature of the period and it was an enormous success and splendidly organised. The Essex Yeomanry were then billeted at Berguette, moving there on August 10th.

The chief events whilst in this area were the continual air raids by the Germans at night, with a view to bombing the factory at Isbergues, which was producing a quantity of munitions of war. Some horses were killed by these night visitations and some men wounded and many had very narrow escapes, the narrowest, perhaps, being the occasion when a dud shell entered the ground between 2 men of the Orsett troop, Essex Yeomanry, who were using the same blankets; with the exception of a hole in each of the blankets, no damage was done.

Brigadier-General R. B. Colvin, C.B., late commanding the Essex Yeomanry, came over from Acheux to visit the Regiment. A full strength parade was ordered for the occasion. This popular Commanding Officer received a great reception from his old regiment.

Useful Field days and training were constantly carried out here, as was a very useful course of Musketry at a short range, which had been carefully made under the direction of Captain J. C. Chaplin, M.C., Essex Yeomanry; and also a Divisional Musketry course for all men of the Division, under the supervision of Major A. Buxton, D.S.O.

XXI.

HALLOY-LES-PERNOIS AND HAVERNAS, 1917.

The Brigade moved to a new billeting area between Guarbecque and Robecq, where it remained from October 12th till October 17th, and then proceeded to Camblain Châtelain for a second time, where it remained until October 21st, and thence by 2 days' march to Halloy-les-Pernois area, at which place the 10th Hussars were billeted. The Essex Yeomanry were billeted at Havernas and Naours. It was whilst in this area that the Royal Horse Guards were sent to the 7th Brigade, and the Leicestershire Yeomanry, under Lt.-Col. H. Combe, D.S.O., came to the 8th Cavalry Brigade in their place.

At Naours was one of the most interesting underground succession of dwelling caves to be found in France. At a depth of about 100 feet under a hill, and entered by a large arched entrance by the side of the hill, are to be found corridors and passages of varying height and width; on either side are large rooms some 500 in number. In the centre of all this excavation is a chapel with chancel and altar complete, capable of holding some hundreds of worshippers; there is also a stable. Many interesting relics are preserved and can be seen in a museum, which forms part of this interesting underground village.

XXII.

CAMBRAI, 1917.

It was on the 18th of November that the Brigade moved out under secret orders to a Divisional Concentration place at Bray, to take part in the great attack of the 3rd Army, near Cambrai. This attack was the first attack to take place with the absence of any artillery preparation, an enormous quantity of tanks being employed. The Brigade was the reserve Brigade of the Division ; although the attack was an immense success at the commencement, enemy reinforcements were brought up so rapidly that all chances of cavalry exploiting the success of the Infantry and Tanks soon became remote, and ultimately vanished. On November 23rd the Brigade marched via Corbie and Querrieu to the Bertangles area, the 10th Royal Hussars being billeted at Rainneville, and the Essex Yeomanry at Allonville.

CAMBRAI, 1917.

On November 30th the Germans delivered their counter-stroke and retook much of the ground which they had lost during the attack at Cambrai by the 3rd Army on the 19th November. This sudden change caused a Dismounted party to be formed at once, which proceeded by motor busses on December 1st. This Brigade party was under command of Lt.-Col. W. O. Gibbs, 10th Royal Hussars, with Major G. Gold, Essex Yeomanry, as 2nd in command. During the absence of this Dismounted party the Brigade moved into a fresh billeting area, 10th Hussars to Dreuil and the Essex Yeomanry to Picquigny and thence on December 22nd to Havernas and Naours, with Headquarters at Vignacourt. The 10th Royal Hussars moving into La Chaussée.

XXIII.

VADENCOURT, 1917-18.

The Command of the Dismounted party now in the line in front of Vermand was taken over from Lieut.-Col. W. O. Gibbs by Lieut.-Col. Whitmore, D.S.O., on December 8th, with Capt. A. Winter Rose, M.C., as Adjutant, Lieut. A. Lowther, 10th Royal Hussars, Intelligence Officer, Lieut. T. Robinson, 10th Royal Hussars, Scout Officer, Lieut. W. J. Brisley, 10th Royal Hussars, Bombing Officer, Capt. E. Stork, D.S.O., Medical Officer and Lieut. F. Balfour, Essex Yeomanry, as Quartermaster.

The snow was deep all the time, and the cold intense beyond comparison. The men holding the line suffered dreadfully from the cold, and many outposts could only be relieved at night, and no fires could be lit. The opposing lines were a long way apart, ranging from 1000 to 2000 yards, with a valley between; this valley was necessarily kept well patrolled every night. These patrols went out clothed in white, being thus less visible in the snow. The familiar objects for reconnaissance by night being " Eleven trees " and " Fisher's Crater." Raids were carried out periodically in order to be certain that such places were not held by the enemy. The " Tumulus " was a familiar land mark in front of the sector and this was continuously being shelled by the enemy, no doubt for the purpose of registration.

The prospect of an early attack by the Germans was by now becoming evident, and the work of putting the front and back lines into a proper state of defence was made increasingly difficult on account of the snow and frost. Vadencourt Chateau, now nothing but a heap of bricks and mortar, was where the second line of defence now existed ; this was once a magnificent residence. Nothing now remained of the house at all but a pile of debris. The garden which must have been very well kept, showed traces of great expenditure in former days ; most of the trees had been cut down and left, not for the purpose of using the timber or even for enabling the position to have been put into a state of defence ; it had been all carried out with one object in view only, and that was for the pure destruction of property, in furtherance of the belief, which the Germans then cherished, that their acts of frightfulness would terrify their enemies into subjection.

The village of Le Verguier was on the left of this Sector; this was a very commanding position and was the position which was held so gallantly by its defenders, the 24th Division, when the great German advance commenced on March 21st.

Lieut.-Col. H. D. Bramwell, 15th Hussars, 9th Brigade, took over from Lieut.-Col. Whitmore on January 15th and the 8th Brigade returned to their horses in the Vignacourt Halloy area, having suffered but few casualties. A party consisting of 1 Officer and 88 other ranks per Regiment were left behind in order to form a Divisional Pioneer Battalion 600 strong. This Battalion was relieved on January 24th.

XXIV.

MONTECOURT, 1918.

On January 27th the Brigade moved into the new Divisional area around Monchy Lagache, the 3 regiments of the Brigade occupying huts at Montecourt. This area was, as was the case for many miles in every direction, absolutely destroyed in every sense of the word. The houses were all demolished, the land was all out of cultivation, magnificent chateaus were lying in heaps of debris; in fact, the whole place was in such a state that it is impossible to give anything like an accurate description of it. The huts were plentiful and in fair condition, the stables were cold and required much attention. It was not long, however, before the Brigade was established in these new quarters.

Large work parties were constantly employed on the defences round Bihecourt and Vermand, and every preparation was being made for the threatened German attack. By the end of February the 3rd Cavalry Division Agricultural Organisation had been formed and was in full working order, and many acres of land became not only ploughed but sown with wheat and other cereals, and some 200 acres were manured and ploughed ready for potato growing.

The Committee of the Organisation consisted of the following :—

Lt.-Col. F. H. D. C. Whitmore, C.M.G., D.S.O., Essex Yeomanry (President).

Brig.-Gen. J. O. G. Longmore, D.S.O., Cavalry Corps.

Major G. G. F. Chomley, 7th Machine Gun Sqdn.

Captain D. E. Wallace, 2nd Life Guards.

Captain E. W. Baker, Army Service Corps.

Lieut. W. G. Wakefield, 8th Machine Gun Squadron.

Lieut. W. Ritchie, Essex Yeomanry.

Lieut. R. D. Holland, Essex Yeomanry.

Lieut. F. Billerey, French Mission.

Lieut. de Vives, French Government.

M. des Logis de Vibraye, French Mission.

The Mayor of Tertry, Representing Land Owners.

Captain R. M. Wootten, D.A.A. and Q.M.G., 3rd Cav. Div. (Secretary)

The work was carried out harmoniously throughout and if it had not been for the German attack on

March 21st, the vast amount of work which had already been carried out would not only have been a great benefit to the French Authorities, but would have been an enormous advantage to the British troops.

The system upon which the Organisation worked was on the principle of labour exchange with the French Government.

The French Authorities who were represented on the Committee possessed many tractors, but had not sufficient horses to carry out the work behind the tractors. On the other hand, the 3rd Cav. Div. Agr. Org. had the use of horses, but no tractors.

It was, therefore, agreed that by an exchange of labour the ploughing should be done by the French, whereas the drilling, sowing, and harrowing should be done by the Organisation, a proper rate of exchange of labour being agreed upon. Some 300 or more horses were employed on the land and many tractors, with the result that by the 3rd week in March some hundreds of acres were already sown and some thousands of tons of manure were spread on the land in preparation for potatoes.

In this connection some 30 to 40 ploughs were repaired by the Cav. Corps Ordnance workshops at Estrées and agricultural implements from all parts were collected with a view to future development of the land. Where possible, arrangements were made with the owners of the land whereby, as regards the land in preparation for potatoes for the British Army, the owners should receive in payment 10 per cent. of the crop, in lieu of rent.

In the case of corn land, the work carried out on the land was entered as a charge against the owner, as was also the cost of the seed. The crop eventually was to be requisitioned and purchased at a price determined by the French Government.

By this system all parties benefited. The owner had his land cultivated and sown and also would have received payment for its product.

On the other hand, the French increased their supply of grain at their own market valuation.

The advance however on the 21st March enabled the Germans to take possession of the agricultural holdings on Lady Day, 1918, and it was not until Michaelmas Day, 1918, that they relinquished tenancy of the land, in which time they were enabled to profit to the full extent by the labours of the 3rd Cavalry Division Agricultural Organisation.

XXV.

TERTRY AND TREFCON, 1918.

About the last day of February, the 10th Royal Hussars moved into Tertry and the Essex Yeomanry went to Trefcon.

It was here that the re-distribution of the Division took place on account of the Indian Cavalry Division being broken up, and the 7th Dragoon Guards, Inniskillings and 17th Lancers coming into the Division to form the 7th Brigade in the place of the Household Cavalry, who were by now ordered to be converted into Machine Gun Battalions.

It was here also that the 4 Yeomanry Regiments—Leicestershire, Bedford, North Somerset and Essex received orders to leave the Cavalry Corps for the purpose of being transferred into Cyclist Companies.

These great changes came as a great blow, not only to the Household Cavalry and Yeomanry Regiments, but to the Cavalry Regiments as a whole, who had by now become so closely connected after $3\frac{1}{2}$ years of war.

Another change which became necessary when the Indian Divisions were broken up, was for the 8th Hussars to find a place in Cavalry Corps, which now consisted of 3 Divisions only. Consequently the 8th Hussars went to the 9th Cavalry Brigade to take the place of the Bedfordshire Yeomanry.

The above changes, together with the introduction of the Canadian Cavalry Brigade into the 3rd Cavalry Division, completed the reduction of the strength of Cavalry Corps, and the Regiments became distributed as follows :

6th Cavalry Brigade :

   1st Royal Dragoons
   3rd Dragoon Guards
   10th Royal Hussars
   " C " Battery, R.H.A.
   6th Machine Gun Squadron.

7th Cavalry Brigade :

   7th Dragoon Guards
   6th Inniskilling Dragoons
   17th Lancers
   " K " Battery, R.H.A.
   7th Machine Gun Squadron

Canadian Cavalry Brigade :

> Royal Canadian Dragoons
> Lord Strathcona's Horse
> Fort Garry Horse
> Battery Royal Canadian Horse Artillery
> Canadian Machine Gun Squadron

The weather early in March was as bad as it could be ; the above re-distribution involved horses having to stand out in the open, and the men of the Essex Yeomanry were crowded into the huts occupied by the 1st Life Guards, and the Leicestershire Yeomanry with the 2nd Life Guards. But of all the hardships which the 3 Regiments of the Household Cavalry and the 4 Regiments of Yeomanry had gone through during the war, no greater hardship had been experienced than this event, when Officers and other ranks had to become parted from their horses.

The distribution of their horses amongst the other Regiments of the Division was a very unhappy day for all concerned.

Eventually the Household Cavalry left the Division and went to Etaples to be trained as Machine Gunners. The 4 Regiments of Yeomanry were under orders to be converted into Cyclist Companies.

These Regiments were under orders to proceed to the back area near Longpre, where this transformation was to take effect, when Lieut.-Col. Whitmore, who had been sent to England to negotiate with the War Office with a view to the Yeomanry Regiments being formed into Machine Gun Battalions instead of Cyclist Companies, was able to wire to Cavalry Corps, saying that his mission had proved successful, and that the Bedfordshire and Essex Yeomanry were to form one Machine Gun Battalion and the Leicestershire and North Somerset were to form another.

It was during this rapid change of procedure that all the arrangements were necessarily cancelled owing to the great German attack, and all the above Regiments of Yeomanry were quickly re-formed as Cavalry and sent into action immediately as such.

It is necessary now to revert to the fortunes of the 10th Royal Hussars, in conjunction with the 6th Cavalry Brigade, which Brigade took so important a part in the events to follow.

In order to make room for the 24th Division, commanded by Major-General Daly, and having regard to the re-distribution of the Cavalry Regiments in the 3rd Cavalry Division, the 10th Royal Hussars moved into Tertry, which place was already occupied by the 1st Royal Dragoons and the 3rd Dragoon Guards.

Discomfort for both men and horses was considerable, owing to the limited amount of accommodation in this area, which consisted of huts and improvised stabling, similar to that which had been previously occupied by the 8th Cavalry Brigade in the Montecourt area, which was close by.

Air raids by now had become constant and the strictest orders had to be given forbidding the least sign of a light showing after dark.

Nevertheless, with every precaution which was taken, the Regiment was unfortunate enough to be the victim of a raid on March 9th. It was about 8 p.m. that a bomb was dropped right into the centre of a large hut which was full of men at the time; they were sitting together in the centre of the hut around a stove on a bitterly cold night. The fearfulness of the unlucky direct hit of the bomb is best appreciated by the fact that 6 men were killed outright, and no fewer than 35 wounded, of whom 4 died of wounds afterwards.

The distressing circumstances were, of course, accentuated by the necessity of dealing with the dying and wounded in the enforced darkness, and it was with the greatest difficulty that the situation could be adequately dealt with.

XXVI.

THE GERMAN ADVANCE, MARCH, 1918.

On March 21st, at 4.30 a.m., the great German attack was launched. It commenced with a terrific bombardment, which extended almost the entire length of the 3rd and 5th Army front, and in depth it surpassed any previous bombardment. The attack covered a front of between 50 and 60 miles, extending between the Sensée River in the 3rd Army front to the Oise river in the South.

At about 9 a.m. orders were received to " stand to," and at about 3.30 p.m. a telegram was received worded " Stand to South." At 5 p.m. the Brigade marched to Beaumont, near Ham, and bivouacked in the open. Early the following day a dismounted Brigade was formed and commanded by Lt.-Col. Burt, D.S.O., Commanding 3rd Dragoon Guards, and a few hours later orders were received for a Brigade mounted party to be formed at once. This party was to act under orders of Brigadier-General Harman, D.S.O., Commanding 3rd Cavalry Division. Major E. Watkin Williams, 10th Royal Hussars, was in command of the 6th Brigade mounted party, about 160 strong.

The led horses of the dismounted party were moved to Carlepont and from there to Ollencourt. The dismounted party rejoined their horses at that place on March 27th, as did Major Irwin's mounted party, which was an additional mounted detachment to that already described, which left the Brigade on the day previous.

By midday, on March 22nd, the Germans were against the Crozat Canal and the 3rd Corps, consisting of the 14th, 18th and 58th Divisions, was reinforced by two dismounted Cavalry Divisions.

It was on March 23rd that the Germans advanced in great force, and the dismounted Divisions were heavily engaged. The 133rd French Infantry Regiment made a counter attack on Tergnier and the Butts; this was, however, met by a counter-stroke delivered by the Germans. This counter-stroke broke the French line and the German masses occupied the Butts.

Further north the position was equally overwhelming, the enemy having already occupied the

entrance to Noureuil. But the village itself was
held until dark.

Throughout that day the Germans continued to
advance in great force. Our troops who had had no
rest for 3 days and nights were nearly exhausted,
but the strain continued day after day, until the
enemy was finally held up at the outer defences
of Amiens.

The mounted party, under Major E. Watkin
Williams, marched from Pontoise to Berlancourt
on March 23rd, and the following morning " stood
to " at 4 a.m. At midday they moved to Collezy
and at about 2 p.m. orders were received for them
to make a mounted attack on the enemy holding
two woods and a hill near Collezy. Major Williams'
detachment was little more than the strength of a
Squadron and they came under heavy machine gun
fire from the direction of Golancourt. No time was
lost and the preparations for the attack were as
follows : The detachment was formed into a Squadron
of three troops : 1st troop, 3rd Dragoon Guards, under
Lieut. P. Vincent; 2nd troop, 10th Royal Hussars,
under Lieut. Viscount Ednam ; 3rd troop, 1st Royal
Dragoons, under Lieut. the Hon. W. H. Cubitt.
Major Watkin Williams accompanied the 2nd troop,
or 2nd wave, of the attacking force. The 1st Royal

Dragoons covered the flanks of the 2 leading troops. The 3rd Dragoon Guards moved in the direction of the enemy holding the woods and soon engaged the enemy, whom they pursued into the wood, dismounting and shooting many at point blank range. They handed over 12 prisoners to the Infantry. The remainder of Major Williams' detachment moved to the West of this wood, and encountered the enemy in considerable strength.

The ground was heavy and all under machine gun fire. The Cavalry charged into the enemy, who fled on hearing the men cheering, and many surrendered. The 10th Royal Hussars rode straight through the enemy's lines, whilst the Royals followed and captured many small parties, who in their panic had run together into groups. The " Rally " was sounded and the Squadrons returned to the Berlancourt-Villeselve road and the wounded were collected. 94 prisoners were brought in by the 10th Royal Hussars and the 1st Royal Dragoons. To this should be added 12 brought in by the 3rd Dragoon Guards. 3 Machine Guns were also captured. About 100 Germans were killed at the point of the sword.

The mounted detachment suffered heavy casualties, including Lieut. the Hon W. H. Cubitt (died

of wounds), who was in command of the Royals
detachment, the total losses being 73 out of 150;
but the attack gave a wonderful moral effect on the
Infantry, who had suffered so severely during the
retreat, and the price the detachment paid was well
rewarded.

On March 25th the mounted party moved before
dawn and bivouacked at Lagny. A dismounted
party, under Lieut. Viscount W. H. E. Ednam,
M.C., 10th Royal Hussars, was sent to support the
Infantry at Catigny, but returned the same evening.

The following day, March 26th, the mounted
party moved to the Bois des Essarts, in support of
the 7th and Canadian Cavalry Brigades, who were
holding the wood from Suzoy to Sceaucourt; a
further retirement was necessary and the party
bivouacked at Elincourt. The composite mounted
troop rejoined the 6th Cavalry Brigade on March
29th.

The dismounted party, under Lieut.-Col. Burt,
D.S.O., arrived at Viry-Noureuil at 5 a.m., on March
22nd, and that night dug a line at Noureuil.

At 11.30 a.m., on March 23rd, the Germans broke
through N. of the Souez-Rouez road. At 1.30 p.m.
orders were received to retire to the West of Noureuil.
The new line was held until 4.30 p.m., when the

left was driven in and the enemy occupied the village, and Capt. E. Palmes, M.C., 10th Royal Hussars, was wounded.

On March 24th the Brigade fell back to Chauny, and at 6 a.m. dug in on a position on the Chauny-Jussy road, with the right $\frac{1}{2}$ mile N.E. of Chauny; this front was held until 8.30 a.m., when the left of the line was driven in. The Brigade then was forced to retire to the Chauny-Caumont road and they again dug in, but were again ordered to retire and take up a position between the canal and the river, arriving there at 4 p.m.

On March 25th, at 3 a.m., the Brigade moved to Quierzy and took up a position at that place and at 10.30 a.m. they retired to take up a position on the high ground about Les Bruyers.

On March 26th the Brigade was relieved by the French and marched back to Tracy-le-Mont and the dismounted party rejoined on the 27th.

On April 1st the Brigade marched out at 6 a.m. to Gentelles wood, in support of the 2nd Cavalry Division and in the evening moved again to a wood South of Blangy-Tronville; and on April 3rd they moved at 4.30 a.m. to Fouilloy and came under the orders of the 1st Cavalry Division as reserve to their line, which extended from the Somme through Hamel to Warfussée Abancourt and in the evening they were relieved by the 14th Division.

On April 4th the enemy delivered a heavy attack soon after dawn and forced the 14th Division to retire. The 6th Cavalry Brigade was ordered to support the 14th Division and in consequence they held a line on the high ground West of Hamel. Lieut. W. S. Murland, 10th Royal Hussars, was sent forward to occupy the East end of the Bois de Vaire, but was forced to fall back, having lost about 50 horses by machine gun fire. The Brigade held on to their ground all day with the 15th Australian Brigade on their left. The Australians took over the whole line that evening.

Lieut.-Col. H. A. Tomkinson, D.S.O., who had only just taken over command of the 10th Hussars, was wounded, as were also Lieuts. R. G. Field, Viscount Ednam, M.C., and H. D. Kelleway; about 4 other ranks were killed and 18 wounded. Lieut. Field died on being received into Hospital.

At 10 p.m. a dismounted party was formed and held the line opposite the S.W. end of the Bois de Vaire. Captain Gosling, M.C., was in command of the X.R.H. dismounted party, and acted on the left of the 3rd Dragoon Guards, with the Australians on the left of the X.R.H.

The enemy heavily shelled the line during April 5th, but no organised attack developed.

The Brigade was relieved by the Australians in the evening, and returned to bivouac near Blangy-Tronville, arriving about 5 a.m. on the 6th April.

On April 6th the Brigade went into billets at Camon, where Lieut.-Col. F. H. D. C. Whitmore, C.M.G., D.S.O., took over command of the 10th Royal Hussars.

As a result of the recent events, in which the 3rd Cavalry Division took so prominent a part, the following order was received by Major-General Harman, D.S.O., from Major-General Cator, commanding the 19th Corps :

" My warmest thanks and congratulations to you, and all ranks of the 3rd Cavalry Division on the splendid work you have done in the 19th Corps. The fighting spirit, and determination displayed, have been beyond all praise, and the results achieved have been of the greatest value."

The casualties incurred by the 10th Royal Hussars from the commencement of the German advance until April 6th were as follows :

KILLED.

2/Lieut. R. G. Field.

THE GERMAN ADVANCE, MARCH, 1918.

WOUNDED.

Lt.-Colonel H. A. Tomkinson, D.S.O.
Major E. H. Watkin Williams.
Captain E. W. E. Palmes, M.C.
Lieut. Viscount W. H. E. Ednam, M.C.
Lieut. W. J. Brisley.
Lieut. F. R. Gaskell.
2/Lieut. H. D. Kelleway.

Other Ranks : 9 killed, 61 wounded, 15 missing.

XXVII.

THE DEFENCE OF VILLERS BRETON-
NEUX, 1918.

In order to appreciate events which led to the 4 Yeomanry Regiments being again horsed, instead of being converted into either Cyclist Companies or Machine Gun Battalions, it is necessary to follow the fortunes of Lieut.-Col. Whitmore in connection with his mission to London for the purpose of persuading, if possible, the Authorities to allow these Regiments to become Machine Gun Battalions. Col. Whitmore took with him Capt. the Hon. T. Hay, Leicestershire Yeomanry and Capt. Ralph Gibbs, North Somerset Yeomanry; time did not admit the inclusion of a representative of the Bedfordshire Yeomanry.

The 3 officers, as above, arrived in London on Sunday evening, March 10th. On Tuesday, March 12th, a Conference was held at 9, Eaton Square, at which meeting, the Presidents, Chairmen and Secretaries of the 4 County Territorial Force Associations concerned were invited to attend. The majority attended the meeting, which was presided over by the Earl of Warwick, Lord-Lieut. of Essex. Major-General F. Johnson, C.B. acted as Secretary of the Conference. The result of the Conference was a decision to the effect that a deputation, consisting of all those present, should represent to Lord Derby, at 4 p.m. that afternoon, at which hour Lord Derby had already kindly consented to receive the deputation, the hope that the above request might be granted. The Duke of Rutland presented the deputation, and, after some discussion, it was agreed by Lord Derby that 2 Machine Gun Battalions should be formed by amalgamation of the Regiments concerned.

On the question as to which two Regiments would in each case amalgamate for this purpose, the decision was arrived at by the names of the 4 Regiments being written on slips of paper and by Lord Derby himself drawing the names from a hat. The result was that the Leicestershire and North Somerset were to form one Battalion, and the Bedfordshire and Essex were to form the other. All was arranged in accordance with this, and had it not been for the great German attack which developed a few days afterwards, these Machine Gun Battalions would have been formed.

However, as it happened, it is safe to say that the Great German Offensive of March 21st was the means of preserving the 4 Yeomanry Regiments as Cavalry, although the critical situation did not allow them to be maintained for long as units in Cavalry Corps.

It was on March 27th that Lieut.-Col. Whitmore, Capt. the Honble T. Hay, and Capt. Ralph Gibbs rejoined their Regiments at Longpré. These regiments were already being re-transformed into Cavalry units to meet the requirements for further Cavalry reinforcements in order to hold up the great German attack which commenced on March 21st. Horses and equipment were hastily provided, and issued preparatory to moving up to support the already depleted Cavalry regiments which had been fighting hard for six consecutive days and nights. The Bedfordshire Yeomanry had already taken their place in the line with their former Brigade.

At 3 a.m., on March 28th, 2 Squadrons, "A" and "C," of the Essex Yeomanry, under Major A. Buxton, D.S.O., marched to Bussy-les-Daours to report to the 1st Cavalry Division for orders, and the following morning, March 29th, Head Quarters and "B" Squadron moved off at the same hour to the same place, arriving at Bussy at 11 a.m.

Villers-Bretonneux, looking East.

Warfusée-Abancourt Church.

Leaving their horses at Fouilloy this Squadron, under Major E. A. Ruggles-Brise, M.C., marched to Villers Bretonneux, where it remained in support of " A " and " C " Squadron Essex Yeomanry and the Bedfordshire Yeomanry, who were already holding the line with the 1st Cavalry Division. Lieut.-Col. Whitmore was then given command of the Sector astride the main Villers Bretonneux-Estrées road on the left to the Marcelcave railway on the right, with the Bedfordshire and Essex Yeomanry as his command. Lieut.-Col. Walker, D.S.O., was in command of the Bedfordshire Yeomanry and Major Eustace Hill assumed command of the Essex Yeomanry, Major A. Buxton, D.S.O., having gone to Hospital sick.

The situation was very obscure ; neither our troops nor the Germans knew how the line on either side had been taken up, although there were only a few yards in some places dividing the opposing forces. Fighting continued throughout the night, but no ground was yielded by either the Bedfordshire Yeomanry or the Essex.

On the following day Villers Bretonneux was heavily shelled, as was also Major Hill's front line. Information soon came in to the effect that the Germans were continuing their advance on the troops

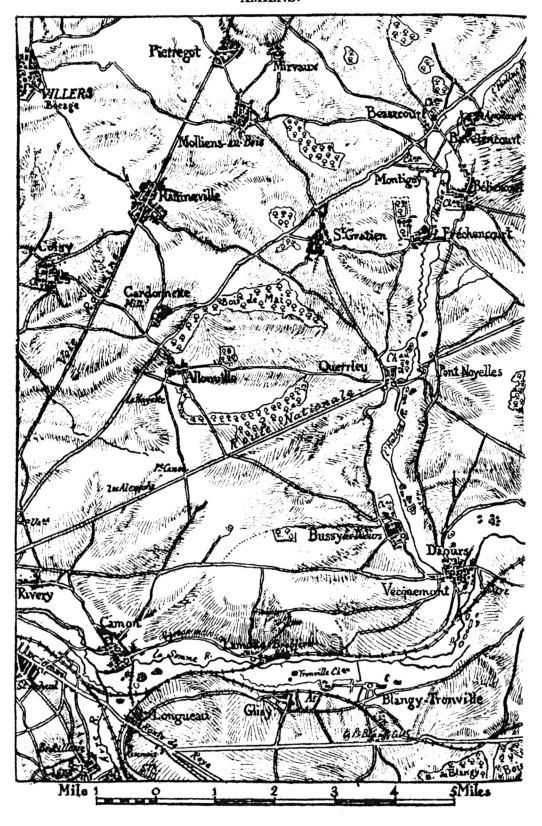

Mile 1   0   1   2   3   4   5 Miles

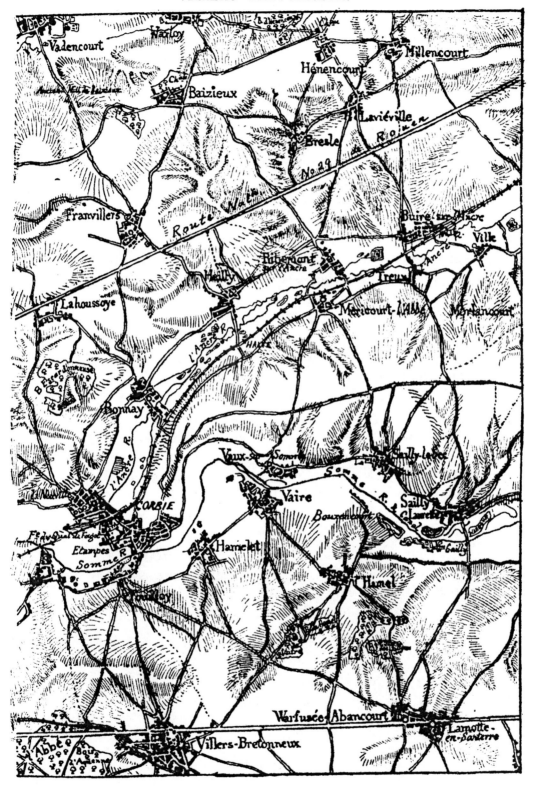

holding the line on the right, and that these troops were falling back. Major Hill sent a message back to Col. Whitmore, whose Headquarters were at Villers Bretonneux, saying that his right flank was becoming seriously exposed owing to the retirement of the Infantry on his right. Col. Whitmore sent a message back to Major Hill, telling him to hold on at all costs and that Major Ruggles-Brise's Squadron, which was in support, was being sent forward to protect his (Major Hill's) right flank.

Villers Bretonneux was by now rapidly being demolished by continuous shell fire. The Chateau at this place, which was renowned for its collection of foreign birds, was suffering dreadful destruction. All the occupants of the vast cages and yards were now running loose in the roads at Villers Bretonneux. It was quite a common occurrence to meet an emu or ostrich in the main road ; all were scared by the tumult of war. Nearly all the inhabitants of the town had now fled west, and many houses were in flames.

Major Ruggles-Brise took his Squadron along the railway towards Marcelcave and protected the flank of Major Hill's Squadron until the situation was restored. Lieut. C. A. Collis, Essex Yeomanry, was wounded.

THE DEFENCE OF VILLERS BRETONNEUX, 1918.

During the night of March 30/31st this Sector was taken over by the Australians and a new Sector was allotted to Col. Whitmore, which extended from Warfusée on the right to Hamel on the left.

This Sector was already held by dismounted parties of the 2nd and 9th Cavalry Brigades and elements of various Infantry and Machine Gun formations known as Carey's Force, who had hurriedly dug a line between the above-named two places.

The formations forming Col. Whitmore's command in this new Sector consisted of :—The 9th Lancers, 18th Hussars, Essex Yeomanry, Bedfordshire Yeomanry, 2nd Machine Gun Squadron, 6th United States Engineers, 3rd Corps School Lewis Gun Detachment, 352nd Electrical Mechanical Company, and details from the 16th Infantry Division. Lieut.-Col. H. Combe, D.S.O., commanding 18th Hussars, acted as 2nd in Command of the Sector. Major Hill, commanding the Essex Yeomanry, was relieved by Major E. A. Ruggles-Brise, M.C.

On April 2nd the 9th Lancers had some casualties, but the enemy showed no desire to resume the attack. Major Fetherstonhaugh, 4th Dragoon Guards, relieved Lieut.-Col. Combe, D.S.O.

The Head Quarters of the Sector were established in a small red brick shed in the Bois de Vaire. The

Bois de Vaire was consistently shelled by the enemy, but no serious casualties occurred. Reports were received during the day, April 3rd, that the enemy were concentrating in the valley at Warfusée and a bombardment of this village was accordingly arrranged and carried out with all the available Artillery behind the Sector. All Carey's Force and the Americans were eventually withdrawn. Consequently the line was very thinly held by the 9th Lancers, 18th Hussars, Essex and Bedfordshire Yeomanry and the 2nd Machine Gun Squadron, with 4th Dragoon Guards in reserve.

The 14th Division took over the line on the night of April 3rd, Brigadier-General Windus, commanding the 47th Brigade taking over the Sector from Col. Whitmore. The relief was not complete until nearly dawn on the 4th April. It was necessary to leave the 2nd Machine Gun Squadron, which was commanded by Capt. G. Dent, in the line, in order to strengthen the 47th Brigade.

At dawn the Germans made a determined attack on the whole line and the 14th Division were forced to retire, giving up the Bois de Vaire and Warfusée to the enemy, and it was then that the 6th Cavalry Brigade were ordered to restore the situation as already described.

XXVIII.

BREAKING UP OF 4 YEOMANRY REGIMENTS, 1918.

In the meanwhile the Essex Yeomanry returned to their horses at Fouilloy and subsequently marched to Bussy les Daours, where orders were received to send a Squadron as reinforcements to each of the Regiments in the 1st Brigade.

All the 4 Regiments of Yeomanry were used in a similar way and as a result Cavalry Corps, which was now only 3 Divisions, was by this means nearly made up to its proper strength.

In consequence " C " Squadron, Essex Yeomanry, went to the 11th Hussars, " B " Squadron to the 2nd Dragoon Guards and " A " Squadron to the 5th Dragoon Guards.

The Senior Officers of the Regiment underwent constant changes, but eventually were posted as follows :—Lieut.-Col. F. H. D. C. Whitmore, C.M.G., D.S.O., to command 10th (P.W.O.) Royal Hussars;

Major Gold, Royal Air Force; Major Buxton, D.S.O., Musketry Instructor Cavalry Corps; Major E. Hill, D.S.O., 2nd in Command, 15th Hussars; Major E. A. Ruggles-Brise, M.C., 2nd in Command, 4th Dragoon Guards.

The breaking up of the Regiment on this occasion was, perhaps, the Regiment's saddest day during the war. It was however fortunate that every Officer and man in the Regiment was more than dog-tired, having been constantly engaged day and night for nearly a fortnight. The time also allowed for the move to be carried out did not admit of much sentimental consideration.

Nevertheless, the 4th April, 1918, will always be remembered as a parting of the ways. The sadness of the parting of old comrades who had fought side by side for $3\frac{1}{2}$ years showed clearly the extent of the esprit de corps which had existed in the Regiment and it showed, above all, the unbounded friendship, together with common respect, which was shared equally by Officers and other ranks.

It would not be out of place to insert here a paragraph of the despatch of Field-Marshal Sir Douglas Haig, K.T., G.C.B., G.C.V.O., referring to the work of the Cavalry and Yeomanry Regiments in the preservation of the defences of Amiens.

BREAKING UP OF 4 YEOMANRY REGIMENTS, 1918.

Extract of Despatch.

" The work of the mounted troops, in particular, was invaluable, demonstrating in marked fashion the importance of the part which Cavalry have still to play in modern war.

" So urgent was the demand for more mounted men, that arrangements were made during the progress of the battle to provide with horses several regiments of Yeomanry, who had but recently been dismounted for employment with other arms.

" In common with the rest of the Cavalry, these Yeomanry did excellent service. Without the assistance of mounted troops, skilfully handled and gallantly led, the enemy could scarcely have been prevented from breaking through the long and thinly held front of broken and wooded ground before the French reinforcements had had time to arrive."

XXIX.

SUMMER, 1918.

Lieut.-Col. F. Whitmore, C.M.G., D.S.O., took over command of the 10th Royal Hussars on April 7th, whilst the Regiment was in billets at Camon. At the same time many reinforcements, both in men and horses, came from the North Somerset Yeomanry.

On April 11th, 12th and 13th the Regiment marched to Aumerval, halting at Buire-au-Bois and Hestrus on the way. The Divisional Head Quarters moved to Pernes.

During the time the Division was in this area one Brigade was always detailed and kept in readiness to move forward to support the 11th Corps.

During the first period up to April 25th the Brigade was to hold the rear defences East of St. Venant, and after that date it was to hold the bridges over the Aire Canal, East of Busnes, also the switch trench line Steenbecque-Busnes.

The Division remained in this area until the 1st week in May, when it moved to Contay, where all the Regiments of the Division were bivouacked in this valley. Much bombing at night by enemy aircraft took place, but Contay itself was never shelled until after the Division had moved. Whilst in this area defensive preparations were made West of Albert.

On May 17th the Brigade marched to Belloy-sur-Somme, where it remained until May 31st, when it returned to Béhencourt, near Contay, as a mobile reserve to the 3rd Army, each Brigade doing duty in turn, bivouacking in a wood. Night bombing by enemy aircraft was for a time a serious matter.

The 4th of June was celebrated in this wood by a regimental Old Etonian dinner party. The following Officers were present:

Brigadier-General A. Seymour, D.S.O.

Capt. E. A. Fielden, M.C.

Lieut.-Col. F. H. D. C. Whitmore, C.M.G., D.S.O.

Major G. E. Gosling, M.C.

Capt. R. Gordon Canning, M.C.

Capt. V. Greenwood, M.C.

Lieut. Lord William W. M. Douglas Scott, M.C.

Lieut. F. C. Drake, M.C.

Lieut. B. A. Wilson, M.C.

SUMMER, 1918.

On June 14 the 6th Cavalry Brigade was relieved by the 7th Cavalry Brigade and consequently the 10th Royal Hussars marched back to their former bivouac at Belloy. The Brigade suffered severely from the epidemic of influenza and the Medical Authorities were in considerable difficulties in dealing with the ever increasing number of cases, with the result that a large camp had to be erected to accommodate the hundreds of cases which required isolation and treatment.

From Belloy the Brigade moved into the next valley south west to Le Mesge, Soues and Reincourt. The 10th Hussars were billeted at Reincourt.

The shooting of the Regiment was immensely improved whilst in this area, because of an admirable range, which the regiment made, which consisted of 15 targets and a range of 200 yards was able to be obtained.

Perhaps the chief event, as far as the Regiment was concerned, was the Brigade Horse Show, at which the 10th Hussars won nearly all the prizes, the greatest achievement being to win both the 1st and 2nd prize for the best conditioned troop of 30 horses. The two troops which received the 1st and 2nd prizes really looked magnificent, and they won the admiration of all who saw them. It is fair to say also that all the troops in the Regiment looked in splendid condition.

At the Regimental eliminating competition prior to the Brigade Horse Show the judges had no easy job to determine which were the best 2 troops in the Regiment.

There was a polo ground and a race course close at hand and both these were frequently used. Troop and Squadron drill, also tactical exercises, were carried out.

The weather was generally fine and it may be said that the Brigade benefited much by the period occupied in this area.

XXX.

THE ATTACK IN AUGUST, 1918.

The attack and Capture of the line of the Amiens outer defences commenced on August 8th.

In preparation for this attack the 3rd Cavalry Division moved East on August 6th.

The 6th Brigade marched from Reincourt at 10.45 p.m. to a concentration area about Pont de Metz. The 10th Hussars were billeted at Renancourt, arriving at 3 a.m. on August 7th.

At 9 p. m., on August 7th, the Brigade marched through the outskirts of Amiens to an assembly area about 2 miles east of Longueau.

The concentration of such a vast quantity of troops in this area in preparation for the great attack of the Fourth Army, in conjunction with the French, was one of the greatest achievements of the war. It was necessary to get the whole of the Cavalry Corps, not to speak of countless Tanks, and Guns of all descriptions, also masses of Infantry over the bridge at Longueau, which was but a few miles from the enemy lines—this necessarily had to be done during the darkness of a very short night. The Cavalry, closed right up head to croup, crossed the bridge in sections. Columns of Tanks were to be seen moving to their allotted positions of readiness. It was well before the appointed hour that all the formations were ready for the attack, which was timed to commence at dawn.

The last few moments before the great attack was launched on August 8th can never be forgotten by those who witnessed it. There was a slight mist, which made the advancing tanks look like great battleships in line, and the weird noise of their advance just before the first gun was fired at zero hour made one think that the suspicion of the enemy would be aroused: but what wind there was happened to be favourable, and the surprise was complete.

No sooner had the first of the hundreds of batteries opened fire on that eventful morning, than every battery pounded its contents into the ever weakening stronghold of the enemy; the tanks moved steadily along, and the infantry the same. And from that moment the great tide had turned against the fortunes of the German power, and afterwards, day by day, our continual successes not only put fresh life and hope into the armies of the Allies, but the morale of the enemy became daily more exhausted.

August 8th is referred to by General Ludendorff as " Germany's Black Day." He writes that six or seven divisions were over-run by tanks; and that the Second Army's defeat reacted upon the Eighteenth Army, the whole Western front being thereby shattered.

The attack of the Fourth Army extended from Dernancourt in the North to the River Luce in the South, a distance of approximately eleven miles. The Australian Corps, with the 5th Tank Brigade, were attacking on the left of the British line and the Canadian Corps, with the 4th Tank Brigade, on the right, and the French were attacking on the right of the Canadians.

The role of the 3rd Cavalry Division was to support the Canadian attack, and to exploit their success.

The attack was launched at 4.20 a.m., at which hour a very heavy bombardment opened, and over 300 Tanks took part in the primary stages of the attack.

The infantry gained their objectives with little opposition, and the Canadian Cavalry Brigade, being the leading Brigade of the 3rd Cavalry Division, was soon in touch with the enemy at Beaucourt. The 7th Cavalry Brigade was in touch with the enemy on the left, and the 6th Cavalry Brigade was in reserve, advancing by way of Cachy—Démuin and N. of Beaucourt.

Towards evening the 10th Royal Hussars were ordered to support the 7th Cavalry Brigade south of Caix and N.E. of Quesnel; the 1st Royal Dragoons, who had already been sent in support of this Brigade, were engaged and were held up by artillery and machine gun fire from the direction of Quesnel.

Lieut.-Col. F. H. D. C. Whitmore, Commanding 10th Royal Hussars, thereupon decided to push on towards Warvillers and Beaufort, and so relieve the pressure on Lieut.-Col. F. W. Wormald, D.S.O., Commanding the 1st Royal Dragoons, arrangements having been made for the co-operation of the 4th Dragoon Guards on the left of the 10th Royal Hussars.

At that moment Lieut.-Col. Whitmore, C.M.G., D.S.O., was ordered to take over command of the 6th Cavalry Brigade from Brig.-General A. Seymour, D.S.O., who was too unwell to continue in command of the Brigade. Capt. R. Gordon Canning, M.C., thereupon assumed command of the 10th Royal Hussars, in the absence of Major Gosling, M.C., who was acting as Liaison Officer.

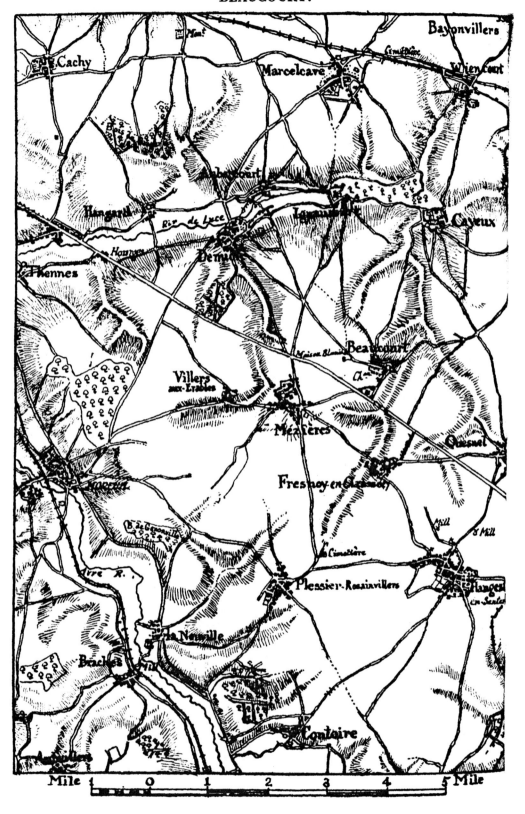

Mile 1   0   1   2   3   4   5 Mile

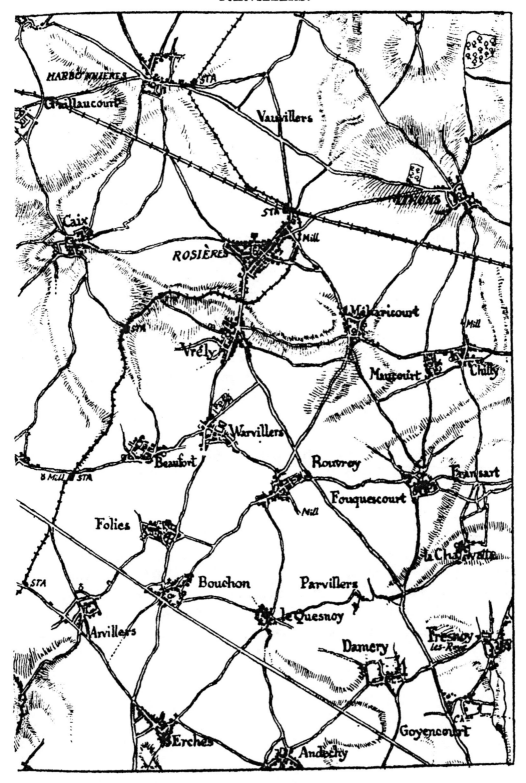

THE ATTACK IN AUGUST, 1918.

Orders were then received from Major-General A. E. W. Harman, D.S.O., Commanding 3rd Cavalry Division, that the line, as then occupied, was to be held without further advance being effected that day. Outposts were thereupon established on the line captured, " A " Squadron, 10th Royal Hussars, under Capt. the Earl of Airlie, M.C., and " B " Squadron, under Lord William Scott, M.C., covering Quesnel from the head of a narrow valley running due South of Caix. The remainder of the Regiment was in reserve about the centre of the valley.

During the night the Regiment suffered some casualties in killed and wounded from shell fire, Lieut. G. H. Perrett being killed, and Lieut. T. Robinson, M.C., wounded, and about 90 horses were lost.

At 10 a.m., on 9th August, the Regiment was withdrawn to the West of Caix, at which place the Division came into Corps Reserve. This gave an opportunity of a much needed rest for the men, and there was a plentiful supply of water for the horses. In the meantime further progress was being made, and it was evident that the Germans were carrying out an extended retirement. Quesnel was already in our hands. Very encouraging reports came to hand from the First Cavalry Division, which was operating on the left, including the report of the capture of an entire train containing Officers and men returning from leave to rejoin their Regiments in the line. This Division alone had captured 11 Officers and 1,350 other ranks prisoners.

On August 9th the 1st and 2nd Cavalry Divisions were ordered to support the attacking Infantry closely and seize any opportunity of passing through and moving forward to the objective, which was the line Roye—Chaulnes.

At 1 p.m. the Canadians attacking in front of the 2nd Cavalry Division were held up by machine gun fire from Beaufort Wood. A Company of Whippet tanks was then put at the disposal of the 2nd Canadian Infantry Brigade and the attack was successful, with the result that at 2.45 p.m. the advanced Squadrons of the 2nd Cavalry Division were able to push forward.

The situation at 4 p.m. was as follows :—

Folies and Beaufort were offering strong resistance. The former was, however, taken by the Canadians, and large numbers of the enemy were seen retiring towards Warvillers.

At 5.30 p.m. the 5th Cavalry Brigade had reached Beaufort and Folies and the Infantry had passed through Warvillers.

In the meanwhile the French attack south of the Roye road had been entirely successful and they had occupied Arvillers.

. On 10th August, at 5.30 a.m., the 6th Cavalry Brigade moved East, the 3rd Cavalry Division relieving the 2nd Cavalry Division. The general advance was taken up with the 6th Cavalry Brigade operating on the right, and the 7th Cavalry Brigade on the left, the Canadian Cavalry Brigade being in reserve.

The Brigade moved up past Beaufort to Folies, with the 3rd Dragoon Guards on the right via Bouchoir, and the 1st Royal Dragoons on the left via Rouvroy. A Company of Whippet Tanks, under Major R. West, D.S.O., was placed at the disposal of Lieut.-Col. Whitmore.

On arrival at the above-named line, it became evident that the situation at Parvillers was obscure and that the high ground between Damery and Andechy was strongly held by the enemy. The nature of the country, owing to old trench systems and barbed wire entanglements of the old battle ground of 1916, rendered the possibilities of cavalry advance impracticable in front of the 6th Cavalry Brigade.

The Canadian Cavalry Brigade was ordered to seize Hill 100, this being the highest point of the road between Quesnel and Roye. Lieut.-Col.

Whitmore, commanding the 6th Cavalry Brigade, was ordered to support this attack. Orders were thereupon issued for the 10th Royal Hussars to keep in close support of the Canadian Cavalry Brigade and the 1st Royal Dragoons were brought into reserve at Folies.

The 10th Royal Hussars in consequence moved to a point just south of the road due South of le Quesnoy and the 3rd Dragoon Guards remained East of le Quesnoy. The Canadian Cavalry Brigade attempted to carry the hill by attacking up the main road, the country on either side being quite impassable for Cavalry. The attack failed and they had many casualties.

The Headquarters of the 6th Cavalry Brigade were, during this operation, just West of le Quesnoy, and suddenly became subjected to a very heavy bombardment, causing casualties in the Brigade Headquarters, and many horses were killed or wounded. The Brigade subsequently concentrated at Folies for the night.

On August 11th the 3rd Cavalry Division marched back to the Boves area, and the 10th Royal Hussars were billeted at Fouencamps.

Whilst in this area the Commander-in-Chief visited all the Regiments in the Division, and he was accorded a great reception.

During the 3 days fighting, August 8th, 9th and 10th, the Cavalry Corps as a whole captured no fewer than 3,000 prisoners, in addition to two trains and a large quantity of supplies and transport.

Between August 8th and 12th the Fourth Army captured 21,850 prisoners and 400 guns; the safety of Amiens had been restored and the Amiens—Paris railway had been freed.

The success thus achieved did not stop there: it was but a forerunner to the series of victories which were gained by all the armies along the western front; victories which, in three months from that date, exhausted the resources of what was once the world's most powerful military organisation, and thus brought about peace.

On August 15th Lieut.-Col. Ewing Paterson, D.S.O., Inniskilling Dragoons, assumed command of the 6th Cavalry Brigade, and the Brigade marched back to Riencourt. In the short time available in this area refitting was carried out as quickly as possible. Reinforcements, remounts, arms and equipment were all necessary to bring the Regiments up to their proper strength. The fighting efficiency of the Brigade was restored in a very few days, and on August 22nd the Brigade marched to Fieffes area and from here to Sibiville, halting for one night at Vitz Villeroy on August 25th.

XXXI.

DROCOURT—QUÉANT LINE, 1918.

Whilst the Brigade was billeted in this area the Canadian Corps were rapidly moved up from the South and they made their magnificent attack on the German line East of Arras, recapturing Monchy-le-Preux; Rœux, Pelves, Vis-en-Artois and all the country well known to those regiments of the Cavalry which took so prominent a part in the capture and defence of Monchy-le-Preux in April, 1917.

It was in continuation of this advance by the Canadian Corps that on August 30th the 10th Hussars were ordered to march to Wailly, South-West of Arras, to be attached to the Canadian Corps for the time being, in order to form part of an independent force, consisting of Cavalry, armoured cars, motor machine gun batteries, field batteries, trench mortars mounted on lorries, and a cyclist battalion.

This mobile Independent Force was to exploit the success of the attack on the strongly held trench system known as the Hindenburg line, particularly the Drocourt—Quéant and Buissy Switch, West of Marquion, and, if possible, to capture the canal crossing at Marquion and form a bridgehead East of that place.

The 10th Hussars bivouacked in the valley of Wancourt, on the night prior to the attack. This valley was already packed with troops, and guns of all calibre. The valley was systematically bombed by enemy aircraft throughout the whole night and many casualties were caused in the Independent Force. An observation balloon was shot down by an enemy aeroplane just on the arrival of the Regiment in the valley; this balloon fell in flames in the middle of a battery horse lines and many horses stampeded in consequence.

By midnight all troops were in readiness for the attack at dawn, all guns were ranged on the once famous Drocourt—Quéant line. Two hours before zero, on that eventful morning, the valley of Wancourt was astir. The various units of the Independent Force pressing their way in the darkness into their proper positions of readiness, the head of the column being on the main Arras—Cambrai road at

St. Rohart Factory, at which place was the Head-quarters of the Independent Force, Brigadier-General Brutinel, C.M.G., D.S.O.

The attack opened at dawn, when every gun in the Canadian Corps poured its shells into the German defences. The whole sky was lit up by the volumes of fire, and the German S.O.S. signals could be seen all along the line. Retaliation, however, was ineffective and it soon became apparent that the Canadian Corps had broken through the great Hindenburg defences. Prisoners came through from the front in large numbers, and our own wounded came back in the best of spirits. Although the casualties in the Canadian Corps were exceedingly heavy in numbers, the majority were only slight wounds, mostly caused by machine gun fire.

This was not the case with the Germans who suffered very heavy casualties indeed, and a very large number were killed.

The following narrative, as prepared immediately after the event, describes the part taken by the 10th Royal Hussars. It is true to say that although the opportunity never occurred when it was possible to make proper use of the Independent Force, the ultimate result of the attack by the Canadian Corps was far reaching and the strong resistance up to that time offered by the Hindenburg line was shattered beyond recovery and another door was thrown open to Cambrai.

Narrative of the Operations East of Arras,

in which the 10th (P.W.O.) Royal Hussars took part, on September 2nd, 1918.

1. Friday, August 30th. The 10th Royal Hussars received orders to march to Wailly, to take part in the operations of the Canadian Corps, organised for the purpose of breaking through the Drocourt—Quéant line astride the Cambrai road, and thence swinging outwards, rolling up the line to North and South.

2. Sunday, September 1st. At a Conference held at the Citadel, Arras, Lieut.-Col. F. H. D. C. Whitmore, C.M.G., D.S.O., commanding 10th Royal Hussars, received orders to command the Leading Group of the Independent Force. This Independent Force, commanded by Brig.-Gen. R. Brutinel, C.M.G., D.S.O., consisted of the following troops :—

10th Royal Hussars
Canadian Light Horse
1st and 2nd Canadian M.M.G. Brigade
Canadian Cyclist Battalion

1 Battery C.F. Artillery
2 Sections Medium Trench Mortars
6 Heavy Armoured Cars (17th Tank Battalion)
2 Light Armoured Cars (2nd Can. M.M.G., Bde.)
1 Wireless Section
1 Supply Column

The role of this Force was as follows :—

As soon as the Red line was captured by the 1st Canadian, 4th Canadian and 4th British Divisions, the Force was to advance through the Red Line and seize the Canal crossing at Marquion and form a bridge head on the high ground, East of that place.

The protective barrage, proceeding onwards from the Red line at Zero + 180 minutes, i.e. 8.0 a.m., being tabled to be clear of Marquion at Zero + 6½ hours, having advanced at the rate of 2,000 yards per hour. At the same time a rectangular area 1,000 yards astride the main Cambrai road was provided, along which the barrage moved at the rate of 1,000 yards per 10 minutes, thus allowing the Independent Force to proceed at the rate of 6,000 yards in one hour in this rectangular area.

The rectangular area included 500 yards on either side of the main road as shown in Canadian Corps Barrage Map " A."

189 .

3. (*a*) The Leading Group, under Lieut-Col. Whitmore, C.M.G., D.S.O., consisted of the following troops :—

10th Royal Hussars
Canadian Light Horse
1 Section Canadian Field Artillery
1 Section 6th M.G. Squadron (Cavalry)
6 Heavy Armoured Cars
2 Light Armoured Cars
10 Motor Cyclists for inter-communication.

(*b*) The 2nd Group, under Lieut.-Col. Walker, D.S.O., consisted of the following :—

4 Light Armoured Cars-
Canadian Cyclist Battalion, less 1 Platoon
5 M.M.G. Batteries
20 Motor Cyclist Scouts
1 Section Canadian Field Artillery
2 Sections Medium Trench Mortars

(*c*) The 3rd Group, under Lieut.-Col. Murling, M.C., consisted of :—

5 M.M.G. Batteries
20 Motor Cyclists

(d) The Supply column, under Major Arnold, consisted of the following :—

    1 Motor lorry
    1 Supply lorry
    1 Ammunition lorry
    1 Fuel and Oil lorry
    Train of 1st and 2nd C.M.M.G. Bde.
    5 Motor Cyclists for inter-liaison

4. *Concentration.*

The Independent Force was assembled at zero (5.0 a.m., September 2nd) on the Wancourt—Guémappe road with the head of the column on the Arras—Cambrai road.

The 10th Royal Hussars, having bivouacked on the night of September 1st in the valley N.W. of Wancourt, formed the head of the column, together with the 2 light and 6 heavy armoured cars.

The column was ready to move off at zero.

5. *Order of March. Leading Group.*

    2 Light Armoured Cars
    6 Heavy Armoured Cars
    " A " Sqdn. X.R.H., Capt. the Earl of Airlie, M.C.
    1 Section 6th M.G. Sqdn.
    1 Sqdn. Hotchkiss A.R., Canadian Light Horse.

"B" Sqdn. X.R.H., Capt. R. C. Gordon
    Canning, M.C.
"C" Sqdn., X.R.H., Capt. W. S. Murland.
1 Section Canadian Field Artillery.
Canadian Light Horse, less H.A.R. Sqdn.
Maltese and Water Carts. Fighting limber.

6. At Zero + 3 hours, 20 minutes, 8.20 a.m.,
Lieut.-Col. Whitmore received orders to move.

> NOTE.—In order to save time in the initial stage of the advance,
> Colonel Whitmore had already moved the column to a
> position of readiness with its head at St. Rohart Factory,
> tail extending parallel to and North of the main Cambrai
> road, 1,500 yards East of the point of assembly referred
> to in para. 4.

7. The Armoured Cars preceding the column
moved off at once, followed by the remainder of
the Force. The mounted troops were obliged to
keep to the main road the whole way, the land on either
side being impassable, until about 2,000 yards East
of Vis-en-Artois.

At 9.10 a.m. a verbal message was received from
Capt. the Earl of Airlie, saying that his leading
patrols were up with the Infantry on the Red line,
who could not proceed any further owing to heavy
Machine Gun fire, that the cross roads on crest
P.26 d.o.2. was being heavily shelled, that the Eastern
slope of the hill was being swept by Machine Gun

Vis-en Artois, looking East

Ruins of St. Rohart Factory, looking West.

fire, also that the Armoured Cars were unable to get on, on account of strong resistance at the cross roads P.34 d.9.2.

Orders were therefore issued for the patrols to keep in touch with the Infantry and report at once any development. At this time one armoured car (heavy) was reported out of action. The leading troops of the 10th Royal Hussars were now distributed in groups on the South of the Cambrai road, about P.25.d. together with the 2 sub-sections, 6th M.G. Sqdn. and Hotchkiss Sqdn. of the Canadian Light Horse. The remainder of the Leading Group, less Section Canadian Field Artillery, on both sides of the road in O.24.d. and O.30.b. 1 Section Canadian Field Artillery was ordered to come into action about P.25.d. against the cemetery P.34.d. and Villers lez Cagnicourt. This Section remained in action throughout the day.

8. The strong resistance at these two places and also from the direction of the Buissy Switch rendered further advance of Cavalry impracticable until these machine guns had been dealt with, and for this purpose the Medium Trench Mortars were brought into action, firing from their lorries.

9. In the event of the resistance at the Cemetery and Villers lez Cagnicourt being overcome by this

bombardment, a further advance by the Leading Group, Independent Force, was prepared, which involved artillery preparation and support, the purpose of this artillery preparation being as follows :—

0 + 10   East end of Villers lez Cagnicourt.
0 + 10   Buissy Switch.
0 + 10   Baralle Wood.
0 + 60   Saudemont.
0 + 60   Rumancourt.
0 + 60   Strong point in Q.31.a.

The objective of the Cavalry being to seize the ridge extending in a N.E. direction from about P.12 central to W.2.c. overlooking Baralle to the S.E. and the Green line to the North.

At 5.0 p.m. the following orders were issued by Lieut.-Col. Whitmore to the formations concerned :—

1. " *The operations of 2nd Group are progressing favourably, which may result in capture of Cemetery and X roads in P.34.d.9.2. and Villers lez Cagnicourt. In this event 2 Squadrons will attack and seize high ground, Gibraltar Hill and lane leading from there to V.12. central and spur through W.7.a and b also W.2.c.*

2. " *The Squadrons detailed for the operation will be " B " Squadron, 10th Hussars, under Capt. Gordon*

Canning, and 1 Squadron, C.L.H., under Major Dawson ; 1 Sub-section 6th M.G. Sqdn. will be attached to each Sqdn. ; one half Sqdn. of Hotchkiss Sqdn. of C.L.H. will also be attached to each Sqdn."

The reconnaissance referred to in the above orders was carried out, the result of which caused any further attempt at advance to be abandoned, and the various formations of the Group received orders to withdraw.

The 10th Royal Hussars thereupon marched to Wailly, where they remained under two hours notice, until orders were received from Cav. Corps to rejoin the 6th Cav. Bde. on Sept. 5th.

Casualties : X.R.H. 1 O.R. wounded.

2 O.R.'s. wounded at duty.

6 horses.

(Sgd.) F. H. D. C. WHITMORE.

Lieut.-Col.,

Commanding 10th (P.W.O.) Royal Hussars.

10.9.18.

XXXII.

ST. QUENTIN, 1918.

After the capture of the Drocourt—Quéant line the 10th Hussars remained at Wailly until September 5th, when they returned to Sibiville to rejoin the 6th Cavalry Brigade.

On the following day, September 6th, the Brigade moved West to the area near Vieil Hesdin, the 10th Hussars being billeted at Vieil Hesdin.

The Cavalry Corps manœuvres took place on September 17th, which necessitated the Regiment moving to the village of Grigny on September 16th and to spend the night after the manœuvres at Boisbergues. The whole of Cavalry Corps and also the Household Cavalry Machine Gun Brigade took part in these manœuvres at which the Commander-in-Chief, Sir Douglas Haig, attended.

On September 19th the Brigade moved into a new Divisional area near Frévent and the 10th

Hussars were billeted at Ligny-sur-Canche, where they remained until September 25th.

On that date Cavalry Corps moved forward to take part in the operations near St. Quentin. The 6th Cavalry Brigade marched from Ligny-sur-Canche at 7.45 p.m. and billeted at Couin, and the following night the Brigade marched through the area only recently vacated by the Germans, through Bouzincourt and Albert, which in the darkness only showed heaps of broken debris, the houses absolutely destroyed and the Cathedral no longer recognisable as a Cathedral at all, merely the outside walls of the ruin left, which showed where the building once stood.

That night, September 26th, the Brigade bivouacked in the open, near the ruined village of Méaulte. Quantities of German war material lay strewn about the place and there was not a house standing. The Church had been completely destroyed since the British evacuation the previous April.

The march was continued on September 27th, during the night passing through Fricourt and the country familiar to all in the battles of the Somme in 1916. On arrival at Hem the Brigade billeted in huts, which had originally been built by the British but occupied recently by the Germans.

ST. QUENTIN, 1918.

On 29th September the Brigade marched in the evening to Vermand.

During all this period the constant and continual attacks of the 3rd and 4th Armies were breaking the morale of the enemy, and every day brought better news.

During the march from Hem to Vermand many hundreds of prisoners were passed on the way. The Brigade marched at dusk over the land, which during the spring had been cultivated and sown by the 3rd Cavalry Division Agricultural Organisation. The crops had been reaped and cleared by the enemy, and from the appearance of the stubble a fair crop must have been taken.

The 10th Hussars were bivouacked in a field close to Bihecourt Station, the Headquarters of the Regiment being situated in what was once the Station Master's house. and after a little patching up, these Headquarters, in comparison with what was to follow, formed a very comfortable home.

XXXIII.

HONNECHY, 1918.

On October 2nd, at 8 a.m., the Brigade moved forward to an assembly area near Bellenglise, the 3rd Cavalry Division being in a position of readiness to exploit the success of the Fourth Army. However, at 10.30 a.m. orders were received to return to Bihecourt.

On October 3rd at 10.30 a.m. the Brigade moved up again to Bellenglise and from there to an assembly area, S.W. of Joncourt, arriving at that place at about 3 p.m.

Lieut. J. B. Bickersteth, 1st Royal Dragoons, Intelligence Officer to the 6th Cavalry Brigade, rendered excellent service by ascertaining the situation at this place, and as a reward for his careful reconnaissance and gallantry in obtaining his information he received the Military Cross.

The 3rd Dragoon Guards were ordered to advance towards Ramicourt, but they could make no progress, being held up by artillery and machine gun fire. The 10th Royal Hussars in support came under heavy machine gun fire from many aeroplanes, also some gas shelling, and were forced to find a fresh position of readiness at Joncourt.

In the evening the Brigade returned to bivouac near Pontru and were subjected to considerable bombing by enemy aircraft during the night. During the march to Pontru an enemy bomb, intended for the column on the march, fell right into the middle of a column of German prisoners and about 70 were killed.

On October 5th the Brigade moved back to Trefcon.

On October 8th the Brigade moved forward to an assembly area at Magny-la-Fosse, marching out from Trefcon at 4.45 a.m.

The role of the 3rd Cavalry Division was to support the 1st Cavalry Division in exploiting the success of the Third and Fourth Armies, attacking in the direction of Caudry—Bohain, the 6th Cavalry Brigade being in Corps Reserve, At 9 a.m. the Brigade moved up to just N. of Wiancourt and returned to Magny-la-Fosse for the night.

On October 9th the Brigade moved off at 5 a.m. to an assembly area E. of Ponchaux. The role of the Division was to keep close touch with the infantry, and, if the opportunity occurred, to push through and occupy the high ground W. and S.W. of Le Cateau.

The 6th Cavalry Brigade moved along the line of the main Estrées—Le Cateau road to a position South of Maretz.

" C " Squadron, 10th Hussars, under Captain Murland, acted as right flank guard to the Division. This Squadron came under machine gun fire from the outskirts of La Sablière Wood (South of Maretz) and it became evident that the enemy were holding the line of the railway, West of Honnechy.

At 1 p.m. orders were received that in the event of the infantry capturing Honnechy, the Canadian Cavalry Brigade would advance via Maurois and the 6th Cavalry Brigade would advance South of Honnechy.

After stubborn resistance Honnechy was captured, the 1st Royal Dragoons advanced on Reumont, and the 3rd Dragoon Guards to the Eastern outskirts of Honnechy. The 10th Royal Hussars in reserve followed the 3rd Dragoon Guards.

The 10th Hussars had suffered many casualties in killed and wounded, prior to this advance, by shell fire, also by enemy aircraft machine guns, and many horses had been killed.

HONNECHY, 1918.

Heavy artillery and machine gun fire were met with by the Regiment at Honnechy, coming under direct observation from the high ground near Escaufourt. "C" Battery R.H.A., under Major Scott, D.S.O., was able to come into action against German batteries which were plainly visible in the open.

Enemy machine gun fire was especially severe against the Southern slopes of the hill, South of Honnechy, and it was here that many casualties occurred.

The village of Honnechy was inhabited by many civilians and many lost their lives in the bombardment that followed. Red Cross flags were flying from most of the houses and also from the church : this was the signal used by the civilian population to draw our attention to the fact that they were there, prior to our occupation of the village. Their bravery under shell fire was much to be admired and the assistance which they rendered to the wounded was beyond praise.

They were all so delighted to be delivered from the yoke of German rule that they were almost beyond themselves with delight. It was in the town of Maretz, close to Honnechy, that a man of the 11th Hussars reported himself, having been living there under the protection of the civilian inhabitants ever since the first battle of Le Cateau in 1914.

HONNECHY and LE CATEAU.

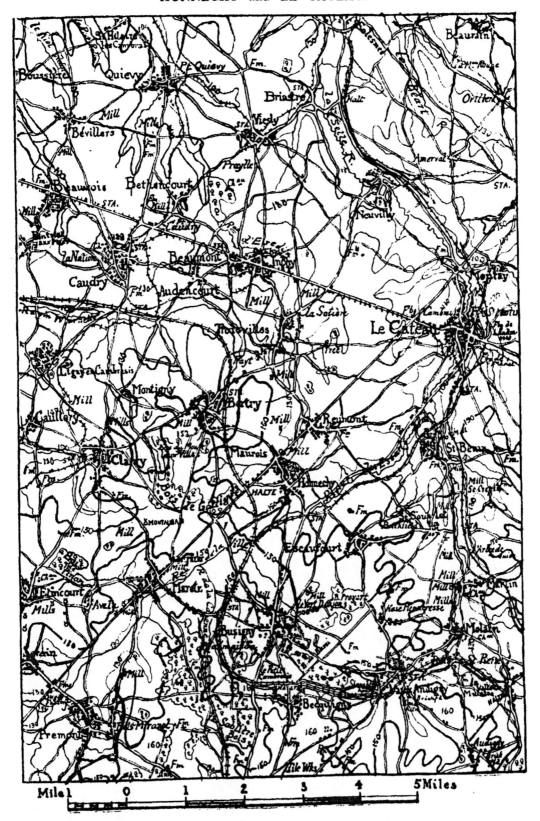

Mile 1   0   1   2   3   4   5 Miles

Honnechy itself was very heavily shelled, as was the entire neighbourhood of the village, casualties becoming constant in the Brigade, and it was here that Lieut.-Col. Rome, D.S.O., commanding the 3rd Dragoon Guards, was wounded.

The 1st Royal Dragoons continued the advance on Reumont, but the high ground East and North-East of that village was strongly held, the enemy holding positions all along the West bank of the river protecting Le Cateau.

The 10th Royal Hussars were in support of the 1st Royal Dragoons and suffered again heavily from enemy aircraft bombs.

At nightfall the situation was that Le Cateau was still held by the enemy in force, as was the West bank of the river, and the Brigade bivouacked on the ground it had captured between Reumont and Maurois, establishing outposts overlooking the river. The line was taken over during the night by the 18th Corps Cyclists.

The casualties of the Regiment were as follows :—

Captain W. S. Murland ..	Wounded.
Lieut. S. J. Tufnell ..	Wounded.
Lieut. W. Ritchie ..	Wounded.
Lieut. F. C. Drake, M.C. ..	Wounded.
Lieut. S. A. Ralli ..	Wounded.

7 Other Ranks   .. Killed.

58 Other Ranks   .. Wounded.

Also 106 horses

Total Casualties : 70 Officers and O.R.'s, 106 horses.

During the night shelling continued intermittently, but diminished towards the early hours of the morning.

On October 10th the Brigade was concentrated by 6 a.m. in the Valley, South of Troisvilles. Very little progress was possible, and the line then ran from the Western outskirts of Neuvilly and Western outskirts of Le Cateau.

The Regiment bivouacked for the night just N.E. of the village of Montigny.

The Brigade marched back to Elincourt on October 11th, billeting there for two nights.

The village of Montigny possessed many inhabitants and they were all very anxious to do something for the British troops. Very little damage had been done in this village, either by friend or foe ; everywhere showed evidence of a hasty retreat.

Elincourt was a larger village altogether, and must have contained a large number of inhabitants. This was one of the unfortunate places which was necessarily included in our area for bombardment prior to its occupation by the Australians. The destructive power of preliminary bombardment was amply illustrated by the fact that there was probably not a single house which had not been either struck or destroyed by our bombardment. The horrors of war were painfully depicted in this small town, and it is to the credit of the enemy that they compelled the inhabitants to evacuate the place prior to the advance of the British troops, knowing that their own resistance at this place would attract a heavy bombardment.

In consequence, when the 6th Cavalry Brigade entered the village, there appeared no evidence of anybody living in the place. It soon became known, however, that there were still a few, and also that there were some bodies of dead civilians. This proved to be only too true. A systematic search was made and some 4 or 5 bodies were found unburied and also the body of a dead German soldier was found lying on the floor of the Church, which had been used as a dressing station.

The story told by one civilian inhabitant to the writer of this narrative was, indeed, a sad story to listen to.

The writer visited a small cottage, containing 3 small rooms; and on rapping at the door, a middle-aged woman with trouble written all over her face opened the door. In the corner of the room sat a very old woman, her mother, aged 87. On being asked whether it was true that the body of a woman was lying unburied in the house, the middle-aged woman opened another door leading into what was evidently the only bedroom. The room presented a terrible sight, for it was obvious that a shell had burst in the room; everything lay about broken and in confusion, tables, chairs, china, and glass, clothes, bricks and timber. In the centre of the room on the floor lay the body of a very old woman on her back, arms stretched out, just as she had been killed, perhaps 4 days before.

The pitiful story was this—that the inhabitants, young and old, received orders to evacuate the village in anticipation of the bombardment; all were told to walk to Honnechy. The old woman of 87, her two daughters, and the woman whose body now lay in the cottage, started to tramp to Honnechy. The two old women could not get as far and remained the night in the open, in the rain, the two daughters went on to their destination carrying what things they could with them, and one of them returned to look for the old ladies, and not finding them, she returned to her old home at Elincourt to find they had crawled back to their house and that no sooner had they got back than a shell burst in the house and killed the unfortunate old friend of the family.

The Church at Elincourt was thoroughly cleaned out by a Brigade fatigue party. Tons of filth and debris were removed, the seats replaced in their position, and the body of the old lady was removed from the cottage and laid on the steps of the altar pending opportunity for burial.

The above story is only one instance of the many similar sad stories which might be told and which illustrate the dreadful hardships which have been suffered by the unfortunate people whom Providence has arranged should become the victims in this terrible war.

XXXIV.

MANANCOURT, 1918.

The Brigade remained at Elincourt until October 13th, when it marched West to Manancourt, halting for one night, the night of the 13th, at Banteux.

Banteux was not far from Vendhuille and the famous " Bird Cage " and Ossus Wood. It was, indeed, interesting to see the defences at the " Bird Cage " and Epehy from the enemy point of view. It was evident that a very strong resistance had been put up by the Germans in this locality. Machine gun posts manned by 5 or 6 Germans were distributed along the positions. Some of the Germans were actually in the positions in which they were in before they were killed, with their hands in the act of firing the machine guns. Others were evidently killed whilst running forward with supplies of ammunition in boxes. The whole area was strewn with machine guns, ammunition, rifles, hand grenades and clothing of all sorts; the whole place bearing the traces of very hard fighting.

The billets or rather dug-outs occupied by the Brigade at Banteux may perhaps be described as some of the worst which have been met with during the whole campaign.

The march to Manancourt the following day was interesting, because it was across the battle area of the previous Autumn, when our troops made so splendid a stand at Gouzeaucourt and where the Guards Division made their magnificent counter thrust against the great German counter attack, subsequent to the advance of the 3rd Army on Cambrai. In one place alone it was possible to count no fewer that 6 derelict tanks which had been abandoned during that engagement. All the ground the whole way to Etricourt was littered with war material and countless ammunition dumps abandoned by the enemy. On arrival at Manancourt the 10th Hussars soon made themselves comparatively comfortable in the huts, which had been abandoned by the enemy; the Headquarters being in quite new huts, which had only recently been built by the Germans and left in a state of incompletion.

All the villages were completely destroyed and places such as Sailly, Saillisel and Rocquigny, which had been destroyed during the concluding stages of the Somme Offensive in 1916, were almost indistinguishable as having ever existed at all.

There was much game about, both partridges and hares, and some very good afternoons, partridge driving, were obtained, Officers and N.C.O.'s of Squadrons turning out mounted to act as beaters. 15 to 20 brace of partridges and 7 to 10 hares was by no means an uncommon bag for 6 to 8 guns in an afternoon.

Major Buxton, who now commanded a Squadron of the 10th Hussars, was usually the organiser of the shooting parades.

The Division remained in this area until November 6th, and many very interesting Brigade Field days were organised by Brigadier-General Ewing Paterson, D.S.O., who was quite an expert in arranging short interesting schemes.

It is generally admitted that if the war had been prolonged the 6th Cavalry Brigade would have found itself far more efficient in working with co-operation after this period at Manancourt than, perhaps, it had ever had an opportunity of being before. This may be attributed to the fact that the country itself was a training area such as the Brigade had never been fortunate enough to be in before, and at the same time every opportunity was taken of getting the greatest advantage out of it.

XXXV.

THE LAST WEEK OF THE WAR.

All news that came to hand early in November was most encouraging and it looked as if the war really was nearly at an end. Orders were eventually received for the Division to move North, and on November 6th the Brigade marched in a deluge of rain to Marquion, this being the place which was the objective of the Regiment when forming part of the Canadian Corps Independent Force on September 2nd.

It was a dreadfully wet day and night and everybody got wet through to the skin. Little or no shelter was to be found at Marquion on account of the destructive effect of the shelling of our own guns some weeks before. The horses which were out in the open were up to knees and hocks in mud, and some saddles and equipment had to be dug out of the mud with spades before saddling up for the march on the following day.

THE LAST WEEK OF THE WAR.

On November 7th the march was continued North, via Aubigny-au-Bac, Douai, to Esquerchin.

Douai, although knocked about in places, was not in a bad state of dilapidation and Esquerchin was a very comfortable billet not destroyed at all, but there were no inhabitants in the neighbourhood, and every house had an unexploded shell concealed either in the cellars or lower rooms, which had been placed there for the purpose of blowing up the houses prior to the German retreat, but the retreat had been forced upon them so quickly that they were unable to carry out their intention.

On November 8th the Brigade moved to the area near Fretin, the 10th Royal Hussars being billeted at that place. The inhabitants were all delighted beyond words to do anything for the British troops and were all eagerly awaiting to know what would be the response to the terms of the Armistice offered.

It was during the march from Fretin to Gaurain—Ramecroix that news came through that the German Navy was in a state of mutiny and that the Kaiser had abdicated. Everybody was in the best of spirits and on arrival at Ramecroix the Regiment found the best of billets and everybody delighted to do all in their power to make the troops comfortable.

Early in the morning of November 11th, the reply to the Armistice still being uncertain, orders were received for the Cavalry to press forward as quickly as possible. Brigadier-General Ewing Paterson attended a conference at the Divisional Headquarters at 4 a.m., with the result that the 6th Cavalry Brigade received orders to push ahead as quickly as possible, and occupy the line Enghien—Soignies.

The 1st Royal Dragoons were the leading regiment and the 10th Royal Hussars received orders to send out in advance 2 troops for the purpose of reconnaissance, and gain touch with the enemy who were rapidly retreating.

All along the road the civilian population were crowding back to their homes, hand carts covered with National flags being drawn by old and young. Some had tramped back for miles; all were tired, and everybody cheerful. Many enquired after the safety of their homes, and many gave interesting information as to the deplorable state in which the Germans were carrying out their retreat.

The main roads and railways were blown up at intervals, huge holes had to be filled up before it became possible to organise transport. It is safe to say that the last few hours of the world's greatest war will never be forgotten by those who were fortu-

The Square at Leuze.

The Square at Mons.

nate enough to survive the strain of 4 years and witness the event.

The Brigade reached Leuze at 10.30 a.m. and received the following message, brought by car, from Cavalry Corps :—

" Hostilities will cease at 11.00 to-day, November 11th. Troops will stand fast on positions reached at hour named. Line of outposts will be established and reported to Corps H.Q. Remainder of troops will be collected, organised ready to meet any demand. All military precautions will be preserved. There will be no communication with the enemy. Further instructions will be issued. Cav. Corps. 08.10.

(*Sgd.*) *G. REYNOLDS, Major.*"

It was then arranged that at 11.00 :

(a) The trumpeters of the Brigade would be formed up in the Square at Leuze.

(b) All Officers and Sergeants available, of the Brigade be formed up by the same hour.

(c) That the trumpeters, under the Trumpet-Major X.R.H., should sound—

" Stand Fast "

" Cease Fire."

At this moment an infantry battalion (14th London), with band, was marching through Leuze. This battalion was formed up in the Square without delay with the band in the centre of the Square.

At 11 a.m. precisely the trumpets sounded and the Band played the British National Anthem, followed by the Belgian and French National Anthems, the infantry battalion presenting arms for the occasion. The ceremony concluded with the Mayor of Leuze addressing the assembled troops, thanking the Allies for their deliverance of the town on behalf of the inhabitants, and the 14th London Battalion marched out of the Square, being cheered by the 6th Cavalry Brigade.

The Regiment moved out to the East of Leuze and waited there for further orders. Orders were subsequently received by aeroplane to the effect that the Brigade would return to the previous night's billets. The Regiment arrived back at Ramecroix at 6 p.m.

The two troops of the 10th Royal Hussars employed on reconnaissance had advanced so quickly that difficulty was experienced in recalling them after hostilities had ceased.

The troop under 2/Lieut. Kyte reached within $\frac{1}{2}$ mile of Bassilly, and at 12.30 they were fired on by a light gun, mounted on a motor lorry. Also they encountered machine gun fire from the Western edge of the Bois de Silly. This patrol returned to the Regiment at 8 p.m.

The troop under Lieut. Lockett did not get in touch with the enemy and did not rejoin the Regiment until 8 a.m. the following morning, 12th November, 1918.

So ended the part taken by the 10th Royal Hussars in the Great European War. The front of the Allies on Monday, November 11th, extended approximately along the line Fresnes, Sedan, Mons, Ghent to the North Sea.

The Guards and the 62nd Division had already occupied the fortress of Maubeuge on November 9th, and the 3rd Canadian Division entered Mons just prior to the Armistice.

The name of Mons will perpetuate the memory of both the beginning and the end of the Great War. The traditions of the British Expeditionary Force will always be associated with its name, and one Regiment, at least, the 2nd Battalion of the Royal Irish Regiment, will for ever carry the record of having concluded hostilities at the very spot from which it was forced to retreat in August, 1914.

XXXVI.

AFTER THE ARMISTICE, 1918=19.

The day after the Armistice was accepted, the Brigade went into billets near Willaupuis, the 10th Hussars being billeted in that village. All preparations were at once made for the triumphal march through Belgium to the German frontier and the Rhine. Arms, saddlery and equipment were cleaned and polished and every man entered into the spirit of the desire to exercise the traditions of the Cavalry.

On November 17th the Regiment marched to St. Marcoule, which was not far from where Lieut. Kyte and his patrol encountered the enemy's machine guns at the Bois de Silly after 11 o'clock on the memorable Armistice day, November 11th. An enormous quantity of enemy guns, limbers, tractors and lorries were lying by the roadside just in the positions where the Germans had abandoned them in order to go East, unhampered by war material.

AFTER THE ARMISTICE, 1918–19.

Every town or village gave the troops a most enthusiastic reception. Triumphal arches and bunting adorned every large centre, and every cottage displayed a national flag.

The following day, November 18th, the whole Brigade was billeted near Saintes. It was here that the brass band and Mayor assembled to welcome the General, and the remainder of the day was spent in general holiday and merriment. The band instruments here, like at all other places, had been buried since the commencement of the war in order to avoid their being taken by the enemy for the purpose of the manufacture of shell cases.

From Saintes the whole Brigade marched across the battlefield of Waterloo. This, perhaps, may be considered the most interesting event of the march. Each regiment, with drawn swords, saluted the monument as it passed, one hundred and three years having passed since these famous regiments fought side by side on that great battlefield.

On arrival at Limal on November 21st a great reception awaited the 10th Royal Hussars. The Square was thronged with people. A huge bouquet was presented to the Commanding Officer by a lady; whilst the Mayor and Councillors, with town band, were present in Official State.

Addresses of welcome were read by the Mayor and responded to by Lieut.-Col. Whitmore ; the usual toasts in the Château brought the eventful proceedings to a close.

On November 22nd the Regiment marched to Taviers, where great hospitality was shown by everybody ; and on November 24th the 10th Hussars marched to St. Germain, where they remained until December 10th.

This was not far from where the Germans had built three huge Zeppelin Sheds. These sheds were wonderful erections and measured 300 feet wide by 600 feet long. The inhabitants gave the information that it was from these sheds that the last Zeppelin raid on England took place, when none of the 3 Zeppelins escaped destruction.

The sheds were abandoned by the Germans some days before the arrival of the Cavalry, they contained a very large amount of new Aeroplanes of every description. Alongside one of the sheds was a railway train loaded entirely with new aeroplanes which had never even been unpacked.

The forts of Namur, one of which was close to this Aerodrome, had been completely dismantled of guns. The gun positions showed that the Germans had increased the strength of the fortifications considerably by adding at least 6 feet reinforced concrete to the already very thick roof of the fort.

It was whilst the Brigade was billeted in this area that the writer of this narrative, together with Brigadier-General Paterson and Capt. Fielden, motored through Dinant along the valley of the Meuse in order to visit the Château Royale D'Ardennes, which chateau was formerly built by the father of the present king of the Belgians, and was subsequently used as a Hotel. As a Hotel in former days it was admirably maintained and much used by visitors who toured the beautiful Forest of Ardennes. The writer of this narrative spent several days here with his wife in the year 1900. The contrast in the aspect of the whole of the surroundings, wrought by over 4 years' occupation by German troops, was deplorable indeed.

The entrance into Dinant, the once beautiful and prosperous little town with its citadel high up on the rocks overlooking the river, was lined with trench mortars and machine guns, many hundreds in number, waiting to be taken over by the Allied troops from the Germans. The dome of the church had disappeared, as had many houses adjacent to the old bridge over the river; the bridge itself was not the old bridge, but a wooden structure erected after the destruction of the former bridge at the commencement of the war in 1914.

The country between Dinant and the Château Royale D'Ardennes looked the same in 1919 as it did in 1900, but the Château itself was a sorry sight. On arrival at the Château the caretaker was interested in the fact that one of the party had stayed there long ago; he exhibited great enthusiasm in showing all the wanton destruction and filth which the Germans had left behind them in their retreat.

The Château had been used as a Hospital for the greater part of the war, but during the latter stages it had been used as a rest camp for the retreating armies. The whole of the ground floor had been used as stables. The dining room, breakfast room, ball room and lounge were full of stable manure, broken harness and indescribable filth of all sorts. The pretty little private chapel adjoining the morning room and winter garden had also been used as a stable. The altar was upside down and being used as a manger, the well finished walls were irreparably damaged by great spikes and staples having been driven in for the purpose of making fastenings for the horses. This was indeed a remarkable contrast to the happiness of former days, which had been enjoyed by many in this beautiful valley of the Meuse, and no greater contrast can be imagined by anybody more so than the writer himself, who had spent many happy days during his honeymoon in this what was then a veritable haven of rest eighteen years ago.

On December 10th the Brigade moved to the area near Huy, the 10th Hussars billeting for 2 nights at Moha, and on December 12th the Brigade continued its march to a new Divisional area near Engis.

The Brigade headquarters being at Warfussee Château, the 1st Royal Dragoons at Fize-Fontaine, the 3rd Dragoon Guards at St. George and the 10th Royal Hussars at Seraing le Château.

Demobilisation of the Allied forces was taken in hand seriously, and many regiments were very soon reduced to cadre strength. Cavalry regiments found great difficulty in looking after their horses owing to the ever diminishing number of men. Horses were classified for sale in the country, or for retention in the Army, and then followed the breaking up of the 6th Cavalry Brigade. The 3rd Dragoon Guards were the first regiment to go; they were reduced to cadre strength and returned to England early in March. The 10th Royal Hussars were the next to leave, being one of the Regiments for the Army of Occupation on the Rhine, likewise the 1st

Royal Dragoons. These two regiments marched to Königshoven and Cologne respectively, no longer being in the same Brigade.

With the breaking up of the 6th Cavalry Brigade so ended the 3rd Cavalry Division. The Divisional Commander, Major-General A. E. W. Harman, D.S.O., and the Brigade Commander, Brigadier-General Ewing Paterson, D.S.O., were on the road to witness the march out of the 10th Royal Hussars on their route to Germany. They will both be remembered by Officers and other ranks as fighters, sympathisers, and above all, the right sort to inspire confidence in all concerned.

The following is a copy of special order issued by Major-General A. E. W. Harman, D.S.O., on the occasion of the breaking up of the 3rd Cavalry Division :—

SPECIAL ORDER OF THE DAY
BY MAJOR-GENERAL A. E. W. HARMAN, D.S.O.,
COMMANDING 3RD CAVALRY DIVISION.

———

Chât: Scheit.
10th March, 1919.

On the break up of the Division, I desire to express to all ranks my sincerest thanks and keen appreciation for the part that each individual Officer, Warrant

Officer, Non-Commissioned Officer and man has taken, and for the very loyal support you have always given me, under all circumstances.

It is entirely due to the spirit of loyalty and comradeship, which you have always shown, which brought the Division to that high state of efficiency which it attained.

Many of you have and are already returning to civilian life ; you will carry with you a record of which you may justly be proud. It is my earnest hope that you will, in whatever sphere of life you may be employed, show that high degree of efficiency, resolution, and courage which you invariably did when with the 3rd Cavalry Division, and which is due to the memory of our comrades who unselfishly gave their lives for their Country and the Cause for which we fought.

I shall always look back with great pride on the time it was my good fortune to command such splendid men, and I wish you all God Speed and Good Luck.

(Sgd.) A. E. W. HARMAN,
Major-General,
Commanding 3rd Cavalry Division.

XXXVII.

SPA AND BERLIN.

Before concluding, reference might be made to two events which it was the fortune of the writer to take part in, and which will always be remembered by him as not the least interesting of the many which he witnessed during the war. As has been already mentioned, one Squadron of the 10th Hussars, " C " Squadron, commanded by Capt. G. E. Gosling, M.C., was acting as the Corps Commanders Escort Squadron at Spa. This Squadron was in admirable quarters. the officers having a house to themselves, and the N.C.O.'s and men had the house of the King of the Belgians for their billet. Great pride was taken by all ranks to keep the rooms spotlessly clean and tidy, and very comfortable they were.

The fact of having one Squadron at Spa brought the writer on several occasions into this town, and at the same time it brought him in touch with his friend and cousin, Capt. Charles Miles, who was on the staff of the British Armistice Commission. Through the kindness of Capt. Miles he was introduced to the President of the British Armistice Commission, General Sir R. C. B. Haking, K.C.B., K.C.M.G., who kindly introduced him to General Nudant, who was President of the entire Commission, and he had the privilege of sitting and listening to the proceedings of the Commission.

The daily sittings took place in the Grand Hôtel Britannique in the large dining room. The members of the Allies' Commission always assembled in the Hall at the appointed hour. The members of the German Commission being already seated in the room would rise on the entry of General Nudant and his supporters. The proceedings were carried out in three languages, being interpreted in turn into German, French and English. All those who had the privilege of witnessing these events must have been struck by the firmness and dignity of General Nudant in his dealings with the German authorities present.

Spa itself possesses, of course, many places of much interest, and will be for ever renowned for having been the Head Quarters of the German Armies for so long during the war. The Kaiser's house, which is just outside Spa, was then being used by the French Armistice Commission. General von Hindenburg's house was being used by the American Commission, and General Ludendorff's by the British. Strong " Dug Outs " had been excavated in both the Kaiser's and General von Hindenburg's houses for their security, and it is noteworthy that the doors contain strong bolts and fastenings which can only be released from the inside.

General Haking was anxious to open a courier service between Spa and Berlin for the purpose of maintaining better communication with the British Military Mission.

This Mission had been at Berlin from the commencement of the Armistice, and consisted of Major-General Sir R. H. Ewart, K.C.M.G., C.B., C.I.E., D.S.O., and his staff; they resided at the former British Embassy.

It was arranged that the writer, with Major Watkin Williams as interpreter, should proceed to Berlin and carry with them dispatches and rations for the British Military Mission. They proceeded by train on March 15th.

The riots were in progress at Berlin at the time, and it was deemed advisable to go armed. The journey was uneventful and extremely comfortable, both officers travelling in luxurious sleeping berths, with their servants next door, who were able to cook the various meals required on the somewhat long journey. The train was the Berlin express, which was used entirely by the German members of the Commission or those who had special authority to travel by it.

With the exception of the British Military Mission, no British Officers had, up to that time, penetrated as far as Berlin, and, as may be supposed, much curiosity was shown by everybody at the various railway stations where the train stopped on the way.

The whole country, as far as could be seen, had the appearance of prosperity, and every inch of land was cultivated and sown, also the crops looked well for the time of year. On arrival at Berlin in the evening of the second day's journey, instructions were received from the German guards posted at the railway station, that all arms must be concealed; this was easily done and the party proceeded to the Esplanade Hotel, at which Hotel, arrangements had been made to house the two British Officers. The German guards posted at the Hotel saluted the British Officers on their arrival, and they went out of their way to show hospitality to the two servants.

Major Williams and the writer proceeded at once to the British Military Mission in order to hand over the documents; they dined at the Embassy with General Sir R. Ewart, and after an excellent dinner returned to the Hotel for the night.

The usual orchestra was to be heard playing music in the lounge exactly as in peace time.

It was considered advisable to store all the rations and also to conceal the rifles in the two bedrooms during the night; this precaution was advised by the Hotel manager on account of the shortage of food and the drastic means adopted by the rioters to obtain it.

The riots had, to a great extent, subsided, and but for some machine gun fire during the night in the northern quarter of the City, there was little indication of the revolution which existed.

From the appearance of the side table in the dining room at the Hotel, the following morning breakfast time, no one would have guessed that the shortage of food available for the inhabitants was so great that it had been the means of accentuating the riots and distress throughout Germany.

The fact was that the shortage was not in itself the means of the trouble; but the improper distribution between the classes was responsible for the fact that those who could pay for it were able to procure it. The imperfect system did not even cease there; for it became possible and profitable for outside agents to procure food, at a price, and sell it for exorbitant sums of money to those who were willing and able to purchase. The result was that, although the food was there, it was not possible for many to obtain it, and this necessarily increased the discontent already existing.

The City of Berlin presented a very dilapidated appearance. Much damage had been done during the short period of the revolution. The streets were barricaded with barbed wire entanglements. Machine guns and trench mortars were in position, and manned by Hindenburg's new volunteer army. These guns were posted in windows of houses occupying prominent places near important buildings and thoroughfares. Masses of soldiers in uniform, but without arms, were to be seen everywhere; but officers were conspicuous by their absence. The whole of the population might be described as being "on edge," and it was said that all theatres and places of amusement were packed night after night; dancing and recreation of all sorts seemed to prevail.

Many of the large buildings were badly damaged by shell fire, especially the Kaiser's own Schloss; the centre window overlooking the Lustgarten from which he used to address the vast crowds who assembled to hear him, was entirely destroyed. The whole of the Schloss had been pillaged; even the clothes he wore had been removed, and pictures which hung on his walls.

The Hindenburg wooden statue, which was in a prominent position close to the Victory monument, near the west end of Unter den Linden, had been erected to celebrate Hindenburg's 70th birthday in 1916. This statue was entirely made of wood, and by paying one penny people were invited to drive a nail into this statue. The result of the enterprise was that the whole surface of the statue was completely and closely studded with square headed nails; the whole appeared like one colossal iron statue. The rings on his fingers were represented by brass headed nails, and the hilt of his sword was studded with white headed nails.

The proceeds of this undertaking were devoted to the funds of the Red Cross and it was evident that a very vast amount of money must have been raised in this manner.

At the foot of the statue were two British Field Guns captured in 1915; one was marked 123rd Battery, R.F.A., and the other 124th Battery, R.F.A.

This visit to Berlin was full of interest ; the respect, and even hospitality, shown by the inhabitants to these two British Officers was very marked. Their presence in British uniform caused, as may be well imagined, much curiosity. Children would approach and touch some part of the uniform, presumably for the purpose of narrating to their friends that they had actually touched a British Officer.

The mission to Berlin concluded by the return journey to Spa, accompanied by the same comfortable surroundings as on the previous journey. On arrival at Spa, after having handed over the papers to General Sir R. Haking, Major Williams and the writer rejoined their Regiment at Rearan, which was on the march to Königshoven, west of Cologne.

It was from Königshoven that the writer took his departure from the 10th Royal Hussars. All the officers of the Regiment assembled at the Regimental Headquarters to bid him " farewell." He will for ever value the recollection that the Regiment, to which he had become so attached, gave him such a great " send off."

The band played " Auld Lang Syne " as he drove away.

XXXVIII.

DEMOBILISED.

The short narratives contained in this volume are the result of the desire to place on record sufficient events of interest to remind those who took part in them, not only of the hardships of the world's greatest war, but to remind them also of the many pleasant incidents which were constant and recurring, and at the same time to remind them of the many friends whom they have made—a friendship only known to those who have had the privilege of being comrades in arms ; and whose ambition have been to do their duty to their country, and co-operate in the perpetuation of the brave and glorious traditions of their respective Regiments.

The writer personally has had the honour of commanding two Cavalry Regiments, and possibly holds the unique position of not having been in the regular army, but having nevertheless commanded a

Regular Cavalry Regiment for a considerable period of the war. This distinction at least qualifies him to compare without bias the Regular Cavalry with a Yeomanry Regiment. He says at once without hesitation that he was always as proud of the one as he was of the other. The unfailing support of the one can only be compared with the confidence and loyalty of the other; the cordial good friendship which existed between Officers and other ranks in both Regiments was the keystone of the success which has so materially assisted in the maintenance of that essential qualification known as " Esprit de Corps " in the Regiments concerned.

The writer will always be proud of the fact that he was recommended to the command of the 10th Hussars by the Cavalry Corps Commander, Gen. Sir Charles Kavanagh, who was himself a former commanding officer of the Regiment.

General Kavanagh's friendly advice and encouragement were of the greatest assistance at all times. His courage and strength of character set an example to be followed; whilst his will and determination marked him always as a powerful cavalry leader.

It gives the writer the utmost pleasure to put on record his deep sense of appreciation for the manner in which all the serving officers of the 10th Hussars accepted him as their commanding officer, and for the loyalty and whole hearted support which they showed him during the whole period of his command.

He will also take this opportunity of thanking the Colonel of the Regiment, General Lord Downe, also the past officers, including General Sir Julian, now Lord Byng of Vimy, also Colonel Lord Valentia for their kind references to him on relinquishing command of their former Regiment.

APPENDICES.

237

APPENDIX 1.

CAVALRY CORPS COMMANDERS :

1. Lieut.-General Sir EDMUND HENRY HYNMAN ALLENBY, K.C.B., From 10/10/1914 to 6/5/1915.
2. Lieut.-General The Honble. Sir JULIAN HEDWORTH GEORGE BYNG, K.C.M.G., M.V.O. From 7/5/1915 to 18/8/1915.
3. Lieut.-General EDWARD ARTHUR FANSHAWE, C.B. From 19/8/1915 to 22/10/1915.
4. Lieut.-General the Honble. CECIL EDWARD BINGHAM, C.B.. C.V.O. From 24/10/1915 to 8/3/1916.
5. Lieut.-General Sir CHARLES TOLER MacMORROUGH KAVANAGH, K.C.B., C.V.O., D.S.O. From 4/9/1916 to 31/3/1919.

1ST CAVALRY DIVISION.

DIVISIONAL COMMANDERS :

		FROM.
Maj.-Gen.	E. H. H. ALLENBY, C.B.	5/8/14
,, ,,	H. DE B. DE LISLE, C.B., D.S.O.	10/10/14
,, ,,	Hon. C. E. BINGHAM, C.V.O., C.B.	28/5/15
,, ,,	R. L. MULLENS, C.B.	25/10/15

BRIGADE COMMANDERS :

1st Cavalry Brigade.

Brig.-Gen.	C. J. BRIGGS, C.B.	5/8/14
,, ,,	E. MAKINS, C.B., D.S.O.	2/6/15
,, ,,	H. S. SEWELL, C.M.G., D.S.O.	17/4/18

2nd Cavalry Brigade.

Brig.-Gen.	H. DE B. DE LISLE, C.B., D.S.O.	5/8/14
,, ,,	R. L. MULLENS, C.B.	10/10/14
,, ,,	D. J. E. BEALE-BROWNE, D.S.O.	24/10/15
,, ,,	A. LAWSON, C.M.G.	17/4/18

9th Cavalry Brigade.

Brig.-Gen.	W. H. GREENLY, C.M.G.	14/4/15
,, ,,	S. R. KIRBY, C.M.G.	15/11/15
,, ,,	D' A. LEGARD, C.M.G., D.S.O.	31/10/16

2ND CAVALRY DIVISION.

DIVISIONAL COMMANDERS :

		FROM.
Maj.-Gen.	H. DE LA POER GOUGH, C.B., ..	.. 16/9/14
,, ,,	C. T. McM. KAVANAGH, C.V.O., D.S.O.	.. 15/4/15
,, ,,	Sir P. W. CHETWODE, Bart., C.B., D.S.O.	.. 15/7/15
,, ,,	W. H. GREENLY, C.M.G., D.S.O. ..	.. 16/11/16
,, ,,	T. T. PITMAN, C.B., C.M.G... ..	.. 9/4/18

BRIGADE COMMANDERS :
3rd Cavalry Brigade.

Brig.-Gen.	H. DE LA P. GOUGH, C.B. ..	.. 5/8/14
,, ,,	J. VAUGHAN, C.B., D.S.O.	.. 16/9/14
,, ,,	J. A. BELL SMYTH, C.M.G.	.. 16/10/15

4th Cavalry Brigade.

Brig.-Gen.	Hon. C. E. BINGHAM, C.B., C.V.O. ..	.. 5/8/14
,, ,,	T. T. PITMAN, C.B. ..	.. 30/5/15
,, ,,	C. H. RANKIN, C.M.G., D.S.O. ..	.. 9/4/18

5th Cavalry Brigade.

Brig.-Gen.	Sir P. W. CHETWODE, Bart., C.B., D.S.O.	.. 5/8/14
,, ,,	F. WORMALD, C.B. ..	.. 15/7/15
,, ,,	C. L. K. CAMPBELL, C.M.G... ..	.. 5/10/15
,, ,,	N. W. HAIG, C.B., C.M.G. ..	.. 8/4/18

3RD CAVALRY DIVISION.
DIVISIONAL COMMANDERS :

Maj.-Gen.	Hon. J. H. G. BYNG, C.B., M.V.O. ..	.. 29/9/14
,, ,,	C. J. BRIGGS, C.B., C.M.G. ..	.. 7/5/15
,, ,,	J. VAUGHAN, C.B., D.S.O. ..	.. 15/10/15
,, ,,	A. E. W. HARMAN, D.S.O. ..	.. 15/2/18

BRIGADE COMMANDERS :
6th Cavalry Brigade.

Brig.-Gen.	E. MAKINS, C.B. ..	.. 21/9/14
,, ,,	D. G. M. CAMPBELL, C.B. ..	.. 7/2/15

APPENDIX 1 (*continued*).

		FROM.
Brig.-Gen.	A. E. W. HARMAN, D.S.O.	28/5/16
,, ,,	A. G. SEYMOUR, D.S.O.	15/2/18
,, ,,	E. PATERSON, D.S.O.	2/9/18

7th Cavalry Brigade.

Brig.-Gen.	C. T. McM. KAVANAGH, C.B., C.V.O., D.S.O. .	10/9/14
,, ,,	A. A. KENNEDY, C.M.G.	4/5/15
,, ,,	B. P. PORTAL, C.B., D.S.O.	11/11/16
,, ,,	A. BURT, D.S.O.	18/4/13

8th Cavalry Brigade.

Brig.-Gen.	C. B. BULKELEY-JOHNSON, A.D.C.	13/11/14
,, ,,	A. G. SEYMOUR, D.S.O.	13 4/17

Canadian Cavalry Brigade.

Brig.-Gen.	Rt. Hon. J. E. B. SEELY, C.B., C.M.G., D.S.O., T.D., ...	28/1/15
,, ,,	R. W. PATERSON, D.S.O.	21/5/18

APPENDIX 2.

1ST CAVALRY DIVISION.

1st Brigade	11th Hussars
	2nd Dragoon Guards
	5th Dragoon Guards
2nd Brigade	18th Hussars
	9th Lancers
	4th Dragoon Guards
9th Brigade	15th Hussars
	19th Hussars
	Bedfordshire Yeomanry

In March, 1918, the 8th Hussars replaced the Bedfordshire Yeomanry.

APPENDIX **2** (*continued*).

2ND CAVALRY DIVISION.

3rd Brigade
4th Hussars
5th Lancers
16th Lancers

4th Brigade
3rd Hussars
6th Dragoon Guards
Oxfordshire Hussars

5th Brigade
Royal Scots Greys
20th Hussars
12th Lancers

3RD CAVALRY DIVISION.

6th Brigade
1st Royal Dragoons
3rd Dragoon Guards
North Somerset Yeomanry

7th Brigade
1st Life Guards
2nd Life Guards
Leicestershire Yeomanry

8th Brigade
Royal Horse Guards
10th Royal Hussars
Essex Yeomanry

In November, 1917, the Royal Horse Guards and Leicestershire Yeomanry changed places.

From March, 1918, the 3RD CAVALRY DIVISION consisted as follows :—

6th Brigade
1st Royal Dragoons
3rd Dragoon Guards
10th Royal Hussars

7th Brigade
7th Dragoon Guards
Inniskilling Dragoons
17th Lancers

Canadian Brigade
Lord Strathcona's Horse
Royal Canadian Dragoons
Fort Garry Horse.

APPENDIX A.

DIARY OF MOVEMENTS OF THE 10th ROYAL HUSSARS,
From October, 1914, to April, 1919.

1914.

Oct.	9.	JABBEKE	Nov. 3.	VERLORENHOEK
Oct.	10.	THOUROUT	Nov. 7.	HALTE
Oct.	12.	ROULERS	Nov. 14.	VLAMERTINGHE
Oct.	13.	GHELUVELT	Nov. 15.	HOOGE
Oct.	16.	ZONNEBEKE	Nov. 17.	VLAMERTINGHE
Oct.	18.	PASSCHENDAELE	Nov. 20.	VIEUX BERQUIN
Oct.	19.	POELCAPPELLE	Nov. 21.	LA RUE DU BOIS
Oct.	21.	ZANDVOORDE		FORÊT DE NIEPPE
Oct.	24.	KLEIN ZILLEBEKE	Dec. 14.	BAILLEUL
Nov.	1.	HOOGE	Dec. 16.	LA RUE DU BOIS

1915.

Jan.	28.	SERCUS	May 22.	SERCUS
Feb.	3.	Ypres (dismounted)	May 29.	Hooge (dismounted)
Feb.	8.	ZILLEBEKE	June 6.	SERCUS
Feb.	13.	SERCUS	Aug. 3.	LAIRES
March	11.	LA RUE DU BOIS	Aug. 9.	ERNY-ST. JULIEN
March	13.	SERCUS	Aug. 11.	Armentières (dismounted)
April	23.	ABEELE	Sept. 21.	BOIS DES DAMES
April	24.	VLAMERTINGHE	Sept. 25.	VERMELLES
April	25.	STEENVOORDE	Sept. 26.	NOYELLES-LES
April	26.	VLAMERTINGHE		VERMELLES
April	28.	ABEELE	Sept. 27.	LOOS
May	3.	VLAMERTINGHE	Sept. 29.	GOSNAY
May	4.	HOUTKERQUE	Oct. 1.	LABEUVRIÈRE
May	7.	SERCUS	Oct. 3.	LESPRESSES
May	9.	Brielen (dismounted)	Oct. 13.	ECQUEDECQUES
May	13.	Potijze (dismounted)	Oct. 19.	FAUQUEMBERGES
May	15.	Vlamertinghe	Oct. 21.	ENQUIN-LES-MINES
		(dismounted)	Nov. 29.	SEMPY

APPENDIX A (continued).

1916.

Jan. 1..Hohenzollern Redoubt	.. Aug. 4..DOURIEZ
(dismounted)	.. Aug. 5..AUCHY-LES-HESDIN
May 15..GAPENNES	.. Aug. 13..Bouzincourt (dismounted)
May 21..SEMPY	.. Sept. 10..DOURIEZ
May 24..MERLIMONT	.. Sept. 11..CAOURS
June 10..SEMPY	.. Sept. 12..ARGŒUVES
June 24..MACHY	.. Sept. 14..BUSSY-LES-DAOURS
June 25..ST. OUEN	.. Sept. 15..LA NEUVILLE
June 26..BONNAY	.. Sept. 17..VECQUEMONT
July 5..LIERCOURT	.. Sept. 22..BOUCHON
July 8..CORBIE	.. Sept. 23..CONCHY-SUR-CANCHE
July 9..BONNAY	.. Sept. 24..MARESQUEL
July 25..Contalmaison (dismounted)	Nov. 21..Englebelmer (dismounted)
Aug. 1..HANGEST-SUR-SOMME	Dec. 22..MERLIMONT
Aug. 2..NEUILLY-L'HOPITAL..	

1917.

Feb. 1..ROYON	.. July 3..MÉRICOURT
April 7..FRÉVENT	.. July 4..AMPLIER
April 8..GOUY-EN-ARTOIS	.. July 5..REBREUVIETTE
April 9..TILLOY-LES	.. July 6..CAMBLAIN-CHÂTELAIN
MOFFLAINES	.. July 17..TANNAY
April 10..FEUCHY CHAPEL	.. Aug. 10..MOLINGHEM
April 11..MONCHY LE PREUX	.. Oct. 12..LES AMUSOIRES
April 12..GOUY-EN-ARTOIS	.. Oct. 17..SACHIN
April 18..OCCOCHES	.. Oct. 21..BOUBERS-SUR-CANCHE
April 19..AUBIN-ST. VAAST	.. Oct. 22..HALLOY-LES-PERNOIS
May 13..VITZ VILLEROY	.. Nov. 18..BRAY
May 14..REMAISNIL	.. Nov. 23..PIERREGOT
May 15..NAOURS	.. Dec. 1..Vadencourt (dismounted)
May 16..PONT NOYELLES	.. Dec. 2..DREUIL
May 17..HAMEL	.. Dec. 14..ARGŒUVES
May 19..COURCELLES	.. Dec. 22..LA CHAUSSÉE-
June 1..Epehy (dismounted)	.·. TIRANCOURT
July 2..SUZANNE	

APPENDIX A (*continued*).

1918.

Jan. 27 . HARBONNIÈRES	.. Aug. 8 . . VALLEY S. of CAIX
Jan. 28 . MONTECOURT	.. Aug. 9 . . CAIX
Feb. 28 . TERTRY	.. Aug. 10 . . FOLIES
March 13 . DEVISE	.. Aug. 11 . . FOUENCAMPS
March 21 . BEAUMONT	.. Aug. 15 . . RIENCOURT
March 22 . PONTOISE	.. Aug. 22 . . FIEFFES
Noureuil (dismounted)	.. Aug. 25 . . VITZ VILLEROY
March 23 . CARLEPONT	.. Aug. 26 . . SIBIVILLE
Berlancourt (dismounted)	Aug. 30 . . WAILLY
March 24 . Guiscard, Abbécourt	.. Sept. 1 . . WANCOURT
(dismounted)	.. Sept. 2 . . WAILLY
March 25 . Lagny, Les Bruyers	.. Sept. 5 . . SIBIVILLE
(dismounted)	.. Sept. 6 . . VIEIL HESDIN
March 26 . OLLENCOURT	.. Sept. 16 . . GRIGNY
March 26 . Elincourt (dismounted)	.. Sept 17 . . BOISBERGUES
March 27 . Chevincourt (dismounted)	.. Sept. 18 . . VIEIL HESDIN
March 29 . AIRION	.. Sept. 19 . . LIGNY-SUR-CANCHE
March 30 . RACINEUSE	.. Sept. 25 . . COUIN
April 1 . . BLANGY–TRONVILLE	.. Sept. 26 . . MEAULTE
April 3 . . FOUILLOY	.. Sept. 27 . . HEM
April 5 . . BLANGY–TRONVILLE	.. Sept. 29 . . BIHECOURT
April 6 . . CAMON	.. Oct. 3 . . PONTRU
April 11 . . BUIRE-AU-BOIS	.. Oct. 5 . . TREFCON
April 12 . . HESTRUS	.. Oct. 8 . . MAGNI-LA-FOSSE
April 13 . . AUMERVAL	.. Oct. 9 . . REUMONT
May 4 . . ROUGEFAY	.. Oct. 10 . . MONTIGNY
May 5 . . VILLERS-L'HOPITAL	.. Oct. 11 . . ELINCOURT
May 6 . . CONTAY	.. Oct. 13 . . BANTEUX
May 17 . . BELLOY-SUR-SOMME	.. Oct. 14 . . MANANCOURT
May 31 . . BÉHENCOURT	.. Nov. 6 . . MARQUION
June 14 . . BELLOY-SUR-SOMME	.. Nov. 7 . . ESQUERCHIN
June 25 . . RIENCOURT	.. Nov. 8 . . FRETIN
Aug. 6 . . RENANCOURT	.. Nov. 10 . . GAURAIN RAMECROIX
Aug. 7 . . LONGUEAU	.. Nov. 12 . . WILLAUPUIS

244

APPENDIX A (*continued*).

1918—*continued.*

Nov. 17..ST. MARCOULE   .. Nov. 24..ST. GERMAIN
Nov. 18..SAINTES   .. Dec. 10..MOHA
Nov. 21..LIMAL   .. Dec. 12..SERAING LE
Nov. 22..TAVIERS   ..   CHÂTEAU

1919.

March 15.SPRIMONT   .. March 19.HONGEN
March 17.THEUX   .. March 20.KÖNIGSHOVEN
March 18.RAERAN   .. April   7.TURNICH

On September 13th the Regiment proceeded to England.

APPENDIX B.

DIARY OF MOVEMENTS OF THE ESSEX YEOMANRY,
From November 30th, 1914, to April 4th, 1918.

1914.

Nov. 30..Harbour HAVRE   .. Dec. 11..SEC BOIS
Dec. 1..ST. ADRESSE HAVRE .. Dec. 14..ST. JANS-CAPPEL
Dec. 4..WARDRECQUES   .. Dec. 16..SEC BOIS

1915.

Jan. 28..Mt. CROQUET   .. April 25..WINNEZEELE
Feb. 3..Ypres and Zillebeke   .. April 26..VLAMERTINGHE
          (dismounted) .. April 28..ABEELE
Feb. 12..Mt. CROQUET   .. May 3..VLAMERTINGHE
March 11..Near SEC BOIS   .. May 4..HOUTKERQUE
March 13..Mt. CROQUET   .. May 7..BLARINGHEM
      and BLARINGHEM .. May 9..Brielen (dismounted)
April 23..ABEELE   .. May 13..Potijze (dismounted)
April 24..VLAMERTINGHE

245

APPENDIX B (*continued*).

1915—*continued.*

May 15..Vlamertinghe(dismounted)	Sept. 26..NOYELLES-LÉS
May 22..BLARINGHEM	VERMELLES
May 29..HOOGE	.. Sept. 27..LOOS
June 6..BLARINGHEM	.. Sept. 27..GOSNAY
Aug. 3..MATRINGHEM	.. Oct. 1..LABEUVRIÈRE
Aug. 11..Armentières (dismounted)	.. Oct. 3..HURIONVILLE
Sept.21..BOIS DES DAMES	.. Oct. 21..MATRINGHEM
Sept.25..VERMELLES	.. Nov. 17..EMBRY

1916.

Jan. 3..Hohenzollern Redoubt	.. Aug. 5..BLANGY
(dismounted)	.. Aug. 12..Bouzincourt (dismounted)
May 15..ARGENVILLERS	.. Sept. 10..MOULINEL, RAPECHY
May 21..EMBRY	.. Sept. 11..ST. RIQUIER
May 31..CUCQ	.. Sept. 12..ST. SAUVEUR
June 10..EMBRY	.. Sept. 14..QUERRIEU
June 24..VIRONCHAUX	.. Sept. 15..LA NEUVILLE
June 25..ST. OUEN	.. Sept. 17..VECQUEMONT
June 26..BONNAY	.. Sept. 22..BOUCHON
July 4..BELLIFONTAINE	.. Sept. 23..FILLIEVRES
July 8..CORBIE	.. Sept. 24..ECQUEMICOURT
July 9..BONNAY	.. and PLUMOISON
July 27..Contalmaison (dismounted)	Nov. 11..Englebelmer
Aug. 1..HANGEST-SUR-SOMME	.. (dismounted)
Aug 2..DRUCAT	.. Dec. 22..St.JOSSE
Aug. 4..MOULINEL	

1917.

Feb. 1..FRESSIN	.. April 11..MONCHY LE PREUX
Feb. 4..Doullens (dismounted)	.. April 12..GOUY-EN-ARTOIS
April 7..FRÉVENT	.. April 16..BARLY
April 8..GOUY-EN-ARTOIS	.. April 18..BOIS JEAN
April 9..TILLOY-LES	.. May 12..SAULCHOY
MOFFLAINES	.. May 13..TOLLENT and
April 10..FEUCHY CHAPEL	.. GENNE-IVERGNY

1917—*continued:*

May 14..BARLY	.. July 17..THIENNES
May 15..HAVERNAS	.. Aug. 10..BERGUETTE
May 16..QUERRIEU	.. Oct. 11..BAS HAMEL
May 17..HAMEL	.. Oct. 17..CAMBLAIN-
May 17..COURCELLES	.. CHÀTELAIN
June 2..Epehy (dismounted)	.. Oct. 21..REBREUVIETTE
July 2..SUZANNE	.. Oct. 22..HAVERNAS
July 3..MÉRICOURT	.. Nov. 18..BRAY
July 4..AUTHIEULE	.. Nov. 23..ALLONVILLE
July 5..REBREUVIETTE	.. Dec. 1..Bernes (dismounted)
July 6..CAMBLAIN-	.. Dec. 2..PICQUIGNY
CHÀTELAIN	.. Dec. 23..VIGNACOURT

1918.

Jan. 27..MARCELCAVE	.. March 15.GUIGNEMICOURT
Jan. 28..MONTECOURT	.. March 16.LIERCOURT
Feb. 28..TREFCON	.. March 26.LONGPRÉ
March 13.St.CHRIST and LONGPRÉ	March 28.BUSSY-LES-DAOURS
March 14.LA NEUVILLE	.. March 29.VILLERS-BRETONNEUX

APPENDIX C.

ROLL OF OFFICERS WHO HAVE SERVED WITH 10TH (P.W.O.) ROYAL HUSSARS DURING THE WAR.

	JOINED.	DEPARTED.	CASUALTY.
Lt.-Col. R. W. R. BARNES ..	7/10/14	2/11/14	Wounded (2)
	24/12/14	3/3/15	
Major E. R. A. SHEARMAN ..	7/10/14	13/5/15	Killed
Major C. W. H. CRICHTON ..	7/10/14	30/10/14	Wounded
	12/3/15	13/5/15	

	JOINED.	DEPARTED.	CASUALTY.
Major Hon. C. B. O. MITFORD ..	7/10/14	23/10/14	
	28/3/15	13/5/15	Killed
Major Hon. W. G. CADOGAN ..	7/10/14	12/11/14	Killed
Capt. Hon. A. ANNESLEY	7/10/14	16/11/14	Killed
Capt. Sir F. ROSE, Bart.	7/10/14	26/10/14	Killed
Capt. C. H. PETO	7/10/14	17/11/14	Killed
Capt. Hon. H. BARING ..	7/10/14	30/10/14	
	24/12/14	9/1/15	
Capt. G. C. STEWART	7/10/14	30/10/14	
	22/12/14	13/5/15	Killed
Capt. M. A. DE TUYLL.. ..	7/10/14	13/5/15	Killed
Capt. E. W. E. PALMES ..	7/10/14	12/11/14	Wounded
	12/3/15	23/3/18	
Lieut. G. E. GOSLING	7/10/14	11/4/17	Wounded
	29/7/17		
Lieut. R. C. GORDON CANNING ..	7/10/14	28/10/18	
Lieut. V. J. GREENWOOD ..	7/10/14	11/4/17	Wounded
	19/6/17		
Lieut. V. A. P. STOKES ..	7/10/14	23/3/15	
	5/10/15	7/11/17	
Lieut. C. B. WILSON	7/10/14	26/3/15	
Lieut. Baron F. C. O. DE TUYLL..	7/10/14	26/3/15	
	24/5/15	16/9/15	
Lieut. C. R. TURNOR	7/10/14	26/10/14	Killed
2/Lieut. Earl of AIRLIE ..	7/10/14	11/4/17	Wounded
	7/8/17	6/10/17	
	29/7/18	7/10/18	
2/Lieut. J. C. Lord CHESHAM ..	7/10/14	13/5/15	Wounded
	21/10/15	4/9/16	
2/Lieut. W. S. MURLAND ..	7/10/14	11/4/17	Wounded
	4/9/17	9/10/18	
2/Lieut. R. F. DRAKE	7/10/14	17/11/14	Killed

	JOINED.	DEPARTED.	CASUALTY.
2/Lieut. R. H. PETO	7/10/14	26/3/15	
Hon. Lt. & Qmr. W. H. DRUCE .	7/10/14	26/5/18	
Capt. Hon. D. R. A. PELHAM ..	4/11/14	11/14	
Capt. W. O. GIBBS	20/10/14	1/11/14	Wounded
	12/3/15	13/5/15	
	21/8/15	16/3/18	
Capt. E. A. FIELDEN		30/10/14	Wounded
Lieut. H. P. CHAPLIN		26/3/15	
	17/9/15	21/5/18	
Lieut. T. BOUCH		18/7/15	
Lieut. Sir B. S. BROOKE, Bart. ..	4/11/14	22/3/16	
2/Lieut. LANE	7/11/14	14/11/14	
Major S. St. G. P. ARMSTRONG ..	7/11/14	14/11/14	
Lieut. O. MOWATT	7/11/14	23/3/15	
	24/5/15	11/4/17	Killed
2/Lieut. G. ALEXANDER ..	17/11/14	13/5/15	Wounded
	6/11/16	25/2/18	
2/Lieut. J. S. M. WARDELL ..	17/11/14	13/5/15	Wounded
2/Lieut. R. G. BORTHWICK ..		8/12/15	
Lieut. H. C. BROCKLEHURST ..	22/11/14	6/9/16	
Lieut. R. G. GODSON	29/11/14	14/3/15	
Major W. R. CAMPBELL ..	3/12/14	9/5/15	Killed
			(N.S.Y.,13/5/15)
Capt. L. HUNTER-JONES ..	3/12/14	23/3/15	
Lieut. R. H. C. THOMAS ..	3/12/14	13/5/15	
Capt. A. L. CAVE	30/12/14	23/3/15	
2/Lieut. A. L. MAYNARD ..	30/12/14	14/3/15	
2/Lieut. H. W. R. BLAKENEY ..			
2/Lieut. E. R. BENNETT ..	23/12/14	14/3/15	
	24/5/15	21/3/16	
2/Lieut. S. B. C. FERRIS ..	8/12/14	14/3/15	
Capt. Hon. F. W. STANLEY ..	3/1/15	16/10/15	
2/Lieut. W. H. E. Visct. EDNAM .	12/3/15	4/4/18	Wounded

	JOINED.	DEPARTED.	CASUALTY.
2/Lieut. H. L. FRAZER.. ..	14/3/15	27/3/15	
2/Lieut. E. W. BOVILL ..	17/3/15	23/3/15	
2/Lieut. C. HUMBERT	27/4/15	13/5/15	Wounded
	18/5/16	29/1/19	
2/Lieut. C. B. HODGSON ..	21/5/15	16/10/15	
2/Lieut. Lord W. W. M. D. SCOTT	24/5/15		
2/Lieut. D. M. GARSTIN ..	24/5/15	29/2/16	Killed
			(Russia, 1918)
2/Lieut. H. A. TWEEDIE ..	24/5/15	22/12/15	
2/Lieut. A. A. FRANKLIN ..	24/5/15	13/10/15	
2/Lieut. S. C. DEED	24/5/15	22/2/17	
2/Lieut. J. C. NEWMAN ..	24/5/15	3/9/15	
2/Lieut. F. M. BALL	12/6/15	17/9/16	
Major E. H. W. WILLIAMS ..	16/6/15	10/9/16	Wounded
	17/9/17	27/3/18	
	23/11/18		
2/Lieut. W. J. BRISLEY ..	21/7/15	23/3/18	Wounded
	15/1/19		
Lt.-Col. H. F. WICKHAM ..	10/9/15	23/5/16	
2/Lieut. Hon. C. J. F. WINN ..	21/10/15	11/4/17	Wounded
2/Lieut. Hon. G. E. D. C. GLYN..	22/10/15	6/16	Wounded
	6/5/17	17/6/17	
	27/8/18		
2/Lieut. H. C. FEWSTER ..	24/11/15	29/2/16	
2/Lieut. W. BURDETT	31/11/15	30/10/17	
2/Lieut. C. W. D. BELL ..	6/2/16	30/10/17	
2/Lieut. D. H. GOUGH	6/2/16		
2/Lieut. F. R. GASKELL ..	6/2/16	8/4/17	Wounded
	25/10/17		
2/Lieut. J. C. HANBURY WILLIAMS	6/2/16	28/8/16	Wounded
2/Lieut. F. C. DRAKE	26/2/16	12/4/17	Wounded
	25/10/17	9/10/18	
2/Lieut. A. N. LOCKETT ..	18/5/16	6/1/19	

		JOINED.	DEPARTED.	CASUALTY.
Lt.-Col. P. E. HARDWICK	..	5/6/16	11/4/17	Wounded
2/Lieut. D. D. STEWART	..	6/6/16	28/11/17	
		8/9/18		
2/Lieut. Hon. G. S. DAWSON DAMER	.. .. ..	23/9/16	11/4/17	Killed
2/Lieut. A. E. LOWTHER	..	23/9/16	17/2/18	
		2/12/18		Wounded
Lieut. G. D. AYLETT BRANFIELD		6/11/16	12/2/17	
2/Lieut. S. A. RALLI	.. ..	6/1/17	9/10/18	Wounded
2/Lieut. R. G. FIELD	.. ..	22/2/17	4/4/18	Killed
2/Lieut. E. G. PAUL	.. ..	22/2/17	24/4/17	
2/Lieut. R. M. BOURNE	..	22/2/17	8/17	
2/Lieut. E. GUNN	.. ..	20/4/17	24/1/18	
2/Lieut. W. E. MAWLE	..	20/4/17	23/11/17	
2/Lieut. C. K. DAVIS	.. ..	6/5/17	1/12/17	
2/Lieut. T. ROBINSON	.. ..	6/5/17	8/8/18	Wounded
		26/11/18		
2/Lieut. J. W. BOARDMAN	..	6/5/17	24/1/18	
2/Lieut. K. T. BOARDMAN	..	6/5/17	12/4/18	
		2/9/18	5/10/18	
2/Lieut. H. W. TAYLOR	..	6/5/17	16/12/18	
2/Lieut. L. V. HUGHES	..	6/5/17	19/11/17	
2/Lieut. G. L. SALTON	..	6/5/17	9/11/17	
2/Lieut. H. DREWETT	..	6/5/17		Wounded
2/Lieut. E. FARRELL	..	6/5/17	1/11/17	
2/Lieut. J. P. SLIM	..	6/5/17	29/7/18	
2/Lieut. E. R. SCULLY	..	25/10/17	11/10/18	
		16/11/18		
2/Lieut. H. D. KELLEWAY	..	25/10/17	4/4/18	
2/Lieut. A. D. HILLHOUSE	..	25/10/17		
Capt. T. C. KING	.. ..	22/8/17	8/9/17	
2/Lieut. J. J. KANE	.. ..	17/1/18	9/3/18	
		20/10/18		

	JOINED.	DEPARTED.	CASUALTY.
2/Lieut. G. R. FARLEY ..	10/3/18	6/9/18	
Lt.-Col. H. A. TOMKINSON ..	16/3/18	4/4/18	Wounded
Lt.-Col. F. H. D. C. WHITMORE ..	7/4/18		Wounded (2)
Lieut. & Qmr. W. SHAKESPEARE..	8/4/18		
Capt. A. W. PHIPPS	6/4/18	31/5/18	Wounded
	23/1/19		
Lieut. C. S. CAMPBELL ..	6/4/18		
2/Lieut. W. G. M. HAKEMAN ..	6/4/18		
2/Lieut. J. C. LEES	6/4/18		
Lieut. W. RITCHIE ..	7/4/18	9/10/18	Wounded
Lieut. S. J. TUFNELL ..	18/4/18	9/10/18	Wounded
Lieut. R. W. BRUCE ..	17/4/18	21/8/18	
2/Lieut. M. D. MORRISON ..	30/4/18	3/2/19	
2/Lieut. S. H. WAUGH ..	30/4/18	18/1/19	
2/Lieut. B. A. WILSON ..	23/5/18		
2/Lieut. G. H. PERRETT ..	23/5/18	9/8/18	Killed
Lieut. H. H. NEWMAN ..	23/5/18	19/1/19	Wounded
2/Lieut. H. W. CORFIELD ..	23/5/18	9/11/18	
2/Lieut. C. ALDERSON	22/6/18	25/11/18	
2/Lieut. C. DE C. MULLINS ..	10/7/18		
2/Lieut. E. P. AWDRY	18/8/18		
Lieut. P. R. JERMYN	6/9/18		
Major A. BUXTON	16/10/18		Wounded
2/Lieut. P. N. H. GARNETT ..	22/10/18		
2/Lieut. G. V. KYTE	20/10/18		
2/Lieut. R. KELLY	20/10/18	15/1/19	
2/Lieut. C. KNIGHT	20/10/18	21/1/19	
2/Lieut. H. CHAMBERS ..	14/11/18		
2/Lieut. R. V. GARTON ..	17/2/19		
2/Lieut. J. D. WRANGHAM ..	18/2/19		
2/Lieut. C. B. CHURCH ..	6/3/19		
2/Lieut. E. R. KIMBELL ..	7/3/19		
2/Lieut. B. G. BEARMAN ..	10/3/19		

APPENDIX D.

Roll of Officers who Have Served with the Essex Yeomanry Overseas.

	Joined.	Departed.	Subsequently Posted to.	Casualty.
Lt.-Col. E. Deacon ..	29/11/14			Wounded & Missing
Major F. H. D. C. Whitmore	29/11/14 4/9/15	16/5/15	10th Royal Hussars 13/4/18	Wounded (2)
Major A. Roddick ..	29/11/14			Killed
Major G. G. Gold ..	29/11/14 12/7/17	15/4/17	Cav. Corps. 19/4/18	Wounded
Major A. Buxton ..	29/11/14 5/5/17	10/4/17 1/4/18	10th Royal Hussars 14/10/18	Wounded
Major E. Hill	29/11/14 14/8/15	9/5/15 16/4/17	15th Hussars 29/4/18	Wounded
Capt. E. A. Ruggles-Brise .	29/11/14 6/2/16	30/9/15	15th Hussars 29/4/18 4th Dragoon Guards 1/7/18	Wounded
Capt. J. O. Parker ..	29/11/14 13/10/17	9/9/17 Base Depot 11/4/18		Wounded
Capt. R. G. Proby ..	29/11/14	Invalided Home 19/5/17		
Lieut. R. Edwards ..	29/11/14	19/5/15		Wounded
Lieut. E. P. W. Wedd ..	29/11/14	Staff Capt. Heavy Art 22/1/16		Killed
Lieut. V. T. G. Hine ..	29/11/14 11/1/16	14/5/15 20/1/18	4th Dragoon Guards	Wounded
Lieut. G. S. Johnston ..	29/11/14			Killed
Lieut. R. A. Thomson ..	29/11/14	Base Depot 11/4/18	19th Hussars	
2/Lieut. C. N. Gilbey ..	29/11/14	24/5/17		Wounded

	JOINED.	DEPARTED.	SUBSEQUENTLY POSTED TO.	CASUALTY.
2/Lieut. H. P. HOLT	.. 29/11/14 15/2/16	24/5/15 3/1st E.Y. 26/4/16		Wounded
2/Lieut. S. J. TUFNELL	.. 29/11/14 .		5th Dragoon Gds. 5/4/18 10th Royal Hussars 18/4/18	Wounded
2/Lieut. J. W. EGERTON GREEN	.. .. 29/11/14	1st Batt, R.B. 8/7/15		Killed
2/Lieut. A. G. SWIRE	.. 29/11/14	.		Killed
2/Lieut. G. P. N. REID	.. 29/11/14			Killed
2/Lieut. T. F. BUXTON	.. 29/11/14	Xth Corps 26/9/15		
2/Lieut. F. C. MEYER	.. 29/11/14	Signal Officer 8th Cav. Brigade		Wounded
Capt. Adjt. A. R. STEELE	.. 29/11/14	22/5/15		Wounded
Lieut. Q.-M. E. J. SAYER	.. 29/11/14	Invalided Home 5/2/17		Wounded
Capt. J. McARTHUR, A.V.C.	29/11/14	2nd Cav. Bde. 22/8/15		
Lieut. G. F. WHITE, R.A.M.C.	.. 29/11/14	3/9/15		
2/Lieut. C. J. ROUND	.. 15/3/15	14/6/15		United Kingdom
Major H. F. WICKHAM	.. 31/5/15	X.R.H. 10/9/15		
2/Lieut. J. K. SWIRE	.. 7/6/15 20/10/17	20/4/17	Cav. Corps Equitation School 17/3/18	Wounded (2)
2/Lieut. J. C. CHAPLIN	.. 7/6/15		11th Hussars 29/4/18	Wounded
2/Lieut. A. W. ROSE	.. 7/6/15		Cav. Corps 19/4/18	Wounded (since died)
Lieut. T. PRESTON	.. 14/6/15	8th M.G. Sqdn. 3/3/16		

APPENDIX D (*continued*).

	JOINED.	DEPARTED.	SUBSEQUENTLY POSTED TO.	CASUALTY.
Lieut. C. C. TOWER ..	14/6/15	A.D.C. 12th Div. 14/6/15		Killed
Capt. M. DUDDING ..	14/6/15	att. 30th Lancers Indian 14.6.15		Wounded
2/Lieut. D. MORGAN ..	14/6/15	A.D.C., R.A., 49th Div. 24/7/16		Wounded Prisoner of War
2/Lieut. F. D. BALFOUR ..	14/6/15 24/12/16	10/7/16	Cav. Corps 19/4/18	
2/Lieut. E. P. L. PELLY ..	14/6/15	30/9/15		Wounded
2/Lieut. R. C. WEATHERBY .	14/6/15	16/4/17		Wounded
Capt. Adjt. M. L. YEATHERD	13/6/15	Invalided Home 22/7/15		United Kingdom
2/Lieut. W. A. TUCZEK ..	29/9/15	4 Sig. Sqd. 5/8/17		
Capt. E. STORK, R.A.M.C. ..	3/9/15 27/4/16	30/10/15		
Capt. Adjt. T. KNOWLES JACKSON	1/10/15	Invalided Home 15/11/16		United Kingdom
2/Lieut. E. G. WINDLE ..	11/10/15	3rd Cav. Div. 24/10/15		
2/Lieut. G. L. HORSEFALL ..	16/10/15 28/4/17	4/4/17	18th Hussars 29/4/18	
2/Lieut. W. P. BATTERS ..	16/10/15	8th M.G. Sqdn. 3/3/16		Wounded
2/Lieut. R. W. BRUCE ..	16/10/15		15th Hussars 5/4/18 10th Royal Hussars 17/4/18	
2/Lieut. L. C. CHAPLIN ..	16/10/15	7/9/16		United Kingdom

255

	Joined.	Departed.	Subsequently Posted to.	Casualty.
Capt. A. H. Benson, R.A.M.C.	30/10/15	2/12/15		
Capt. Grove White, R.A.M.C.	16/12/15	19/1/16		
Capt. R. Marshall, R.A.M.C.	19/1/16	23/4/16		
2/Lieut. B. F. Wilmer	..	15/2/16	Base Depot 11/4/18	
2/Lieut. A. Richardson	..	15/2/16		United Kingdom
2/Lieut. G. Wear	..	26/3/16 10/3/17 20/10/17	7/11/16 16/4/17	2nd Dragoon Guards 6/4/18	Wounded
2/Lieut. W. Ritchie	..	9/6/16		10th Royal Hussars 7/4/18	Wounded
2/Lieut. R. D. Holland	..	3/6/16	Invalided Home	United Kingdom
2/Lieut. C. G. W. A. Charters	27/6/16	22/11/16		United Kingdom
2/Lieut. K. C. Herron	..	24/7/16	R.A.F. 1/7/17	Killed
2/Lieut. S. White	..	30/8/16	16/4/17		Wounded
2/Lieut. W. C. V. Schwier	.	7/11/16		2nd Dragoon Guards 5/4/18	
2/Lieut. L. Abraham	..	11/11/16	R.A.F. 13/5/17	
2/Lieut. H. W. Newman	..	19/11/16		10th Royal Hussars 29/4/18	Wounded
2/Lieut. J. F. Lingeman	..	11/1/17	28/4/17		Died of Wounds
2/Lieut. L. B. Hore	..	30/3/17	Tank Corps 31/1/18	Prisoner of War
2/Lieut. C. A. Collis	..	13/3/17	2/4/18		Wounded
2/Lieut. H. N. Long	..	13/3/17	Leave to U.K. indefinitely 2/9/17	United Kingdom

APPENDIX D (*continued*).

	JOINED.	DEPARTED.	SUBSEQUENTLY POSTED TO.	CASUALTY.
2/Lieut. C. W. H. RIDLEY ..	13/3/17		2nd Dragoon Guards 29/4/18	
2/Lieut. S. N. TAYLOR ..	7/5/17		11th Hussars 5/4/18	
2/Lieut. P. R. JERMYN ..	7/5/17		5th Dragoon Guards 1/4/18 10th Royal Hussars 6/9/18	
2/Lieut. E. K. COLLINS ..	7/5/17	1/1st H.A.C. 10/9/17		
2/Lieut. J. BROWN ..	7/5/17		9th Lancers 5/4/18	
2/Lieut. W. H. NAISH ..	7/5/17		Conducting Officer 1/10/17	
2/Lieut. C. A. HALL-HALL ..	7/5/17		11th Hussars 5/5/18	
2/Lieut. A. D. LIPPETT ..	7/5/17	U.K. for duty 23/3/18		United Kingdom
2/Lieut. W. H. POLKINHORNE	7/5/17	Invalided 1/10/17		United Kingdom
2/Lieut. W. BROWN ..	7/5/17		9th Lancers 5/4/18	
2/Lieut. L. SOLAINI ..	7/5/17		2nd Dragoon Guards 5/4/18	
2/Lieut. B. W. GREEN ..	7/5/17		11th Hussars 5/4/18	
2/Lieut. E. J. McFADDEN ..	20/10/17	Labour Coy. 5/2/18		
2/Lieut. F. G. DOE ..	20/10/17		5th Dragoon Guards 5/4/18	
2/Lieut. C. H. DEVIN ..	20/10/17		4th Dragoon Guards 5/4/18	

257

S

APPENDIX E.

10TH (P.W.O.) ROYAL HUSSARS.

LIST OF OFFICERS AND OTHER RANKS WHO HAVE RECEIVED HONOURS
OR AWARDS SINCE THE COMMENCEMENT OF THE CAMPAIGN.

	NATURE OF AWARD.	DATE.
Major the Hon. W. G. CADOGAN, M.V.O.	Mentioned in Despatches	18/2/15
Major the Hon. C. B. O. MITFORD	Mentioned in Despatches	18/2/15
Captain C. H. PETO	Mentioned in Despatches	18/2/15
Lieut. C. B. WILSON	Mentioned in Despatches	18/2/15
1603 L./Cpl. W. BARNES	Mentioned in Despatches	18/2/15
5380 L./Cpl. G. HEARN	Distinguished Conduct Medal	28/3/15
128 Pte. A. BUTCHER	Distinguished Conduct Medal	28/3/15
3646 Pte. R. SAVAGE	Distinguished Conduct Medal	28/3/15
Major C. W. H. CRICHTON	Distinguished Service Order	26/5/15
Major the Hon. C. B. O. MITFORD	Distinguished Service Order	26/6/15
Major the Hon. C. B. O. MITFORD	Mentioned in Despatches	26/6/15
Lieut. C. B. WILSON	Military Cross	23/6/15
1603 L./Cpl. W. BARNES	Cross of the Order of St. George, 4th Class	25/8/15
239 Sgt. E. COX	Medal of St. George, 2nd Class	25/8/15
25683 L./Cpl. A. MARTIN	Medal of St. George, 3rd Class	25/8/15

	NATURE OF AWARD.	DATE.
4987 Pte. P. HODGES	Medal of St. George, 4th Class ..	25/8/15
Lt.-Col. C. W. H. CRICHTON, D.S.O.	Mentioned in Despatches	31/12/15
Lieut. the Earl of AIRLIE ..	Mentioned in Despatches	31/12/15
Lieut. G. A. ALEXANDER ..	Mentioned in Despatches ..	31/12/15
Lieut. S. C. DEED	Military Cross ..	3/3/16
Captain V. J. GREENWOOD ..	Military Cross ..	2/6/16
Lieut. the Earl of AIRLIE ..	Military Cross ..	2/6/16
Captain G. E. GOSLING ..	Mentioned in Despatches ..	2/6/16
4004 S.S.M. RAWSON	Mentioned in Despatches	2/6/16
3701 Pte. P. O'KEEFE ..	Military Medal ..	2/6/16
1088 L/Cpl. JENKINS	Mentioned in Despatches	2/1/17
6107 I./Sgt. A. J. WARD ..	Mentioned in Despatches	2/1/17
6107 L/Sgt. A. J. WARD ..	Military Medal ..	22/1/17
4290 Cpl. W. C. BROAD ..	Military Medal ..	22/1/17
3183 Sgt. J. HARWOOD.. ..	Military Medal ..	22/1/17
5016 L./Cpl. J. WIGLEY ..	Military Medal ..	22/1/17
591 Cpl. (L./Sgt.) J. W. H. SIMPKINS	Military Medal ..	22/1/17
Major W. O. GIBBS	Mentioned in Despatches	15/5/17
2021 Cpl. W. E. DUNCE ..	Mentioned in Despatches	15/5/17
47075 Sgt. C. ALDERSON ..	Military Medal ..	26/5/17
15182 Pte. W. AYRES	Military Medal ..	26/5/17
6446 L./Cpl. G. W. DAVIES ..	Military Medal ..	26/5/17

	NATURE OF AWARD.	DATE.
19789 Pte. A. GODDEN ..	Military Medal ..	26/5/17
5361 Sgt. F. JONES ..	Military Medal ..	26/5/17
20029 Pte. A. LYNN ..	Military Medal ..	26/5/17
2272 Far./Sgt. J. MANSER ..	Military Medal ..	26/5/17
2130 Pte. T. MARKEY ..	Military Medal ..	26/5/17
47017 Far./Sgt. F. MARTIN ..	Military Medal ..	26/5/17
8445 Cpl. R. PAYNE ..	Military Medal ..	26/5/17
47010 L./Cpl. T. ROGERS ..	Military Medal ..	26/5/17
4184 Pte. J. S. SCOTT ..	Military Medal ..	26/5/17
7219 Pte. J. W. SPICE ..	Military Medal ..	26/5/17
1075 Cpl. S./S. H. S. STEWART ..	Military Medal ..	26/5/17
12188 Pte. F. WALKER..	Military Medal ..	26/5/17
923 Pte. A. WHITE ..	Military Medal ..	26/5/17
Captain WOOD, R.A.M.C.	Distinguished Service Order	18/6/17
Lieut. Viscount EDNAM	Military Cross ..	18/6/17
Captain R. C. GORDON CANNING ..	Military Cross ..	18/6/17
Lieut. F. C. DRAKE ..	Military Cross ..	18/6/17
A/Major E. W. E. PALMES	Military Cross ..	18/6/17
12159 Pte. J. P. DUNN ..	Distinguished Conduct Medal	18/6/17
11558 Pte. H. W. GREEN	Distinguished Conduct Medal	18/6/17
M. DE LOGIS TINAN, Interpreter (attached)	Distinguished Conduct Medal	14/7/17
M. DE LOGIS TINAN, Interpreter (attached)	Croix de Guerre (France) ..	14/7/17
47068 L/Cpl. E. T. BAKER ..	Military Medal ..	16/8/17
7974 Sgt. A. PICKERSGILL ..	Military Medal ..	16/8/17
Captain G. E. GOSLING ..	Chevalier, Order de Leopold, Croix de Guerre (Belgium) ..	24/9/17

APPENDIX E (*continued*).

	NATURE OF AWARD.	DATE.
2/Lieut. A. N. LOCKETT	Mentioned in Despatches	11/12/17
4871 Sgt. H. DUNK	Mentioned in Despatches	11/12/17
47074 A./Sgt. T. M. LOADER	Meritorious Service Medal	1/1/18
25542 L./Cpl. P. B. ENGLISH	Military Medal	15/3/18
47013 R.M.S. F. MASON	Good Conduct Medal	1/4/18
47009 Sgt. A. WALKUP	Good Conduct Medal	1/4/18
47011 Sgt. W. HOPKINS	Good Conduct Medal	1/4/18
2950 Pte. W. SAVAGE	Good Conduct Medal	1/4/18
47017 Far./Sgt. F. MARTIN	Good Conduct Medal	1/4/18
Lieut. Lord WILLIAM W. M. D. SCOTT	Mentioned in Despatches	7/4/18
20783 L./Cpl. G. COTTINGHAM	Croix de Guerre (Belgium)	15/4/18
28500 L./Cpl. D. GARNER	Croix de Guerre (Belgium)	15/4/18
12825 L./Cpl. A. T. FLACK	Croix de Guerre (Belgium)	15/4/18
913 Sgt. G. W. HAWKINS	Military Medal	16/4/18
5905 Cpl. B. BAXTER	Military Medal	16/4/18
20047 Pte. T. P. MORGAN	Military Medal	16/4/18
3609 Pte. G. H. KNIGHT	Military Medal	16/4/18
28603 Pte. A. E. COOKE	Military Medal	16/4/18
Major E. H. W. WILLIAMS	Distinguished Service Order	20/4/18
Lieut. D. H. GOUGH	Military Cross	20/4/18
2947 Pte MALSTON	Military Medal	23/4/18
Lt.-Col. H. A. TOMKINSON, D.S.O.	Bar to Distinguished Service Order	28/4/18
Captain G. E. GOSLING	Military Cross	28/4/18
4871 Sgt. H. DUNK	Croix de Guerre (France)	28/4/18

	NATURE OF AWARD.	DATE.
Lieut. A. N. LOCKETT	Croix de Guerre (France)	28/4/18
2962 Sgt. S. J. NELSON	Military Medal	28/4/18
Lieut. Lord WILLIAM W. M. D. SCOTT	Military Cross	5/5/18
31377 Pte. J. R. HALL	Distinguished Conduct Medal	5/5/18
Lieut. T. ROBINSON	Military Cross	3/6/18
959 Pte. H. BLAKEMORE	Bar to Distinguished Conduct Medal	3/6/18
47007 R.S.M. W. A. MITCHELL	Meritorious Service Medal	17/6/18
Lieut. P. R. JERMYN	Military Cross	24/10/18
D/16144 Tptr. W. GREGORY	Croix de Guerre (France)	30/10/18
Lt.-Col. F. H. D. C. WHITMORE, C.M.G., D.S.O.	Mentioned in Despatches	8/11/18
Major E. H. W. WILLIAMS, D.S.O.	Mentioned in Despatches	8/11/18
Lieut. W. S. MURLAND	Mentioned in Despatches	8/11/18
Lieut. S. J. TUFNELL	Mentioned in Despatches	8/11/18
963 Pte. C. CAVANAGH	Distinguished Conduct Medal	12/1/19
1682 Cpl. C. BANKS	Meritorious Service Medal	18/1/19
19280 Pte. W. F. PEACOCK	Military Medal	14/5/19
Lieut. W. S. MURLAND	Military Cross	3/6/19
47013 R.Q.M.S. F. MASON	Meritorious Service Medal	3/6/19
47032 S.Q.M.S. A. J. DENNIS	Meritorious Service Medal	3/6/19
H/47030 Farr.Sgt. (A. Farr. Q.M.S.) W. R. TREASURE	Meritorious Service Medal	3/6/19

	NATURE OF AWARD.	DATE.
2809 Sgt. F. BARKER	Meritorious Service Medal	3/6/19
2139 Pte. R. R. BALMER ..	Meritorious Service Medal	3/6/19
Lt.-Col. F. H. D. C. WHITMORE, C.M.G., D.S.O., T.D. ..	Mentioned in Despatches ..	5/7/19
47040 S.S.M. W. SMEED ..	Mentioned in Despatches	5/7/19
47009 Sgt. A. WALKUP	Mentioned in Despatches	5/7/19

OFFICERS AND OTHER RANKS OF THE 10TH (P.W.O.) ROYAL HUSSARS WHO RECEIVED HONOURS OR AWARDS WHILST SERVING AWAY FROM THE REGIMENT.

	NATURE OF AWARD.	DATE.
Col. (temp. Brig.-Gen.) R. W. R. BARNES, D.S.O.	Mentioned in Despatches	30/4/16
Brig.-Gen. R. W. R. BARNES, D.S.O.	Mentioned in Despatches, and C.B...	13/11/16
Brig.-Gen. R. W. R. BARNES, C.B., D.S.O.	Mentioned in Despatches	7/11/17
Maj.-Gen. R. W. R. BARNES, C.B., D.S.O.	Croix de Guerre (France)	28/1/19
Capt. C. H. POTTER	Mentioned in Despatches ..	8/11/18
Capt. C. H. POTTER	Order of British Empire	1/1/19
Capt. the Hon. E. B. MEADE ..	Mentioned in Despatches	8/11/18
Capt. the Hon. D. H. PELHAM ..	Distinguished Service Order	2/6/16
Capt. the Hon. F. W. STANLEY ..	Distinguished Service Order	29/12/16
Capt. A. H. C. KEARSLEY, D.S.O...	Mentioned in Despatches ..	1/7/16

	NATURE OF AWARD.	DATE.
Capt. A. H. C. KEARSLEY, D.S.O.	Order of the Star of Kara-George of Servia, 4th Class with Swords ..	15/2/17
Capt. A. H. C. KEARSLEY, D.S.O.	Mentioned in Despatches	16/1/18
Capt. A. H. C. KEARSLEY, D.S.O.	Order of the Nile, 3rd Class	9/11/18
Capt. W. L. PALMER	Mentioned in Despatches ..	20/10/14
Capt. W. L. PALMER	Military Cross ..	23/6/15
Capt. E. A. FIELDEN	Mentioned in Despatches ..	9/4/17
Capt. E. A. FIELDEN	Military Cross ..	3/6/18
Major J. F. NEILSON	Order of St. Vladimir, 4th Class with Swords	24/9/15
Major J. F. NEILSON	Brought to notice of Secretary of State for War	23/1/17
Major J. F. NEILSON	Order of St. Anne, 2nd Class	26/9/16
Major J. F. NEILSON	Distinguished Service Order	/10/16
2/Lieut. D. N. GARSTIN	Distinguished Service Order	
2/Lieut. D. N. GARSTIN	Military Cross ..	8/3/19
A/Capt. J. C. Lord CHESHAM ..	Military Cross ..	3/6/18
A/Capt. W. M. ARMSTRONG ..	Mentioned in Despatches	20/10/14
A/Capt. W. M. ARMSTRONG ..	Mentioned in Despatches	11/12/15
A/Capt. W. M. ARMSTRONG ..	Military Cross ..	2/8/16

	NATURE OF AWARD.	DATE.
A/Capt. W. M. ARMSTRONG ..	Mentioned in Despatches ..	11/7/16
A/Capt. W. M. ARMSTRONG ..	Mentioned in Despatches ..	9/4/17
Lt. Sir B. S. BROOKE, Bart. ..	Military Cross ..	2/6/16
Lt. Sir B. S. BROOKE, Bart. ..	Mentioned in Despatches ...	11/7/16
Lt. Sir B. S. BROOKE, Bart. ..	Croix de Guerre (France)	10/10/18
Capt. C. R. MOLYNEUX ..	Military Cross ..	1/1/18
Lieut. J. S. M. WARDELL ..	Member of Order of British Empire ..	22/3/19
977 Cpl. S. ECKERS	Military Medal ..	28/4/18
Lieut. (A/Capt.) W. BURDETT ..	Mentioned in Despatches	5/7/19
21096 Pte. (A./Sgt.) E. WILLIAMS	Mentioned in Despatches	5/7/19

APPENDIX F.

ESSEX YEOMANRY.

LIST OF OFFICERS AND OTHER RANKS WHO HAVE RECEIVED HONOURS OR AWARDS SINCE THE COMMENCEMENT OF THE CAMPAIGN.

	NATURE OF AWARD.	DATE.
Capt. E. A. RUGGLES-BRISE ..	Military Cross ..	3/7/15
174 Sgt. W. C. HOWARD ..	Distinguished Conduct Medal	5/8/15
1064 Pte. G. WEAR	Cross of the Order of St. George, 4th Class	25/8/15
Major A. RODDICK	Mentioned in Despatches	31/12/15
Major A. BUXTON	Mentioned in Despatches ..	31/12/15

	Nature of Award.	Date.
Capt. E. A. Ruggles-Brise, M.C.	Mentioned in Despatches	31/12/15
Capt. R. A. Thomson ..	Mentioned in Despatches	31/12/15
174 S.S.M. W. C. Howard ..	Mentioned in Despatches	31/12/15
780 Sgt. A. Frost	Mentioned in Despatches ..	31/12/15
624 Sgt. H. R. Wardill ..	Mentioned in Despatches	31/12/15
1110 Cpl. W. C. V. Schwier ..	Mentioned in Despatches	31/12/15
1555 L./Cpl. F. Smy	Mentioned in Despatches	31/12/15
1370 L./Cpl. L. G. Cook ..	Distinguished Conduct Medal	15/3/16
753 Sgt. A. E. Abbott	Distinguished Conduct Medal	10/3/16
Major A. Buxton	Distinguished Service Order	3/6/16
Major A. Buxton	Mentioned in Despatches	15/6/16
2/Lieut. T. F. Buxton	Mentioned in Despatches ..	15/6/16
3217 R.S.M. C. Farrell ..	Mentioned in Despatches	15/6/16
4779 S.S.M. E. G. Bidie ..	Long Service and Good Conduct Medal ..	16/12/16
Lt.-Col. F. H. D. C. Whitmore ..	Mentioned in Despatches	29/12/16
Lt.-Col. F. H. D. C. Whitmore ..	Distinguished Service Order	1/1/17

APPENDIX F (*continued*).

	NATURE OF AWARD.	DATE.
Lieut. E. J. SAYER	Military Cross ..	1/1/17
1665 Pte. E. D. DORRINGTON ..	Military Medal ..	19/1/17
1650 Pte. G. PLAYER	Military Medal ..	19/1/17
895 Pte. A. E. ROLPH	Military Medal ..	19/1/17
1555 Sgt. F. SMY	Military Medal ..	19/1/17
606 Sgt. R. D. TURNELL ..	Military Medal ..	19/1/17
767 Sgt. E. W. WALKER ..	Military Medal ..	19/1/17
1628 Pte. L. G. HOWARD ..	Military Medal ..	22/1/17
Lieut. R. A. THOMSON	Croix de Guerre (France)	1/5/17
Major J. O. PARKER	Mentioned in Despatches	15/5/17
4779 S.S.M. E. G. BIDIE ..	Mentioned in Despatches	15/5/17
80586 Pte. A. D. PAGE ..	Military Medal ..	26/5/17
80270 Cpl. G. E. ROWELL ..	Military Medal ..	26/5/17
81192 Pte. W. ROPER ..	Military Medal ..	26/5/17
80123 Pte. H. THORN ..	Military Medal ..	26/5/17
80027 Sgt. G. G. CREES ..	Military Medal ..	26/5/17
80244 Cpl. G. E. PETTITT ..	Military Medal ..	26/5/17
80333 Sgt. L. G. COOK, D.C.M. ..	Military Medal ..	26/5/17
80139 Cpl. B. G. STEWARD ..	Military Medal ..	26/5/17
80180 S.S.M. G. S. J. REX ..	Military Medal ..	26/5/17
80169 Pte. E. H. FINCH ..	Military Medal ..	26/5/17
80593 L./Cpl. F. LAST ..	Military Medal ..	26/5/17
80161 Pte. W. C. SAVILLE ..	Military Medal ..	26/5/17
80937 L./Cpl. J. N. BUCKNELL ..	Military Medal ..	26/5/17
Capt. E. STORK (R.A.M.C. T.) ..	Distinguished Service Order	18/6/17
Capt. E. STORK (R.A.M.C. T.) ..	Mentioned in Despatches	18/6/17
Lieut. J. C. CHAPLIN	Military Cross ..	18/6/17
2/Lieut. A. WINTER ROSE ..	Military Cross ..	18/6/17

	Nature of Award.	Date.
80047 S.S.M. W. W. McKellar ..	Distinguished Conduct Medal	18/6/17
80075 Sgt. J. Brown	Distinguished Conduct Medal	18/6/17
10557 Pte. J. Graham	Military Medal ..	3/7/17
3217 R.S.M. C. Farrell ..	Long Service and Good Conduct Medal ..	12/7/17
M. De Logis P. Vernot, Interpreter (attached) ..	Military Medal ..	14/7/17
M. De Logis P. Vernot, Interpreter (attached) ..	Croix De Guerre (France) ..	14/7/17
Major G. G. Gold	Legion of Honour, Croix de Chevalier	14/7/17
3217 R.S.M. C. Farrell ..	Medaille Militaire ..	14/7/17
80017 R.Q.M.S. H. B. Joscelyne	Territorial Force Efficiency Medal ..	1/11/17
163 S.S.M. E. W. Robins ..	Territorial Force Efficiency Medal ..	1/11/17
Lt.-Col. F. H. D. C. Whitmore, D.S.O.	Mentioned in Despatches ..	11/12/17
Lieut. R. D. Holland ..	Mentioned in Despatches ..	11/12/17
Lt.-Col. F. H. D. C. Whitmore, D.S.O.	Companion of the most Distinguished Order of St. Michael and St. George ..	1/1/18
Capt. R. G. Proby	Military Cross ..	1/1/18
80348 Pte. E. W. Bewers ..	Mentioned in Despatches	7/4/18
Major J. O. Parker	Croix de Guerre .. (Belgium)	15/4/18
80391 S.Q.M.S. L. A. Skipper ..	Croix de Guerre .. (Belgium)	15/4/18

	NATURE OF AWARD.	DATE.
80611 Cpl. H. C. CORDELL ..	Croix de Guerre .. (Belgium)	15/4/18
81033 Pte. C. WOOD	Croix de Guerre .. (Belgium)	15/4/18
Lieut. G. WEAR	Mentioned in Despatches	20/5/18
Major E. HILL	Distinguished Service Order	3/6/18
Major E. HILL	Mentioned in Despatches	3/6/18
80017 R.Q.M.S. H. B. JOSCELYNE	Meritorious Service Medal	16/6/18
170147 A./Sgt. G. D. T. SLADE .	Meritorious Service Medal	16/6/18
80289 L./Cpl. H. S. WHITCHER ..	Meritorious Service Medal	16/6/18
11573 Sgt. F. H. JENKINS ..	Mentioned in Despatches	22/6/18
80523 L./Cpl. A. J. HALL ..	Military Medal ..	18/7/18
80027 Sgt. G. C. CREES, M.M ..	Bar to Military Medal	18/7/18
80970 L./Sgt. J. T. LOWE ..	Military Medal ..	18/7/18
2/Lieut. W. C. V. SCHWIER ..	Military Cross ..	26/7/18
80020 Sgt. A. SPRAKE	Distinguished Conduct Medal	4/9/18
Lieut. C. A. COLLIS	Mentioned in Despatches ..	20/12/18
Lt.-Col. F. H. D. C. WHITMORE, C.M.G., D.S.O.	Territorial Decoration	31/12/18
Major G. G. GOLD	Territorial Decoration	30/5/19
Major E. HILL, D.S.O.	Territorial Decoration	15/7/19
Major E. A. RUGGLES-BRISE, M.C.	Territorial Decoration	18/8/19
Major A. BUXTON, D.S.O. ..	Territorial Decoration	16/1/20

OFFICERS AND OTHER RANKS OF THE ESSEX YEOMANRY WHO RECEIVED
HONOURS OR AWARDS WHILST SERVING AWAY FROM THE REGIMENT.

	NATURE OF AWARD.	DATE.
Capt. E. P. W. WEDD ..	.. Mentioned in Despatches	4/1/17
Lieut. W. P. BATTERS ..	.. Military Cross ..	28/7/17
80078 Sgt. C. A. CURTIS..	.. Military Medal ..	28/7/17
Lieut. F. C. MEYER ..	.. Mentioned in Despatches ..	11/12/17
80160 Pte. C. V. RIGGS	.. Distinguished Conduct Medal	3/6/18
2/Lieut. A. J. COCKRILL	.. Military Cross ..	16/8/18
2/Lieut. L. SOLAINI ..	.. Military Cross ...	16/8/18
Capt. L. M. WOODHOUSE	.. Military Cross ..	25/8/18
Lieut. L. B. HORE ..	.. Military Cross ..	16/9/18
Capt. E. P. W. WEDD ..	.. Military Cross ..	16/9/18
Lieut. D. MORGAN ..	.. Croix de Guerre (France)	10/10/18
80647 S./S. B. CHAPMAN	.. Distinguished Conduct Medal	30/10/18
Capt. L. M. WOODHOUSE, M.C.	.. Distinguished Flying Cross	2/11/18
81239 Pte. D. G. PERRY	.. Military Medal ..	13/11/18
80178 Ptc. F. J. LEVEY	.. Military Medal ..	13/11/18
80101 Sgt. C. W. BUGG	.. Military Medal ..	13/11/18
80087 Cpl. P. J. GREEN......	.. Military Medal ..	11/12/18
Lt.-Col. F. H. D. C. WHITMORE, C.M.G., D.S.O. ..	.. Mentioned in Despatches ..	20/12/18
Lieut. S. J. TUFNELL ..	.. Mentioned in Despatches ..	20/12/18
D/16144 Tptr. W. GREGORY	.. Croix de Guerre (France)	29/1/19
2/Lieut. P. R. JERMYN ..	.. Military Cross ..	1/2/19
Lieut. W. A. TUCZEK ..	.. Military Cross ..	3/6/19
D/16307 A/S.S.M. W. E. WINKLEY	Meritorious Service Medal	3/6/19

	NATURE OF AWARD.	DATE.
Lt.-Col. F. H. D. C. WHITMORE, C.M.G., D.S.O., T.D.	Mentioned in Despatches	5/7/19
Lieut. (T./Major) S. DAY	Mentioned in Despatches	5/7/19
A./Capt. M. DUDDING	Order of the Nile, 4th Class	13/1/20

SUPPLEMENTARY LIST APPENDIX F.

OFFICERS AND OTHER RANKS, FORMERLY OF THE ESSEX YEOMANRY, WHO RECEIVED HONOURS OR AWARDS AFTER BEING TRANSFERRED TO OTHER UNITS.

	NATURE OF AWARD.	DATE.
L./Cpl. H. MUGFORD, 8th M.G. Squadron	Victoria Cross	11/4/17
Lieut. W. P. CONNOLLY, 16th Royal Warwickshire Regiment	Military Cross	7/11/18
Sgt. J. R. TOZER, 8th M.G. Sqdn.	Military Medal	11/4/17
Sgt. N. HARRISON, 8th M.G. Sqdn.	Military Medal	11/4/17
Pte. D. W. L. WARREN, 8th M.G. Squadron	Military Medal	6/4/18
Sgt. F. W. COTTIS, 8th M.G. Sqdn.	Croix de Guerre (Belgium)	11/4/17
Sgt. W. H. BATEMAN, 9th Battn. Essex Regiment	Military Medal	9/6/17
Lieut. W. H. BATEMAN, 1st Battn. Essex Regiment	Military Cross	2/4/19
Lieut. E. POOLE, City of London Yeomanry	Military Medal	3/6/19
Lieut. C. B. PRIOR (Chaplain), 66th Div. R.F.A.	Military Cross	30/9/18
Pte. M. G. MALE, 1st Battn. Essex Regiment	Military Medal	9/10/18
Pte. F. SUTTON, Tank Corps	Military Medal	31/8/18

	Nature of Award.		Date.
Pte. G. Hewett, 4th Battn. Essex Regiment	Military Medal	..	28/5/18
Pte. G. Hewett, 4th Battn. Essex Regiment	Croix de Guerre	..	28/5/18
Gnr. P. D. Manning, Tank Corps	Military Medal	..	31/8/18
Pte. F. W. Larrett, 6th Cav. Field Ambulance	Military Medal	..	16/8/18

Officers of the Essex Yeomanry who have Received Honours or Awards, or who have been Mentioned in Despatches by the Secretary of State for War for Valuable Services Rendered in Connection with the War.

	Nature of Award.	Date.
Lt.-Col. the Hon. A. H. F. Greville, M.V.O.	Commander of the Royal Victorian Order	3/6/18
Lt.-Col. the Hon. A. H. F. Greville, C.V.O.	Territorial Decoration	31/12/18
Hon. Brig.-General R. B. Colvin, C.B., T.D.	Mentioned in Despatches	28/8/19
Capt. R. Edwards	Mentioned in Despatches ..	28/8/19
Lieut. (A./Capt.) R. R. Archer,	Mentioned in Despatches ..	28/8/19
Lieut. F. Gingell	Mentioned in Despatches ..	28/8/19

APPENDIX G.

List of Casualties incurred by the 10th (P.W.O.) Royal Hussars during the War.

Date.				Casualty.
13/10/14	2956 L./Cpl. W. Beckwith	..		Wounded and Missing
15/10/14	5595 S. S. E. Cox	..	..	Wounded
,,	9646 Pte. C. Selby	..	..	,,

APPENDIX G (*continued*).

DATE.			CASUALTY.
17/10/14	11295 Pte. C. WORBOYS..	..	Wounded and Missing (believed dead)
,,	5130 Pte. W. COOPER ..	..	Wounded
,,	3161 Pte. F. BURCHELL	..	,,
,,	4532 Pte. A. RAY ..	..	,,
,,	966 Pte. J. GILLINGHAM	..	,,
19/10/14	259 Pte. T. HUNT ..	..	,,
,,	5584 Pte. FAHRLANDER	..	,,
22/10/14	6986 L/Cpl. L. HAIGH..	..	,,
23/10/14	5147 Pte. A. HALL ..	..	Killed
,,	7987 Pte. E. CARRETT..	..	,,
,,	Lt.-Col. R. W. W. BARNES, D.S.O.		Wounded
,,	Major Hon. C. B. O. MITFORD	..	,,
,,	Capt. G. C. STEWART, ..	..	,,
,,	2228 L./Cpl. W. BARRETT	..	,,
,,	1716 Pte. J. JORDAN ..	..	,,
,,	2005 Pte. E. SMITH ..	..	,,
,,	7457 Pte. E. HART ..	..	,,
,,	1369 Pte. F. BALDWIN..	..	,,
,,	914 Pte. J. SAGAR ..	..	,,
,,	3035 Pte. G. HOGARTH..	..	,,
,,	5411 Pte. J. NOCK ..	..	,,
,,	808 Pte. T. BELL ..	..	Died of Wounds
,,	8672 Pte. G. BUCKLEY..	..	,,
,,	6952 Pte. W. CHADWICK	..	Wounded and Missing (believed dead)
26/10/14	Capt. Sir FRANK ROSE, Bt.	..	Killed
,,	Lieut. C. R. TURNOR ..	..	,,
,,	2975 Pte. R. McKENZIE	..	,,
,,	Pte. J. STARKEY ..	..	,,
,,	8499 Pte. T. WAREHAM	..	,,
,,	1368 L./Cpl. J. WAUGH	..	,,
,,	9298 Pte. W. R. GREEN	..	Wounded

Date.				Casualty.
26/10/14	1290	Pte. J. Williamson	..	Wounded
,,	10156	Pte. A. Rowledge	..	,,
,,	1603	L./Cpl. E. Barnes	..	,,
,,	7092	Pte. W. Riley ..	..	,,
,,	2962	L./Cpl. S. J. Nelson	..	,,
,,	6541	L./Cpl. W. Swales	..	,,
,,	2726	Pte. T. Bell ..	..	Died of Wounds
27/10/14	5565	Cpl. W. Ovenden	..	Wounded
,,	2277	Pte. E. Ibbotson..	..	,,
,,	7958	Pte. E. Barden ..	..	,,
,,	4046	Pte. H. Gale ..	..	,,
,,	12295	Pte. F. Tharrett	..	,,
29/10/14	5609	Pte. B. Churchyard	..	,,
,,	7348	Pte. J. W. Wilson	..	,,
,,	2760	Pte. E. Cummings	..	,,
31/10/14		Capt. Kinkhead, R.A.M.C.	..	Killed
,,	1296	L./Cpl. C. Fennell	..	,,
,,	2957	L./Cpl. G. Prowse	..	,,
,,	7730	L./Cpl. L. Pattle	..	,,
,,	1309	Pte. W. Henwood	..	,,
,,		Capt. Hon. H. Baring ..	..	Wounded
,,		Major C. W. H. Crichton, D.S.O.		,,
,,		Capt. E. A. Fielden ..	..	,,
,,		Capt. G. C. Stewart ..	..	,,
,,	4486	Saddler T. Williams	..	,,
,,	749	Pte. J. Durman ..	..	,,
,,	4097	Cpl. T. Pollock ..	..	,,
,,	6496	Pte. F. Brown ..	..	,,
,,	1491	Pte. H. Strangeway	..	,,
,,	8482	Pte. E. J. Hicks ..	..	,,
,,	4357	Sgt. C. Foster ..	..	,,
,,	4136	Sgt. W. Hopkins..	..	,,
,,	7106	Pte. S. Brown ..	..	,,

APPENDIX G (*continued*).

DATE.				CASUALTY.
31/10/14	4220	Pte. P. GARRETT	..	Wounded
,,	62	Pte. E. REEVES	..	Wounded and Missing (believed dead)
,,	5210	Pte. A. McFARLANE	..	,,
,,	4364	Sgt. F. CURL	..	Died of Wounds
,,	9707	Pte. W. DEVEREUX	..	,,
,,	78	Trptr. P. HOLMES	..	Wounded (subsequently died)
1/11/14	5544	L./Cpl. L. HOLLISTER	..	Killed
,,	958	Pte. E. GOMERSALL	..	,,
,,		Capt. W. O. GIBBS	..	Wounded
,,	2447	L./Cpl. W. GREAVES	..	,,
,,	4972	Cpl. E. G. COOMBS	..	,,
,,	954	Pte. F. C. MAYES	..	,,
,,	1500	L./Cpl. W. BEECH	..	,,
,,	5284	Pte. H. BOND	..	,,
,,	2422	Pte. E. DALBY	..	,,
,,	4623	Pte. H. SMITH	..	,,
2/11/14		Lt.-Col. R. W. R. BARNES, D.S.O...		,,
,,	5217	L./Sgt. F. BLANCHARD	..	,,
6/11/14	421	L./Cpl. W. NORTON	..	,,
,,	962	L./Cpl. C. HOTINE	..	,,
,,	4176	Pte. C. GENT	..	,,
,,	1340	Pte. T. WIKE	..	,,
,,	2269	Pte. H. ELLIS	..	,,
,,	1417	Pte. F. WATERHOUSE	..	,,
,,	8507	Pte. H. NEWBURY	..	,,
,,	7212	Pte. BENTLEY	..	,,
11/11/14	1117	S.S. J. FRASER	..	,,
,,	5539	Pte. E. BAKER	..	,,
,,	11655	Pte. H. W. DAWSON	..	,,
,,	711	Pte. A. MILDRED	..	,,
,,	4997	Pte. H. WILLIAMS	..	,,

DATE.			CASUALTY.
11/11/14	59 Pte. P. REYNOLDS	..	Wounded
,,	3798 Pte. J. EATON	..	,,
,,	4409 Pte. D. HIGGINS ..	..	,,
,,	6648 Pte. W. FOXWELL	..	,,
,,	7342 Pte. G. REYNOLDS	..	,,
;,	5587 Pte. R. MORRIS ..	..	Died of Wounds
,,	926 Pte. P. RIDGEWAY	..	,,
12/11/14	Major Hon. W. G. CADOGAN, M.V.O.		Killed
,,	3351 R.S.M. W. KING ..	..	,,
,,	Capt E. W. E. PALMES ..	..	Wounded
,,	5498 Cpl. H. HARDY ..	..	,,
,,	4695 Pte. E. SABIN ..	..	,,
,,	2469 Pte. W. SUGDEN ..	..	,,
,,	8412 Pte. C. UPTON ..	..	,,
,,	4576 Pte. J. E. BALKWILL	..	,,
,,	5422 Pte. J. WILLIAMS..	..	,,
,,	3268 Sgt. R. BELL ..	..	,,
,,	4991 Cpl. J. PHILLPOT ..	..	,,
,,	312 Pte. W. ROSE ..	..	,,
,,	4536 Pte. W. WORTH ..	..	,,
,,	4995 Pte. C. HENNIGAN	..	,,
,,	967 Pte. H. MAY ..	..	,,
,,	7994 Pte. W. DIBLEY ..	..	,,
,,	6646 Pte. H. GALLAND..	..	,,
,,	3236 Pte. W. RIX ..	..	,,
,,	2830 Pte. G. ADAMS ..	..	Died of Wounds
,,	5035 Pte. H. BUCKLEY..	..	,,
,,	7713 Pte. H. TONKS ..	..	,,
,,	7191 Pte. W. BURGESS..	..	,,
13/11/14	5214 Sgt. G. GILMORE ..	..	,,
,,	1819 Pte. R. BOWNS ..	..	Wounded
16/11/14	Capt. Hon. A. ANNESLEY	..	Killed
17/11/14	Capt. C. H. PETO ..	..	,,

DATE.			CASUALTY.
17/11/14	2/Lieut. R. F. DRAKE	.. ..	Killed
,,	4897 Sgt. H. STRUDWICK	..	,,
,,	1924 L./Cpl. A. MURRAY	..	,,
,,	5087 L./Cpl. W. TWINING	..	,,
,,	5738 Pte. W. HILLARD..	..	,,
,,	17 Pte. H. SMITH	.. ..	,,
,,	6467 Pte. E. MORRIS	.. ..	,,
,,	9349 Pte. A. SHEPPARD	..	,,
,,	1544 Pte. C. HEPBURN..	..	,,
,,	9060 Pte. J. SMEATON	..	,,
,,	6333 Pte. S. SAGE	.. ..	,,
,,	4048 S.S.M. W. A. MITCHELL	..	Wounded
,,	894 Pte. H. STOCKTON	..	,,
,,	5052 Pte. J. WHEELER..	..	,,
,,	7081 Pte. T. GREAVES ..	..	,,
,,	5837 Pte. T. WALLER ..	..	,,
,,	6499 Pte. P. DEVLIN ..	..	,,
,,	3035 Pte. F. KAPPLER ..	..	,,
,,	865 Pte. H. ELLIOTT ..	..	,,
,,	9925 Pte. F. STOCKWELL	..	,,
10/2/15	4898 Pte. W. WALLACE	..	Died of Wounds
12/2/15	28313 Pte. R. TATTERSALL	..	Killed
27/4/15	4802 Sgt. H. J. PASKELL	..	Wounded
,,	963 Pte. C. P. CAVANAGH	..	,,
13/5/15	Lt.-Col. E. R. A. SHEARMAN	..	Killed
,,	Major Hon. C. B. O. MITFORD	..	,,
,,	Capt. G. C. STEWART	.. ..	,,
,,	Capt. M. A. de TUYLL ..	..	,,
,,	3941 S.S.M. A. KEATS	..	,,
,,	5610 Sgt. J. DICKS	.. ..	,,
,,	4524 Sgt. A. KEELEY ..	..	,,
,,	5413 Sgt. E. LURCOTT ..	..	,,
,,	5238 Cpl. S. HADDINGTON	..	,,

APPENDIX G *(continued)*.

Date.			Casualty.
13/5/15	396	Cpl. A. Bayston ..	Killed
,,	5453	Cpl. T. Chamberlain ..	,,
,,	18	Cpl. H. Nepean ..	,,
,,	4563	L./Cpl. G. Guyver ..	,,
,,	5171	L./Cpl. H. Meads ..	,,
,,	5369	L./Cpl. H. Scales ..	,,
,,	3507	L./Cpl. T. Mason ..	,,
,,	5601	L./Cpl. H. Johnson ..	,,
,,	14789	L./Cpl. A. Masters ..	,,
,,	7998	L./Cpl. F. Smith ..	,,
,,	3205	Pte. W. Fewster ..	,,
,,	7972	Pte. B. Senior	,,
,,	1110	Pte. A. McBryde ..	,,
,,	5119	Pte. J. Cooper	,,
,,	3472	Pte. C. Chatten	,,
,,	4899	Pte. A. Walker	,,
,,	5469	Pte. F. Fletcher ..	,,
,,	4310	Pte. C. Hope	,,
,,	7371	Pte. T. Sole	,,
,,	14479	Pte. A. Cobb	,,
,,	5042	Pte. P. Cole	,,
,,	28430	Pte. W. Kimmens ..	,,
,,	5230	Sgt. G. Hyland	Wounded
,,	1484	Sgt. R. Lloyd	,,
,,	8152	Sgt. F. Hibble	,,
,,	8756	Sgt. A. Mitchell.. ..	,,
,,	5550	Sgt. R. Stone	,,
,,	10791	L./Sgt. F. Lock	,,
,,	2280	Cpl. K. Swadling ..	,,
,,	2809	Cpl. S. Eckers	,,
,,	11294	Cpl. W. Penfold ..	,,
,,	4290	Cpl. W. Broad	,,
,,	537	Cpl. C. Portway ..	,,

Date.				Casualty.
13/5/15	1500	Cpl. W. Beech	.. ..	Wounded
,,	391	Cpl. J. Parfrement	..	,,
,,	8277	Cpl. A. Price	.. ..	,,
,,	4698	Cpl. C. Wilson	.. ..	,,
,,	4650	Cpl. W. Snell	.. ..	,,
,,	61	Cpl. A. Stevens	.. ..	,,
,,	2292	Cpl. J. Brown	.. ..	,,
,,	2280	Cpl. F. Warren	..	,,
,,	7361	Cpl. P. Hargreaves	..	,,
,,	491	Tptr. J. Jones	.. ..	,,
,,	7960	Pte. A. Dickenson	..	,,
,,	22563	Ptc. H. Sharpe	.. ..	,,
,,	3353	Pte. C. Barker	.. ..	,,
,,	14191	Pte. R. Straight	..	,,
,,	2823	Pte. J. Allison	.. ..	,,
,,	6141	Pte. A. Hobbins	.. ..	,,
,,	923	Pte. W. Hayday	..	,,
,,	25475	Pte. W. Rowntree	..	,,
,,	10552	Pte. H. Meredith	..	,,
,,	4414	Pte. A. Tee	.. ..	,,
,,	11296	Pte. H. Page	.. ..	,,
,,	22521	Pte. E. Fallon	.. ..	,,
,,	2603	Pte. G. Thompson	..	,,
,,	25376	Pte. E. Auston	.. ..	,,
,,	5199	Pte. G. Baines	.. ..	,,
,,	1087	Pte. W. Colville	.. ..	,,
,,	6807	Pte. D. Roberts	.. ..	,,
,,	10698	Pte. H. Smith	.. ..	,,
,,	6424	Pte. E. Scott	.. ..	,,
,,	5037	Pte. J. Whittakbr	..	,,
,,	25376	Pte. J. Clay	.. ..	,,
,,	29042	Pte. H. Glucksman	..	,,
,,	7952	Pte. J. Holmes	.. ..	,,

Date.		Casualty.
13/5/15	838 Pte. W. Quarton ..	Wounded
,,	253 Pte. T. Bentall	,,
,,	25381 Pte. W. Furniss ..	,,
,,	2809 Cpl. F. Barker	,,
,,	7082 Pte. M. Reading ..	,,
,,	5285 Pte. W. Gillard ..	,,
,,	7459 Pte. W. Spriggs	,,
,,	2791 Pte. F. Bellwood ..	,,
,,	10857 Pte. G. Lancaster ..	,,
,,	7720 Pte. A. Atkinson ..	,,
,,	3034 Pte. E. Burke	,,
,,	3736 Pte. W. Derrington ..	,,
,,	5057 Pte. T. Glazebrook ..	,,
,,	12270 Pte. A. Marples	,,
,,	6289 Pte. A. Jennings ..	,,
,,	9350 Pte. T. Wallis	,,
,,	6816 Pte. S. Whatmore ..	,,
,,	6434 Pte. A. Barrett	,,
,,	12089 Pte. A. Farrell	,,
,,	4952 Pte. B. Tansey	,,
,,	10825 Pte. E. Evans	,,
,,	7706 Pte. A. Frith	,,
,,	6343 Pte. A. Lockwood ..	,,
,,	17114 Pte. A. Pilkington ..	,,
,,	20795 Pte. G. Chapman.. ..	,,
,,	7219 Pte. J. Spice	,,
,,	25262 Pte. H. Smith	,,
,,	20502 Pte. A. Attwell.. ..	,,
,,	10412 Pte. A. Hicks	,,
,,	954 Pte. H. Mayes	,,
,,	10427 Pte. H. Pearcy	,,
,,	1954 Pte. D. Arscott	,,
,,	5016 Pte. J. Wigley	,,

DATE.			CASUALTY.
13/5/15	7194 Pte. T. WRIGHT	..	Wounded
,,	2574 Pte. W. MORTON	..	,,
,,	4533 Pte. T. WILSON	..	,,
,,	17388 Pte. J. WIDDAMSON	..	,,
,,	5218 Pte. J. KELLY	..	,,
,,	1818 Pte. R. HOLDSWORTH	..	,,
,,	7656 Pte. H. WYATT	..	,,
,,	12052 Pte. T. SWIFT	..	,,
,,	10694 Pte. H. NOBLE	..	,,
,,	12776 Pte. J. BURNELL	..	,,
,,	8384 Pte. P. FOUNTAIN	..	,,
,,	25764 Pte. F. EGERTON	..	,,
,,	Major C. W. H. CRICHTON, D.S.O.		,,
,,	Major W. O. GIBBS	..	,,
,,	Lieut. J. C. Lord CHESHAM	..	,,
,,	Lieut. G. ALEXANDER	..	,,
,,	Lieut. J. S. M. WARDELL	..	,,
,,	Lieut. C. HUMBERT	..	,,
,,	622 Sgt. F. PORTER	..	Died of Wounds
,,	3610 Cpl. E. JOEL	..	,,
,,	882 Cpl. B. SYKES	..	,,
,,	1353 Cpl. W. FETROL	..	,,
,,	1358 Cpl. W. ROSE	..	,,
,,	7128 L./Cpl. W. TREASURE	..	Missing (believed killed)
,,	8423 Pte. F. ARMSTRONG	..	,,
,,	4891 Pte. S. HOILE	..	,,
,,	8200 Pte. W. DRAPER	..	,,
,,	2291 Pte. A. BATTYE	..	,,
,,	5561 Sadd. Cpl. E. POLLIKETT	..	Wounded and Missing
31/5/15	6499 Pte. P. DEVLIN	..	Killed
,,	710 Pte. W. JOHNSON	..	Wounded
,,	5465 L./Cpl. J. HILL	..	,,
2/6/15	5284 Pte. H. BOND	..	,,

Date.		Casualty.
2/6/15	4619 Pte. L. Strudwick ..	Wounded
,,	5298 Pte. G. Biddle	Died of Wounds
4/6/15	5894 Pte. R. Bloomer	Killed
5/6/15	4368 Pte. G. Wilson	Wounded
6/6/15	17992 Ptc. F. Frances	Killed
,,	3636 Sgt. H. Gibbons	Wounded
16/8/15	8184 Pte. A. Bird..	,,
,,	1330 Pte. G. Summers	,,
,,	868 Pte. R. Doig	,,
27/9/15	Capt. R. O'Kelly (R.A.M.C.) ..	,,
,,	25898 Pte. L. Faithfull ..	Killed
,,	7102 Pte. F. Whitbread ..	Wounded
,,	10860 L./Cpl. H. Tweedale ..	,,
,,	7977 Pte. W. Whittingham ..	,,
,,	14478 Pte. W. Ingram	,,
,,	20188 Pte. F. Cattle	Wounded (Gassed)
9/1/16	12159 Pte. J. Dunn	Wounded
,,	28768 Pte. A. Quarton	,,
,,	12114 Pte. W. Stones	,,
10/1/16	12173 Pte. W. Richards ..	,,
,,	12308 Pte. W. Johnson.. ..	,,
,,	22159 Pte. C. Hayes	Killed
11/1/16	28499 Pte. D. Partridge ..	Wounded
,,	28549 Pte. B. Hutchinson ..	,,
,,	7735 Pte. S. Warren	,,
,,	8142 L./Cpl. C. Upton	Killed
,,	9177 L./Cpl. S. Kingman ..	Wounded
,,	838 Pte. H. Quarton.. ..	Wounded (Shell Shock)
,,	2312 Pte. E. Wraye	,,
18/1/16	2469 Pte. W. Sugden	Wounded
,,	12004 Pte. H. Walton	,,
,,	2227 Pte. E. Ibbotson.. ..	,,
,,	6491 Tptr. T. Green	,,

Date.		Casualty.
18/1/16	22566 Pte. D. Fox	Wounded
21/1/16	1874 Pte. W. Loach	,,
,,	7263 Pte. J. Phillips	,,
,,	6788 L./Cpl. G. Scarisbrick	,,
22/1/16	591 Sgt. W. Simpkins	,,
,,	22580 Pte. F. Adcock	Died of Wounds
23/1/16	603 Sgt. E. Bradley	Wounded
,,	11593 Pte. R. Lucas	,,
,,	929 Pte. F. Stockwell	,,
2/2/16	907 Pte. F. Strange	Killed
,,	5036 Pte. W. Grinsell	Died of Wounds
3/2/16	5280 Pte. W. Jasper	Wounded
,,	7959 L./Cpl. J. Garside	Killed
,,	6452 Pte. J. Ley	Wounded
,,	22435 Pte. J. Timson	,,
4/2/16	8173 Pte. J. McFadden	Died of Wounds
,,	25984 Pte. J. Wagster	,,
5/2/16	14592 Pte. N. E. Bates	Wounded
,,	2245 L./Cpl. R. Wilson	,,
26/7/16	17332 Pte. A. Elliott	Wounded (Shell Shock)
28/7/16	15103 Pte. P. Parkes	Killed
24/7/16	15234 Pte. D. Johnson	Wounded (accidental)
30/7/16	10528 Pte. A. Whittington	Killed
,,	4508 Pte. A. Winter	Wounded
,,	19283 Pte. J. H. Beardmore	,,
,,	19278 Pte. V. Ellis	,,
,,	11467 Pte. J. Prior	,,
,,	13132 Pte. A. L. Webb	,,
,,	28327 Pte. W. McVeigh	,,
,,	22113 Pte. W. Auton	,,
,,	14641 Pte. C. Parsons	,,
,,	14474 Pte. W. Stevenson	,,
16/8/16	275 L./Cpl. H. Shaw	,,

DATE.		CASUALTY.
20/8/16	17297 Pte. J. THOMSON	Killed (accidental)
31/8/16	2/Lieut. J. HANBURY WILLIAMS ..	Wounded
17/9/16	25759 Pte. A. NIXON	,,
,,	10857 Pte. G. LANCASTER ..	,,
,,	25322 Pte. J. H. FERGUSON ..	,,
,,	28898 Pte. E. ROLPH	,,
,,	28837 Pte. S. FITZGERALD ..	,,
10/10/16	12056 Pte. DAVISON	Killed
,,	5420 Pte. W. HODGSON ..	,,
,,	31183 Pte. A. E. MATTHEWS ..	,,
,,	5659 Pte. W. SIMMONDS ..	,,
,,	31400 Pte. C. WHITE	,,
,,	22754 Pte. E. WAITE	,,
,,	8532 Pte. H. WHITE	,,
,,	12431 Pte. H. ARTHURS	Wounded
,,	12838 Pte. W. BLAKENEY ..	Died of Wounds
,,	5629 Pte. W. BODILL	,,
,,	28974 Pte. F. CROSSBY	Wounded
,,	28976 Pte. R. HESLOP	,,
,,	10708 Pte. S. HOYLE	Died of Wounds
,,	20861 Pte. O. SMEDLEY.. ..	,,
,,	17828 L./Cpl. E. WALKER ..	Wounded
11/4/17	2/Lieut. Hon. G. S. DAWSON DAMER	Died of Wounds
,,	Lieut. O. MOWATT	,,
,,	Lt.-Col. P. E. HARDWICK, D.S.O. ..	Wounded
,,	Capt. V. J. GREENWOOD ..	,,
,,	Capt. G. E. GOSLING	,,
,,	Lieut. D. L. G. W. O. Earl of Airlie, M.C.	,,
,,	Lieut. W. S. MURLAND	,,
,,	Lieut. Hon. C. J. F. WINN ..	,,
,,	Lieut. D. H. GOUGH	,,
,,	4358 S.S.M. H. LANGDON ..	Killed

APPENDIX G (*continued*).

Date.				Casualty.
11/4/17	5542	Cpl. S. S. R. Norman	..	Killed
,,	1935	Cpl. T. Marchant		,,
,,	7310	L./Cpl. E. Mayes..	..	,,
,,	5342	Pte. F. Green ..	..	,,
,,	11087	L./Cpl. Sanderson	..	,,
,,	12300	Pte. G. Grey ..	..	,,
,,	11559	Pte. H. Twiddy ..	..	,,
,,	4544	Pte. G. Jackson ..	..	,,
,,	19617	Pte. J. Long ..	..	,,
,,	5596	Pte. A. Salmon ..	..	,,
,,	11866	Pte. H. W. Willis	..	,,
,,	4499	Sgt. H. Harding..	..	,,
,,	4940	Cpl. D. Knight ..	..	,,
,,	243	L./Cpl. W. Smith..	..	,,
,,	25466	S. S. Courtman ..	..	,,
,,	14545	Pte. G. Titchener	..	,,
,,	19788	L./Cpl. T. Fairbairn	..	,,
,,	27868	Pte. J. Holliday	..	,,
,,	12220	Pte. G. Chase ..	..	,,
,,	3511	Pte. S. Jarvis ..	..	,,
,,	25929	Pte. Parry ..	..	,,
,,	1417	Pte. J. Waterhouse	..	,,
,,	603	Sgt. E. Bradley..	..	Died of Wounds
,,	28999	Pte. R. Sutton ..	..	Missing, believed Killed
,,	4004	S.S.M. W. Rawson	..	Wounded
,,	4821	Sgt. W. Goodwin	..	,,
,,	3183	Sgt. R. Harwood	..	,,
,,	7953	Cpl. H. Hansell ..	..	,,
,,	8533	Cpl. R. White ..	..	,,
,,	15161	L./Cpl. H. Woods	..	,,
,,	20628	S.S. H. Tregay ..	..	,,
,,	3635	Pte. J. Burgess ..	..	,,
,,	28993	Pte. W. Dunn ..	...	,,

DATE.			CASUALTY.
11/4/17	4272 S.S. J. MANSER	.. ..	Wounded
,,	4531 Sgt. S. ROBINSON..	..	,,
,,	2560 Cpl. J. FOWLER	.. ..	,,
,,	961 Cpl. J. W. TAYLOR	..	,,
,,	204 L./Cpl. W. MOORES	..	,,
,,	6434 L./Cpl. A. BARRETT	..	,,
,,	31397 S.S. H. G. COLEMAN	..	,,
,,	5570 Pte. T. CROMBIE	.. ..	,,
,,	15282 Pte. C. DOWSON	..	,,
,,	31203 Pte. A. R. DEAVES	..	,,
,,	7706 Pte. A. FRITH	.. ..	,,
,,	1728 Pte. J. GAFFNEY ..	..	,,
,,	10844 Pte. A. GRANGER..	..	,,
,,	748 Pte. W. HAMMOND	..	,,
,,	2227 Pte. E. IBBOTSON..	..	,,
,,	840 Pte. E. LONG	.. ..	,,
,,	6285 Pte. J. RICHARDS..	..	,,
,,	6500 Pte. E. RAY	.. ..	,,
,,	6721 Pte. F. VAUGHAN..	..	,,
,,	19251 Pte. J. GROCUTT	.. ..	,,
,,	7253 Pte. W. BRADBURY	..	,,
,,	1958 Pte. J. PRESTON	.. ..	,,
,,	2420 Pte. T. A. SIMPSON	..	,,
,,	2735 Pte. J. JOHNSON ..	..	,,
,,	30303 Pte. H. WILKINSON	..	,,
,,	258 Sgt. W. ROYS	.. ..	,,
,,	262 L./Cpl. E. R. BREADMORE ..		,,
,,	421 L./Cpl. W. NORTON	..	,,
,,	1726 S.S. J. COYLE	.. ..	,,
,,	20188 Pte. F. CATTLE	.. ..	,,
,,	10557 Pte. J. C. COONEY	..	,,
,,	31313 Pte. W. H. FOSTER	..	,,
,,	21881 Pte. C. GENT	.. ..	,,

APPENDIX G (*continued*).

DATE.				CASUALTY.
11/4/17	28493	Pte. J. E. MILLS	..	..	Wounded
,,	4542	Pte. J. NORTH	..	..	,,
,,	6204	Pte. W. ROWSON	..	..	,,
,,	25555	Pte. J. A. SMITH	..	..	,,
,,	31297	Pte. J. STANSFIELD	..	..	,,
,,	2312	Pte. H. WRAYE	..	..	,,
,,	17616	Pte. G. BARRAS	..	..	,,
,,	15230	Pte. W. GALLAGHER	..	..	,,
,,	11655	Pte. H. W. DAWSON	..	..	,,
,,	5487	Sgt. W. BULLEN	..	..	,,
,,	25542	L./Cpl. P. S. ENGLISH	..	..	,,
,,	28892	Pte. T. ASHTON	..	..	,,
,,	4993	Pte. J. C. BUSH	..	..	,,
,,	12783	Pte. C. COMBER	..	..	,,
,,	544	Pte. R. DINE	..	..	,,
,,	31238	Pte. G. ELDERS	..	..	,,
,,	25780	Pte. H. EVERITT	..	..	,,
,,	25198	Pte. E. GARROD	..	..	,,
,,	28456	Pte. L. HALLAM	..	..	,,
,,	31399	Pte. D. HARWOOD	..	..	,,
,,	12341	Pte. G. H. HOCKING	..	..	,,
,,	31248	Pte. F. PARKIN	..	..	,,
,,	4695	Pte. E. SABIN	..	..	,,
,,	1427	Pte. H. SKIPPER	..	..	,,
,,	4755	Pte. S. SMITH	..	..	,,
,,	25364	Pte. W. WEEDON	..	..	,,
,,	7102	Pte. F. WHITBREAD	..	..	,,
,,	4997	Pte. H. WILLIAMS	..	..	,,
,,	31192	Pte. F. ROWLEY	..	..	,,
,,	10828	Pte. W. A. TURNER	..	..	,,
,,	19752	Pte. W. WARFIELD	..	..	,,
,,	7120	Pte. E. GRUNDY	..	..	,,
,,	6687	Cpl. L. D. PEARSON	..	..	,,

Date.			Casualty.
11/4/17	4942 Pte. W. Dillon	.. ..	Wounded
,,	15250 Pte. H. Fulton	..	,,
,,	12960 Pte. C. E. Garrod	..	,,
,,	15227 Pte. J. Holmes	.. ..	,,
,,	20007 Pte. W. Hodgson	..	,,
,,	28604 Pte. H. Johnson	.. ..	,,
,,	679 Pte. G. Marshall	..	,,
,,	19256 Pte. H. Shelton	.. ..	,,
,,	14486 Pte. J. Roache	.. ..	,,
,,	1428 Pte. J. Glencross	..	,,
,,	5418 Pte. H. Wakefield	..	,,
,,	19748 Pte. T. Arrowsmith	..	,,
,,	879 Pte. A. Reilly	.. ..	,,
,,	8498 Pte. R. Wilkins	.. ..	,,
,,	17792 Pte. J. Lakin	.. ..	,,
,,	983 Sgt. G. Oliver	.. ..	,,
,,	5540 Sgt. E. Davies	.. ..	,,
,,	17130 L./Cpl. F. W. Tompkinson		,,
,,	6491 Tptr. T. Green	.. ..	,,
,,	8184 Pte. A. H. Bird	.. ..	,,
,,	25376 Pte. J. Clay	.. ..	,,
,,	25221 Pte. E. Fallon	.. ..	,,
,,	1987 Pte. J. Gauton	.. ..	,,
,,	40 Pte. C. Gladwell	..	,,
,,	11881 Pte. H. Montgomery	..	,,
,,	2626 Pte. A. Pallister	..	,,
,,	6946 Pte. P. Smith	.. ..	,,
,,	12414 Pte. W. Swainston	..	,,
,,	5603 Pte. F. Thomas	.. ..	,,
,,	3996 Pte. R. E. Wraye	.. ..	,,
,,	15276 Pte. W. Garfat	.. ..	,,
,,	4945 Cpl. H. B. Webb	.. ..	,,
,,	6655 Pte. D. Moriarty	.. ..	,,

DATE.			CASUALTY.
11/4/17	391	Cpl. J. PARFREMENT ..	Wounded
,,	14476	Pte. M. G. ANDREWS ..	,,
,,	28880	Pte. G. M. BROWN ..	,,
,,	28899	Pte. J. W. CLEMENTS ..	,,
,,	7118	Pte. J. CROMBIE	,,
,,	28986	Pte. G. DIXON	,,
,,	22086	Pte. H. ENNION	,,
,,	12136	Pte. J. FRANKS	,,
,,	6558	Pte. T. GREEN	,,
,,	7457	Pte. E. HART	,,
,,	19635	Pte. S. HEMBLYS.. ..	,,
,,	948	Pte. C. McCORMACK ..	,,
,,	464	L./Cpl. C. REDGRAVE ..	,,
,,	1646	Pte. W. SCOTT	,,
,,	4623	Pte. H. SMITH	,,
,,	8193	Pte. S. T. SMITH	,,
,,	19616	L./Cpl. A. WELCH ..	,,
,,	31188	Pte. S. WILLEY	,,
,,	20920	Pte. J. WOODWARD ..	,,
,,	9925	Pte. F. STOCKWELL ..	,,
,,	947	Pte. J. WHITEHEAD ..	,,
,,	7750	Pte. J. BARLOW	,,
,,	5592	Sgt. C. ALDERSON ..	,,
,,	2823	L./Cpl. J. ALLISON ..	,,
,,	15182	Pte. W. AYRES	,,
,,	28641	L./Cpl. R. KING	,,
,,	2924	Pte. T. MALSTON	,,
,,	2870	Pte. J. W. WIGHAM ..	,,
,,	5905	L./Cpl. W. BAXTER ..	,,
,,	128	Sgt. A. FUTCHER	,,
,,	1954	Pte. D. ARSCOTT	,,
,,	12159	Pte. J. P. DUNN	,,
,,	6788	L./Cpl. G. SCARISBRICK ..	,,

DATE.				CASUALTY.
11/4/17	1777	L./Cpl. J. MATHIESON	..	Wounded
,,	144	Pte. M. PURDON ..	..	,,
,,	12825	Pte. A. FLACK ..	..	,,
,,	31148	Pte. J. CARTWRIGHT	..	,,
,,	17550	Pte. P. HUME ..	..	,,
,,	5016	L./Cpl. S. WIGLEY	..	,,
,,	6459	Pte. J. DORWARD..	..	,,
,,	12946	Pte. L. CHERRY ..	..	,,
,,	3609	Pte. D. KNIGHT ..	..	,,
,,	1489	Pte. G. DAY ..	..	,,
,,	4128	L./Cpl. T. ROGERS	..	,,
,,	7729	L./Cpl. P. LARKIN	..	Wounded and Missing
,,	31082	Pte. E. WADDINGTON	..	,,
,,	28901	Pte. J. RANSOME ..	..	.,
,,	25304	Pte. W. FURNISS ..	..	Wounded (Shell Shock)
,,	31034	Pte. J. ROBERTSON	..	,,
10/6/17	9600	Pte. B. ALLEN ..	..	Killed
,,	22363	Pte. A. AUTON ..	..	,,
,,	24724	Pte. R. BROWN ..	..	,,
,,	28989	Pte. A. R. CLAYTON	..	,,
,,	6317	Pte. E. SCOTT ..	..	,,
,,	24957	Pte. W. H. DOLMAN	..	,,
,,	32418	Pte. S. P. WARD ..	..	,,
,,	32421	Pte. F. WILFORD ..	..	,,
,,	22715	Pte. W. WILLIAMS	..	,,
,,	31185	Pte. A. E. TOPHAM	..	,,
,,	21026	Pte. L. BREWER	..	Wounded
,,	19789	L./Cpl. A. GODDEN	..	,,
,,	31038	Pte. G. BATES ..	..	Wounded (accidental)
,,	24721	Pte. H. GOODSON	..	Wounded
,,	4184	L./Cpl. J. S. SCOTT	..	,,
3/6/17	31236	Pte. P. ROBERTSON	..	,,
7/3/17	31191	Pte. D. BELL ..	..	Killed (Accidental)

APPENDIX G (*continued*).

Date.			Casualty.
17/6/17	31031	Pte. E. Shaw	Wounded (Accidental)
18/6/17		2/Lieut. Hon. G. E. D. C. Glyn	Wounded
,,		2/Lieut. A. E. Lowther	Wounded (Shell Shock)
22/6/17	30284	Pte. F. J. Wrighton	Wounded
,,	6804	Sgt. F. Price	,,
,,	1675	Cpl. R. Cattanach	,,
,,	27695	Pte. F. Portch	,,
14/8/17	9395	Pte. H. E. Swain	Wounded (Gassed)
21/8/17	2808	Pte. J. Waters	Killed (Accidental)
17/12/17	28270	Cpl. McIlvride	Died of Wounds
22/12/17	31295	Pte. C. Doyle	Killed (Accidental)
,,	29883	Pte. H. Edwards	Wounded
,,	29658	Pte. G. Varney	Missing
23/3/18	2398	Pte. W. Bass	Killed
,,	32843	Pte. W. Dudley	,,
,,	22671	Pte. K. Constable	,,
,,	29662	Pte. A. Roberts	,,
,,	2331156	Pte. P. Wessen	,,
,,	32979	Pte. W. Williams	,,
,,	47053	Sadd. Cpl. C. Gilbert	Died of Wounds.
,,	15151	L./Cpl. C. Barber	,,
,,	28880	Pte. G. N. Brown	,,
,,	29889	Pte. T. Butcher	,,
,,	31020	Pte. R. Green	,,
,,	948	Pte. C. MacCormack	,,
,,	12188	L./Cpl. F. Walker	,,
,,	47069	Sgt. W. Ovenden	Wounded
,,	47088	Cpl. L. Pearson	,,
,,	1494	Cpl. J. Spence	,,
,,	47073	L./Cpl. J. Squires	,,
,,	12000	S.S. J. Tyler	,,
,,	32390	Pte. R. Barnett	,,
,,	2305	Pte. J. Bond	,,

APPENDIX G (*continued*).

Date.		Casualty.
23/3/18	5016 L./Sgt. J. Wigley ..	Wounded
,,	20783 L./Cpl. J. Cottingham ..	,,
,,	24754 Pte. J. W. Wheatcroft ..	,,
,,	15546 Pte. A. Percy ..	,,
,,	8585 Pte. E. G. Atkins	,,
,,	3682 L./Cpl. G. Stewart	.,
,,	47077 Pte. J. Colvin ..	,,
,,	22566 Pte. D. Fox ..	,,
,,	128 Sgt. A. Futcher	.. Missing (believed killed)
,,	Major E. H. W. Williams ..	Wounded
,,	47010 Sgt. Tptr. T. Rogers ..	,,
,,	321523 Pte. B. Price ..	,,
,,	47071 Pte. P. Shortall ..	,,
,,	28729 Pte. P. Jones ..	,,
,,	2755 Pte. H. M. Battram ..	,,
,,	2954 Pte. E. Harris ..	.. Wounded and Missing
,,	5648 Pte. H. W. Anderson ..	Wounded
,,	47015 Pte. A. Gaston ..	,,
,,	31403 Pte. A. Willicombe ..	,,
,,	35891 Pte. W. H. Taylor ..	,,
,,	1716 S.S. J. Jordan ..	,,
,,	32420 Pte. R Wiltshire ..	,,
,,	22317 Pte. A. H. Read..	,,
,,	27848 Pte. C. Shefford	.. Wounded and Missing
,,	3409 L./Cpl. G. Ward..	Wounded
,,	15309 S.S. J. Thompson ..	Killed
,,	47007 R.S.M. W. A. Mitchell ..	Wounded
,,	7218 Pte. W. Paul ..	Missing
,,	1728 Pte. J. Gaffney ..	,,
.,	32176 Pte. J. H. Gale ..	.. Missing (believed killed)
,,	32118 Pte. F. Bowles ..	Wounded
,,	71481 Pte. R. Campbell ..	,,
,,	31391 Pte. R. Dingle ..	,,

APPENDIX G (*continued*).

DATE.				CASUALTY.
23/3/18	256492	Pte. W. CODLING..	..	Wounded
,,	3899	Pte. T. HANNAY..	..	,,
,,	10651	Pte. R. HARDY ..	..	,,
,,	32878	Pte. F. HASTE ..	..	,,
,,	29822	Pte. F. HOPKINS ..	..	,,
,,	305705	Pte. H. LOTT ..	..	,,
,,	19682	Pte. W. MAHONEY	..	,,
,,	31043	Pte. W. MEDCALF	..	,,
,,	1973	Pte. H. MIDDLETON	..	,,
,,	34121	Pte. J. MAXWELL	..	,,
,,	855	Pte. M. NICHOLLS	..	,,
,,	10317	Pte. E. RICHMOND	..	,,
,,	12824	Pte. H. ROSS ..	..	,,
,,	32087	Pte. G. STRATFORD	..	,,
,,	14680	Pte. W. STUART BROWN	..	,,
,,	32974	Pte. J. VIVEASH ..	..	,,
,,	32420	Pte. R. WILTSHIRE	..	,,
,,	32276	Pte. A. DUDLEY	..	,,
12/3/18	1875	Pte. H. ASHDOWN	..	Died
23/3/18	12015	Cpl. E. SCOTT	..	Killed
,,	47090	L./Cpl. O. NOONAN	..	,,
,,	12694	Pte. F. ATKINSON..	..	,,
,,	14496	Pte. C. CLARKE ..	..	,,
,,		Capt. E. W. E. PALMES..	..	Wounded
,,		Lieut. W. J. BRISLEY ..	..	,,
,,	967	Pte. H. MAY ..	..	,,
,,	7646	Pte. J. BODILL ..	..	,,
,,	23185	Pte. A. FISHER ..	..	,,
,,	31376	Pte. C. LOADER ..	..	,,
,,	6500	Pte. E. W. RAY ..	..	,,
,,	31392	Pte. A. HILL ..	..	,,
,,	1340	Pte. T. WIKE ..	..	,,
,,	18492	Pte. R. C. MILLER	..	,,

DATE.		CASUALTY.
23/3/18	1489 Cpl. G. DAY	Wounded
,,	5951 Cpl. T. W. TAYLOR ..	,,
,,	2569 Cpl. P. PORTER	,,
,,	749 Pte. J. DURMAN	,,
,,	20211 Pte. A. HOPLEY	,,
,,	19232 Pte. P. LAWRENCE ..	,,
,,	31034 Pte. J. ROBERTSON ..	,,
,,	10534 Ptc. J. ADAMSON.. ..	,,
,,	31313 Pte. W. FOSTER	Prisoner of War
,,	19281 Pte. J. GREEN	,,
24/3/18	Lieut. F. R. GASKELL	Wounded
,,	19280 Pte. W. PEACOCK ..	,,
,,	11314 Pte. R. LUMLEY.. ..	,,
,,	31029 Pte. J. SQUIRES	,,
,,	866 Pte. J. GILLINGHAM ..	,,
,,	10936 Pte. R. LUCY	Missing
,,	28810 Pte. A. MASON	Wounded
4/4/18	47085 L/Cpl.J. HARRIS	Killed
,,	27920 Pte. J. TALBOT	,,
,,	1288 Pte. J. McQUEEN	,,
,,	7965 Pte. A. COOPER	,,
,,	5293 Cpl. S. S. A. DRINKWATER	Missing (believed killed)
,,	25923 Pte. E. ECCLES	,,
,,	28992 Pte. H. ILEY	,,
,,	Lt.-Col. H. A. TOMKINSON, D.S.O.	Wounded
,,	Lieut. Viscount EDNAM, M.C. ..	,,
,,	2/Lieut. R. G. FIELD	Died of Wounds
,,	2/Lieut. H. D. KELLEWAY ..	Wounded
,,	2/Lieut. A. D. HILLHOUSE ..	,,
,,	5421 Cpl. B. WARREN	,,
,,	1484 Sgt. R. LLOYD	,,
,,	6639 Sgt. J. CAMPBELL.. ..	,,
,,	977 Cpl. S. ECKERS	,,

Date.				Casualty.
4/4/18	28899	L./Cpl. J. Clements	..	Wounded
,,	748	Pte. J. Hammond	..	,,
,,	15176	Pte. G. Leggett	..	,,
,,	230536	Pte. J. Shepperd	..	,,
,,	47060	S. S. W. Lomas ..	..	,,
,,	8482	S.S. E. Hicks ..	..	,,
,,	31397	S.S. J. Coleman ..	..	,,
,,	32393	Pte. J. Cairns ..	..	,,
,,	31150	Pte. H. Alderson	..	,,
,,	12058	Pte. H. Leaf ..	..	,,
,,	19754	Pte. J. Moreton	..	,,
,,	8193	Pte. S. Smith ..	..	,,
,,	9053	Tptr. O. Thorpe	..	,,
,,	31380	Pte. L. Brown ..	..	,,
,,	10870	Pte. D. Keyzor ..	..	,,
,,	80409	Pte. Barber (E.Y.)	..	,,
,,	3117	Cpl. H. Lewis	..	,,
,,	8321	Pte. R. Turner, } A.V.C...		,,
,,	8691	Pte. W. Glasgow	..	,,
8/8/18	165841	Pte. T. Warren (N.S.Y.) ..		Killed
,,	47042	S.S.M. G. Farrant	..	Wounded
,,	47034	Sgt. H. Dunk ..	..	,,
,,	15282	L./Cpl.C. Dowson	..	,,
,,	165783	Pte. C. F. Butt (N.S.Y.) ..		,,
,,	17499	Pte. F. Carter ..	..	,,
,,	42405	Pte, A. G. Dance..	..	,,
,,	31035	Pte. W. Fawcett	..	,,
,,	230535	Pte. W. Shepherd	..	,,
,,	165399	Pte. E. Tilke (N.S.Y.)	..	,,
,,	32077	Pte. H. Wray ..	..	,,
,,	8873	Pte. S. Morris ..	..	,,
9/8/18		Lieut. G. H. Perrett ..	..	Killed
,,	20577	Sgt. C. Allen ..	..	,,

APPENDIX G (*continued*).

DATE.		CASUALTY.
9/8/18	5057 Pte. T. GLAZEBROOK .. ·	Killed
,,	Lieut. T. ROBINSON	Wounded
,,	28810 Pte. A. MASON	,,
,,	12825 Cpl. A. FLACK .. .. ·	,,
,,	28833 Pte. A. GILL	,,
10/8/18	S/16144 Tptr. W. GREGORY (E.Y.)	,,
2/9/18	18468 S.S. F. NOTLEY	,,
,,	175487 L./Cpl. H. FIRTH (N.S.Y.) ..	,,
,,	5189 Pte. C. WOOTON ..	,,
9/10/18	A./Capt. W. S. MURLAND	,,
,,	Lieut. F. C. DRAKE, M.C. ..	,,
,,	Lieut. S. A. RALLI	,,
,,	Lieut. S. J. TUFNELL (E.Y.) ..	,,
,,	Lieut. W. RITCHIE (E.Y.) ..	,,
,,	10883 Sgt. W. EDNEY	Killed
,,	73697 Pte. P. BRENNAN ..	,,
,,	34009 Pte. H. HARVEY	,,
,,	171278 Pte. C. SAYERS	,,
,,	36342 Pte. F. KENDALL ..	,,
,,	165453 L./Cpl. C. H. MAIL (N.S.Y.)	,,
,,	165799 Pte. V. C. FEAR (N.S.Y.) ..	,,
,,	165992 Pte. F. BLACKER (N.S.Y.) ..	,,
,,	9177 Sgt. S. KINGMAN ..	Died of Wounds
,,	6983 Pte. J. McDONALD ..	,,
,,	165896 Pte. H. MILLER (N.S.Y.) ..	,,
,,	1309 Pte. W. THOMAS ..	Wounded
,,	47075 Sgt. C. ALDERSON ..	,,
,,	47039 Sgt. V. J. POINTING ..	,,
,,	47749 Pte. G. STEVENS	,,
,,	74010 Cpl. T. STANNAGE ..	Died of Wounds
,,	10850 Cpl. E. V. HOMES ..	Wounded
,,	47013 Cpl. G. JUDSON	,,
,,	2823 Cpl. J. ALLISON	,,

DATE.				CASUALTY.
9/10/18	36454	Cpl. S. FITZGERALD	..	Wounded
,,	19768	Cpl. J. HALL ..	..	,,
,,	32398	L./Cpl. E. GROOM	..	,,
,,	2377	Tptr. G. NASH ..	..	,,
,,	4559	S.S. W. ROYAL ..	..	,,
,,	47036	S.S. J. SHEPHERD	..	,,
,,	34132	Pte. W. BALLEY ..	..	,,
;,	15273	Pte. W. HUNT ..	..	,,
,,	27695	Pte. F. PORTCH ..	..	,,
,,	17124	Pte. J. STATHAM ..	..	,,
,,	42391	Ptc. L. BENNETT..	..	,,
,,	31395	Pte. F. CHILDS ..	..	,,
,,	34007	Pte. J. POWELL ..	..	Died of Wounds
,,	29572	Ptc. F. BARLEY ..	..	Wounded
,,	32334	Pte. A. FRYER ..	..	,,
,,	16396	Pte. A. FARRANT..	..	,,
,,	35991	Pte. W. TAYLOR ..	..	,,
,,	31372	Pte. F. JACKSON ..	..	,,
,,	10513	Ptc. J. ADAMSON..	..	,,
,,	36361	Pte. H. HARRISON	..	,,
,,	74056	Pte. M. WHITFORD	..	,,
,,	325492	Pte. A. HARRIS ..	..	,,
,,	25198	Pte. F. GARROD ..	..	,,
,,	206286	Pte. C. REEVE ..	..	,,
,,	31297	Pte. J. STANSFIELD	..	,,
,,	17346	Pte. J. WHITTAKER	..	,,
,,	165221	Cpl. S.S. E. J. SPRATT (N.S.Y.)		,,
,,	165756	L./Cpl. C. BRINKWORTH	..	,,
,,	165774	L./Cpl. W. POWELL	..	,,
,,	105616	S.S. A. PLEDGER..	..	,,
,,	165407	Ptc. A. LAMBERT..	..	,,
,,	165874	Pte. J. DAGGER ..	..	,,
,,	165057	Pte. A. J. BURR ..	..	,,

APPENDIX G (*continued*).

SUMMARY OF CASUALTIES, 10th (P.W.O.) ROYAL HUSSARS.

			Killed in Action or Died.		Wounded.		Prisoners of War.
Officers ..	..	..	15	..	41	..	—
Other Ranks	..	..	199	..	528	..	2
	Total	..	214	..	569	..	2

APPENDIX H.

LIST OF CASUALTIES INCURRED BY THE ESSEX YEOMANRY
DURING THE WAR.

APPENDIX H (*continued*).

DATE.			CASUALTY.
9/2/15	965 Pte. S. F. BRADDY	.. ..	Wounded
,,	1309 Pte. G. E. FOSTER	.. ..	,,
,,	837 Pte. C. J. FRENCH	.. ..	,,
,,	1069 Cpl. J. W. SALMON	..	,,
,,	1564 Pte. H. HUGHES	.. ..	,,
12/2/15	946 Pte. A. WRIGHT	.. ..	,,
24/4/15	702 L./Cpl. C. E. THORN	..	Died
28/4/15	193 Pte. W. MORLEY	.. ..	Wounded
,,	1698 Pte. H. DIGBY	.. ..	,,
,,	1403 Pte. A. W. KING	.. ..	,,
,,	1171 Pte. P. A. D. T. BOWERS	..	,,
13/5/15	Major A. RODDICK	.. ..	Killed
,,	Lieut. G. S. JOHNSON	.. ..	,,
,,	Lieut. A. G. SWIRE	.. ..	,,
,,	2/Lieut. G. P. N. REID	.. ..	,,
,,	26 Sgt. T. CLARK	.. ..	,,
,,	32 Sgt. J. DRAPER	.. ..	,,
,,	476 Cpl. F. E. BIRD	.. ..	,,
,,	621 L./Cpl. A. B. CROXON	..	Died of Wounds
,,	674 Sgt. D. LEDGER	.. ..	Killed
,,	735 Pte. A. T. SOUTH	.. ..	,,
,,	747 Sgt. A. PEARCE	.. ..	,,
,,	839 Pte. A. J. WILD	.. ..	,,
,,	956 Pte. C. TAYLOR	.. ..	,,
,,	964 Cpl. T. ALLEN	.. ..	,,
,,	989 Pte. E. J. PETCHEY	.. ..	,,
,,	990 Pte. E. PROPERT	.. ..	,,
,,	991 Pte. B. SNELL	.. ..	,,
,,	1055 Pte. O. ASKEW	.. ..	,,
,,	1080 L./Cpl. F. SEABROOK	..	,,
,,	1093 Sgt. S. NEWMAN	.. ..	,,
,,	1117 Sgt. L. C. DEAKIN	.. ..	,,
,,	1129 Pte. F. BELL	.. ..	,,

DATE.		CASUALTY.
13/5/15	1135 Pte. W. E. GARDINER	Killed
,,	1207 Pte. M. D. FREE	Died of Wounds
,,	1225 Pte. F. DEIGHTON	Killed
,,	1227 Pte. R. LAGDEN	,,
,,	1246 Pte. J. TRUEFIT	,,
,,	1269 Pte. H. McTURK	,,
,,	1275 Pte. R. RIDGEWELL	,,
,,	1297 Pte. D. TAYLOR	,,
,,	1307 Pte. E. SEABROOK	,,
,,	1314 Pte. D. CHRISTIE	,,
,,	1338 Pte. S. BLENCOE	,,
,,	1401 Pte. W. JONES	,,
,,	1405 Pte. H. SMITH	,,
,,	1114 Pte. C. A. ROBINS	Died of Wounds
,,	1277 Pte. J. RUST	,,
,,	1092 Cpl. V. S. DIGGENS	Killed
,,	53 Sgt. R. C. PACKER	Died of Wounds
,,	1132 Pte. W. BEENEY	,,
,,	838 Pte. W. RAYNER	,,
,,	1252 Pte. H. R. ROWELL	,,
,,	1271 Pte. H. SWANN	,,
,,	1388 Pte. W. DAY	Killed
,,	1149 Pte. E. J. PHARAOH	,,
,,	1331 Pte. H. TAYLOR	,,
,,	723 Cpl. G. C. DEVERELL	Died of Wounds
,,	1632 Pte. B. MANN	Killed
,,	917 Pte. S. E. NEWMAN	,,
,,	870 Pte. E. J. PRIME	,,
,,	1350 Pte. B. W. BEGGIN	,,
,,	1128 Sgt. C. E. BROCK	,,
,,	1189 Pte. W. NUNN	,,
,,	927 Pte. H. MILLAR	,,
,,	1651 Pte. W. R. MILBANK	,,

APPENDIX H (*continued*).

Date.		Casualty.
13/5/15	981 Pte. H. E. Mansfield	Killed
,,	1576 Pte. C. E. Green	,,
,,	686 Pte. L. A. Hill	,,
,,	1261 Pte. J. Barker	,,
,,	977 Pte. J. W. Taylor	,,
,,	1656 Pte. H. G. Wright	,,
,,	1703 Pte. S. Fairhead	,,
,,	710 Sgt. L. E. Butcher	,,
,,	1026 Pte. C. H. Cattell	,,
,,	953 Pte. G. Cottee	,,
,,	1048 Cpl. E. Appleton	,,
,,	1230 Pte. B. Hurst	,,
,,	1681 Pte. J. J. Taylor	,,
,,	1674 Pte. R. C. Williams	,,
,,	625 Cpl. G. E. Glew	Died of Wounds
,,	1281 Sgt. P. Hoare	,,
,,	820 Cpl. E. Ridgwell	,,
,,	Lt.-Col. E. Deacon	Missing (believed killed)
,,	Major F. H. D. C. Whitmore	Wounded
,,	Capt. A. R. Steele	,,
,,	Lieut. V. T. G. Hine	,,
,,	Lieut. R. Edwards	,,
,,	2/Lieut. H. P. Holt	,,
,,	1655 Pte. J. C. Finney	,,
,,	1438 Pte. W. T. Dunmore	,,
,,	1005 Pte. L. H. Jenkyn	,,
,,	650 Pte. L. Hallett	,,
,,	1660 Pte. W. P. Connolly	,,
,,	1738 Pte. F. Last	,,
,,	1697 Pte. G. Austin	,,
,,	764 Pte. A. Smith	,,
,,	1263 Pte. E. G. Newcombe	,,
,,	1203 Cpl. K. S. Grant	,,

APPENDIX H (*continued*).

Date.		Casualty.
13/5/15	1670 Pte. W. H. Pennal	Wounded
,,	1181 Pte. P. Manning	,,
,,	1074 Pte. H. W. Goody	,,
,,	1433 L./Cpl. W. Baker	,,
,,	1043 Pte. K. Holland	,,
,,	923 Pte. P. Harvey	,,
,	1116 Pte. A. Ball	,,
,,	1812 Pte. A. Blyth	,,
,,	1191 Pte. L. Smith	,,
,,	1123 Sgt. H. Mann	,,
,,	910 Pte. N. Leeder	,,
,,	590 Pte. H. Cunningham ..	,,
,,	1678 Pte. E. G. Moss	,,
,,	845 Pte. G. W. Fox	,,
,,	1676 Pte. H. W. Hutton	,,
,,	1228 Pte. T. D. Harvey	,,
,,	1259 Pte. E. Pegrum	,,
,,	761 Cpl. W. J. Hart	,,
,,	891 Pte. G. J. Adams	,,
,,	1665 Pte. E. D. Dorrington ..	,,
,,	862 Pte. W. Butcher	,,
,,	1562 Pte. W. Joyce	,,
,,	448 Sgt. B. Pritchard	,,
,,	1078 Pte. J. K. Franks	,,
,,	1192 Pte. C. Errington	,,
,,	1199 Pte. R. Hall	,,
,,	1652 Pte. H. Waller	,,
,,	1369 Pte. G. A. Rivers	,,
,,	1686 Pte. F. C. Woods	,,
,,	1167 Pte. A. J. Mills	,,
,,	853 Pte. J. Green	,,
,,	963 Pte. H. Cunningham ..	,,
,,	625 Cpl. E. Glew	,,

Date.			Casualty.
13/5/15	1213 Pte. C. Brazier	.. ..	Wounded
,,	461 Pte. E. Hazelton	.. ..	,,
,,	429 Sgt. F. Speakman	.. ..	,,
,,	975 Pte. H. Richards	.. ..	,,
,,	827 Pte. C. A. Curtis	.. ..	,,
,,	1641 Pte. E. C. Caines	.. ..	,,
,,	1079 Pte. G. Scrivener	.. ..	,,
,,	1286 Pte. R. Townsend	.. ..	,,
,,	767 Sgt. E. Walker	.. ..	,,
,,	1648 L./Cpl. F. Chapman	.. ..	,,
,,	1032 Pte. E. H. Finch	.. ..	,,
,,	948 Pte. A. J. Bond	.. ..	,,
,,	1310 Pte. J. Sparrow	.. ..	,,
,,	957 Pte. W. J. Revell	.. ..	,,
,,	639 Pte. A. J. Wyatt	.. ..	,,
,,	490 Sgt. J. H. Moody	.. ..	,,
,,	1121 Pte. G. R. Williams	.. ..	,,
,,	645 Pte. D. W. Steward	.. ..	,,
,,	1151 Pte. A. E. Brice	.. ..	,,
,,	715 Pte. W. T. Bentley	.. ..	,,
,,	1379 Pte. S. J. Curtis	.. ..	,,
,,	877 Pte. J. W. Jordan	.. ..	,,
,,	912 Pte. O. T. Sutton	.. ..	,,
,,	1194 Pte. E. Minns	.. ..	,,
,,	1696 Pte. P. J. Dyer	.. ..	,,
,,	1101 Cpl. S. Brown	.. ..	,,
,,	1393 Pte. E. W. Bewers	.. ..	,,
,,	1083 Pte. O. Hughes	.. ..	,,
,,	640 L./Cpl. G. J. Wyatt	.. ..	,,
,,	866 Pte. J. E. Banks	.. ..	,,
,,	1568 Pte. A. Baynes	.. ..	,,
,,	868 Pte. R. Robinson	.. ..	,,
,,	900 Pte. H. Lang	.. ..	,,

DATE.		CASUALTY.
13/5/15	890 Pte. R. CLARE	Wounded
,,	973 Pte. R. P. BAKER	,,
,,	1453 Pte. C. J. BRUCE	,,
,,	1027 Pte. J. H. SERGEANT ..	,,
,,	904 Pte. C. H. VEALE	,,
,,	1327 Pte. H. W. WHENT	,,
,,	518 S.S.M. H. H. NEWMAN ..	,,
,,	1282 Pte. S. E. THOMPSON ..	,,
3/6/15	670 L./Cpl. J. W. SCOTT	,,
8/6/15	1397 Pte. W. WHITWELL	,,
23/6/15	1218 Sgt. G. SMART	Died
18/7/15	1677 Pte. D. M. HULTON	Wounded
21/7/15	1916 Pte. J. SMITH	,,
27/9/15	1406 Pte. H. G. SQUIRRELL ..	Killed
,,	Capt. E. A. RUGGLES BRISE, M.C.	Wounded
,,	2/Lieut. J. K. SWIRE	,,
,,	2/Lieut. E. T. L. PELLY	,,
,,	891 Pte. G. J. ADAMS	,,
,,	1347 A. WATERMAN	,,
,,	1136 Pte. C. E. GARDINER ..	,,
,,	1749 Pte. H. FIELD	,,
4/10/15	Lieut. C. C. TOWER	Killed
9/1/16	1645 Pte. W. J. BRADFORD ..	Wounded (Accidental)
13/1/16	1727 Pte. J. STOCKWELL	,,
14/1/16	1445 Pte. F. J. PENNALL	Wounded
15/1/16	1970 Pte. J. EADE	Died of Wounds
,,	1855 Pte. H. JOWERS	,,
21/1/16	1412 Pte. S. WREN	Wounded
,,	954 Pte. W. W. FISHER ..	,,
,,	1869 Pte. G. GOSLING	,,
,,	1342 L./Cpl. H. GOSLING	,,
22/1/16	1628 Pte. L. G. HOWARD	,,
,,	2102 Pte. E. T. PARKER	,,

DATE.			CASUALTY.
26/1/16	2243	Pte. W. T. RIDDLE	Wounded
,,	1756	Pte. P. B. BACON	,,
,,	1370	L./Cpl. L. G. COOK	,,
,,	1495	Pte. E. LAW	,,
2/2/16	895	Pte. A. E. ROLPH	,,
,,	1513	Pte. G. PIGGOTT	,,
,,	1708	Pte. F. C. CHAPMAN	,,
,,	2138	Pte. G. GRUNDY	,,
,,	2254	Pte. A. C. DANIEL	,,
,,	2066	Pte. L. H. PASSIFUL	Died of Wounds
3/2/16	988	Pte. T. H. MOORSE	Wounded
,,	1202	Pte. W. R. WOOLLINGS ...	,,
4/2/16	1797	Pte. J. A. MCLOUGHLIN ..	,,
5/2/16	1939	Pte. F. G. GIBSON	,,
,,	2228	Pte. E. ROOKS	,,
,,	1620	Pte. T. CUDMORE	,,
,,	1822	Pte. W. R. GOSLING.. ..	,,
,,	1776	Pte. H. S. WOODS	,,
,,	1439	Pte. G. E. VAINES	,,
14/2/16	2268	Pte. S. A. CAPON	Killed
16/2/16	2166	Pte. G. ETHERDEN	Wounded
9/7/16		Capt. J. C. CHAPLIN	,,
,,	1762	Pte. R. BRIGHT	,,
,,	2146	Pte. S. V. PEARCE	,,
30/7/16	1295	Pte. B. WILLIS	,,
31/7/16	2482	Pte. G. CATTON	Killed
,,	1814	Pte. R. J. BELL	Wounded
,,	2130	Pte. A. W. HAWES	,,
21/8/16	892	Pte. R. GERRARD	Killed
,,	1752	Pte. S. A. LORD	,,
16/9/16	1914	Pte. C. H. CORDEROY ..	Died of Wounds
,,	2652	Pte. J. W. ARGENT	Wounded
5/10/16	1328	Pte. E. Y. WESTCOTT ..	,,

DATE.			CASUALTY.
9/10/16	1465 Pte. W. LAW	.. ..	Wounded
17/11/16	898 L./Cpl. G. PERRY	.. ..	Died
3/12/16	Lieut. and Q.M. E. J. SAYER	..	Wounded
11/4/17	2/Lieut. J. F. LINGEMAN	.. ..	Died of Wounds
,,	80247 Sgt. R. S. GRANT	.. ..	Killed
,,	80403 Cpl. W. G. BAREHAM	..	,,
,,	80567 Pte. H. DIGBY	.. ..	,,
,,	80708 Pte. J. SMITH	.. ..	,,
,,	81173 Pte. F. SMITH	.. ..	,,
,,	80963 Pte. T. A. WRIGHT	.. ..	,,
,,	80630 Pte. E. YOUNG	.. ..	,,
,,	80431 Pte. T. E. CHARLESWORTH	..	,,
,,	80007 S.S.M. W. C. HOWARD	..	,,
,,	80362 Pte. H. BRIGHT	..	,,
,,	81073 Pte. F. E. BUNTING	.. ..	,,
,,	80524 Pte. E. E. ROLLINSON	..	,,
,,	80651 Pte. C. P. GOSLING	.. ..	,,
,,	80600 Pte. S. E. GUIVER	.. ..	,,
,,	80286 S./S. S. THOMPSON	.. ..	,,
,,	80167 Pte. F. C. HOLBROUGH	..	,,
,,	80415 Pte. E. A. HOLLAND..	..	,,
,,	81021 Pte. H. TRAVERS	.. ..	,,
,,	80797 Tptr. A. T. TIBBENHAM	..	,,
,,	80785 Tptr. A. STOWELL	.. ..	,,
,,	80613 Pte. C. STEWARD	.. ..	,,
,,	80240 Pte. D. T. MATTHAMS	..	,,
,,	81194 Pte. C. W. STEWARD	..	,,
,,	80631 Pte. B. SMITH	.. ..	,,
,,	80329 Sgt. A. E. SMITH	.. ..	,,
,,	80185 L./Cpl. F. E. WARREN	..	,,
,,	80668 Pte. F. W. BAYMAN ..	..	,,
,,	80982 Pte. W. H. BAINES ..	. ..	,,
,,	80444 Pte. G. BASSETT	.. ..	,,

DATE.		CASUALTY.
11/4/17	80363 Sgt. E. MAY ..	..Missing (believed Killed)
,,	Lt.-Col. F. H. D. C. WHITMORE,	
	D.S.O.	Wounded
,,	Major A. BUXTON, D.S.O.	,,
,,	Major G. G. GOLD	,,
,,	Major E. HILL	,,
,,	Capt. C. N. GILBEY	,,
,,	Lieut. J. K. SWIRE	,,
,,	2/Lieut. S. WHITE	,,
,,	2/Lieut. A. WINTER ROSE	,,
,,	2/Lieut. R. C. WEATHERBY.. ..	,,
,,	2/Lieut. G. WEAR	,,
,,	2/Lieut. W. RITCHIE	,,
,,	3217 R.S.M. C. FARRELL	,,
,,	80508 Pte. B. J. STONE	,,
,,	80682 L./Cpl. C. D. PACKARD . ..	,,
,,	80123 Pte. H. THORN	,,
,,	80327 Cpl. C. J. MIDGLEY	,,
,,	80536 L./Cpl. H. WALLER	,,
,,	80382 Cpl. F. BRUNWIN	,,
,,	80367 Pte. W. S. CARDY	,,
,,	80658 Pte. T. CHOPPING	,,
,,	81176 Pte. S. WASPE	,,
,,	80116 Sgt. G. SIDDONS	,,
,,	80695 S./S. N. C. DEACON	,,
,,	80674 Pte. W. APPLEBY	,,
,,	80696 Pte. F. PARTRIDGE	,,
,,	80047 S.S.M. W. W. McKELLAR ..	,,
,,	80321 Cpl. E. GLADWELL	,,
,,	80895 Pte. G. ETHERDEN	,,
,,	80944 Pte. E. W. HUME	,,
,,	81208 Cpl. W. C. CHAPPELL.. ..	,,
,,	80957 L./Cpl. H. BENNETT	,,

DATE.				CASUALTY.
11/4/17	81221	L./Cpl. A. J. Brown..	..	Wounded
,,	80904	L./Cpl. E. T. Wakefield	..	,,
,,	80614	Pte. H. S. Woods	..	,,
,,	80751	Pte. G. Andrews	..	,,
,,	81136	Pte. G. E. Benson	..	,,
,,	80618	Pte. W. C. Carter	..	,,
,,	80747	Pte. G. Davis	..	,,
,,	80282	Pte. L. J. Goodwin	..	,,
,,	80151	Pte. W. J. Hatley	..	,,
,,	81088	Pte. S. D. Harvey	..	,,
,,	80588	Pte. W. Hodge	..	,,
,,	81138	Pte. S. J. Jackaman..	..	,,
,,	81196	Pte. A. Jopson	..	,,
,,	80145	Pte. T. H. Moorse	..	,,
,,	80577	Pte. A. T. Peckham..	..	,,
,,	80960	Pte. W. G. Riddle	..	,,
,,	80477	Pte. P. Searles	..	,,
,,	81021	Ptc. H. Travers	..	,,
,,	80214	Pte. F. W. Wilson	..	,,
,,	80324	Pte. D. Wood	..	,,
,,	80465	Pte. H. Warren	..	,,
,,	80060	S.S.M. A. S. Tyler	..	,,
,,	80660	Pte. M. Goodinson	..	,,
,,	80101	Sgt. O. W. Bugg	..	,,
,,	80470	Sgt. G. S. Hodge	..	,,
,,	80711	Cpl. G. W. Payne	..	,,
,,	80056	F./Sgt. T. Meredith..	..	,,
,,	80068	Cpl. S.S. W. S. Woodford	..	,,
,,	80270	Cpl. G. E. Rowell	..	,,
,,	80271	L./Cpl. A. C. Rowell	..	,,
,,	80087	L./Cpl. P. J. Green	..	,,
,,	80100	Pte. G. J. Adams	..	,,
,,	81025	Pte. A. A. Auger	..	,,

Date.				Casualty.
11/4/17	81010	Pte. W. H. BARRETT	..	Wounded
,,	80531	Pte. W. BRADFORD ..	..	,,
,,	80273	Pte. J. J. BRITTON ..	..	,,
,,	80054	Pte. O. J. CATON	..	,,
,,	81007	Pte. C. H. CREES	..	,,
,,	81193	Pte. A. D. DEEKS ..	..	,,
,,	81164	Pte. M. G. DELLOW ..	..	,,
,,	80666	Pte. S. MILLARD	..	,,
,,	80959	Pte. F. J. C. PAGE ..	..	,,
,,	80426	Pte. T. ROGERS	..	,,
,,	80299	Pte. A. J. RIVERS ..	..	,,
,,	81006	Pte. F. SEARLE	..	,,
,,	80817	Pte. A. W. COVILL ..	..	,,
,,	81085	Pte. A. C. SMITH	..	,,
,,	80624	Pte. H. WEBB	..	,,
,,	80115	L./Cpl. W. C. STOCK	..	,,
,,	81170	Pte. L. RADFORD	..	,,
,,	80726	Pte. P. J. MARTIN ..	..	,,
,,	80036	Pte. F. C. SUTTON ..	..	,,
,,	80873	Pte. W. K. WARREN..	..	,,
,,	80168	Pte. A. WRIGHT	..	,,
,,	80433	Pte. H. BARKER	..	,,
,,	81151	Pte. S. R. TAYLOR ..	..	,,
,,	81162	Pte. W. J. BAMBER ..	..	,,
,,	80902	Pte. E. W. FRENCH ..	..	,,
,,	81079	Pte. W. G. TOLHURST	..	,,
,,	80015	Sgt./Tptr. G. OSBORNE	..	,,
,,	80285	Pte. S. E. PEACOCK ..	..	,,
,,	81141	Pte. F. BAKER	..	,,
,,	80628	Pte. W. W. CULLUM ..	..	,,
,,	80259	Pte. T. D. HARVEY ..	..	,,
,,	81183	Pte. A. C. CORRALL ..	..	,,
,,	80308	Pte. N. B. DANIELS ..	..	,,

DATE.		CASUALTY.
11/4/17	81211 Pte. W. W. Deeks	Wounded
,,	81012 Pte. L. Gregory	,,
,,	81074 Pte. A. E. Cracknell ..	,,
,,	80473 Pte. A. G. Burch	,,
,,	80704 Pte. E. Tompkins	,,
,,	81023 Pte. J. T. Gooch	,,
,,	80619 Pte. E. Knight	,,
4/6/17	15086 Pte. J. F. Ashwin	,,
27/6/17	80699 L./Cpl. J. Robertson ..	,,
2/7/17	80124 Sgt. W. Ridgewell.. ..	Died of Wounds
2/9/17	Major J. O. Parker	Wounded
24/10/17	19343 Pte. A. Newton	Killed
18/11/17	80550 Sgt. W. H. Pennal	Died
1/12/17	Capt. M. Dudding	Wounded
22/12/17	81090 Pte. F. M. Pilgrim	Killed
,,	80248 Pte. S. W. Humphries ..	,,
,,	80735 Pte. K. Putland	Wounded
,,	19270 Pte. H. Charters	,,
,,	81092 Pte. F. C. Martin .. ..Missing, Prisoner of War
6/1/18	80578 Pte. C. R. Keene	Wounded
26/2/18	D/16127 L./Cpl. A. H. Stevens ..	,,
21/3/18	Lieut. F. C. Meyer	,,
30/3/18	D/21134 Pte. J. G. Pyle	,,
,,	D/8243 Pte. W. E. Wright ..	,,
,,	80233 Pte. L. Savill	,,
,,	80652 L./Cpl. W. R. Gosling ..	,,
,,	81165 Pte. C. Wise	,,
1/4/18	80976 Pte. G. Bradley	Killed
,,	80966 Pte. G. Searle .. ..Missing, believed Killed
,,	2/Lieut. C. A. Collis	Wounded
,,	80864 L./Cpl. F. R. Austin.. ..	,,
,,	80261 Pte. F. M. Palmer	,,
,,	80119 Pte. G. C. Foster	,,

APPENDIX H (*continued*).

DATE.				CASUALTY.
1/4/18	81146 Pte. J. DOUCE	..	..	Wounded
,,	81050 Pte. E. J. COOK	..	..	,,
2/4/18	81174 Pte. W. C. KIPPING	..	..	,,
,,	81065 Pte. G. CARPENTER	..	..	,,
3/9/18	101966 Pte. H. S. HAWKINS	..	..	,,
,,	81010 Pte. W. H. BARRETT	..	..	,,
4/4/18	80409 Pte. A. H. BARBER	..	..	,,
6/4/18	Lieut. R. D. HOLLAND	..	..	,,
9/4/18	80058 L./Sgt. J. BARBOUR	..	..	,,
28/4/18	Lieut. D. MORGAN		.:	Wounded and Missing (Prisoner of War)
28/4/18	80529 Pte. E. A. GILL	..	..	Wounded & Missing (Prisoner of War)
16/6/18	81183 Pte. A. C. CORRALL	..	..	Wounded
22/6/18	D/16434 Pte. W. T. DEEVES		..	Died of Wounds
18/8/18	80647 S./S. C. CHAPMAN	..	..	Missing (Prisoner of War)
,,	80997 Pte. J. R. BEESON	..	..	Wounded
,,	80740 Pte. T. B. WARD	..	..	,,
,,	80285 Pte. F. E. PEACOCK	..	..	,,
,,	81525 Cpl. G. S. CHANNINGS		..	,,
,,	80420 Cpl. L. W. BARKER	..	..	,,
,,	80856 S./S. A. MATTOCKS	..	..	,,
,,	80502 Pte. L. H. GOLDSMITH		..	,,
,,	80641 Pte. F. CLOUGHTON	..	..	,,
,,	80829 S./S. W. LESTER	..	..	,,
,,	81004 Pte. C. SPELLER	..	..	,,
,,	75518 Pte. S. LEES	..	..	,,
,,	80004 Cpl. F. ATKINS	..	..	,,
,,	80523 L./Cpl. A. J. HALL	..	..	,,
,,	80285 L./Cpl. A. HARDEN	..	..	,,
,,	81005 L./Cpl. L. W. HAMMOND		..	,,
,,	81196 Pte. A. JOPSON	..	..	,,
,,	80577 L./Cpl. A PECKHAM	..	..	,,

APPENDIX H (*continued*).

Date		Casualty
18/8/18	D/16304 Sgt. W. PLOWRIGHT	Wounded
,,	D/16978 Pte. C. ARMOUR	,,
,,	80242 Pte. C. GIDDINGS	,,
,,	81168 Pte. F. W. NICHOLLS	,,
9/8/18	80547 Sgt. J. BRUCE	,,
,,	81018 Pte. S. A. ANDERSON	,,
,,	D/16276 Pte. A. GAYMER	,,
,,	80161 Pte. W. E. SAVILL	,,
,,	D/15085 Pte. L. S. BLACKWELL	,,
,,	80958 Pte. M. C. SAVAGE	,,
10/8/18	80592 Sgt. H. E. BOLLETER	Killed
,,	80704 Pte. E. TOMPKINS	,,
,,	D/16144 Tptr. W. GREGORY	Wounded
,,	81137 Pte. G. A. WHITTEN	,,
,,	80267 Pte. G. ANDREWS	,,
,,	D/14164 Pte. G. SCOTT-BARTIE	,,
,,	80435 L./Cpl. W. MASCALL	,,
14/8/18	81054 Pte. P. BURTON	,,
21/8/18	80518 Pte. P. PRYKE	,,
24/8/18	80972 Pte. F. G. HAPPS	,,
28/9/18	80132 Pte. W. J. REVELL	Died of Pneumonia
8/10/18	80540 L./Cpl. E. SMITH	Wounded
,,	80643 Pte. V. J. GOLDSMITH	,,
,,	D/16993 Pte. W. MANN	,,
,,	80866 L./Cpl. A. W. HAWES	,,
9/10/18	Lieut. S. J. TUFNELL	,,
,,	Lieut. W. RITCHIE	,,
12/10/18	80674 Pte. W. APPLEBY	,,
25/10/18	75261 Pte. W. KENNEDY	Died of Pneumonia
28/10/18	75617 Pte. F. BRADBURY	,,
29/10/18	Capt A. WINTER ROSE, M.C.	Died of Influenza
31/10/18	75626 Pte. H. F. GILLIATT	Died of Pneumonia
21/11/18	D/16364 Pte. S. M. PRATT	,,

APPENDIX H (*continued*).

DATE.		CASUALTY.
28/11/18	D/12809 L./Cpl. L. W. HENLEY ..	Died of Pneumonia
7/12/18	15882 Pte. C. HARRIS	,,
27/12/18	80361 Pte. G. C. GARDINER.. ..	,,
14/2/19	80556 Pte. A. N. WHYMAN ..	,,

SUMMARY OF CASUALTIES, ESSEX YEOMANRY.

	KILLED IN ACTION OR DIED.	WOUNDED.	PRISONERS OF WAR.
Officers	8	28	1 (wounded)
Other Ranks ..	131	296	3 (1 wounded)
Total ..	139	324	4

SUPPLEMENTARY LIST, APPENDIX H.

OFFICERS AND OTHER RANKS OF THE ESSEX YEOMANRY WHO WERE KILLED IN ACTION OR DIED WHILST SERVING WITH, OR AFTER BEING TRANSFERRED TO, OTHER UNITS.

DATE.

13/7/18 Capt. E. P. W. WEDD, R.A.M.C. (Killed).

9/10/17 Capt. J. W. EGERTON-GREEN, 1st Batt. Rifle Brigade (Died of Wounds).

24/4/18 Lieut. K. C. HERRON, 82nd Sqdn., R.A.F. (Killed).

12/4/18 2/Lieut. T. H. CHRISTY, 10th Batt. Essex Regiment (Killed).

27/9/18 Capt. L. M. WOODHOUSE, 59th Sqdn., R.A.F. (Killed).

29/7/16 Capt. H. R. ROBERTSON, 2/1st Essex Yeomanry (Died).

24/12/15 Lieut. M. HEAD, Royal Flying Corps (Killed).

6/8/15 Pte. J. FLUX, 10th Australian Light Horse (Killed in Gallipoli).

10/7/16 Pte. W. P. A. POUND, 9th Essex Regiment (Killed).

20/9/16 L./Cpl. H. M. CHAPLIN, 2nd Batt. Norfolk Regiment (Died of Dysentry in Mesopotamia).

17/10/16 Cpl. L. W. PLANE, R.F.A. (Killed).

Pte. E. CLARKE (Killed).

APPENDIX H (*continued*).

11/4/17 Pte. J. H. ARROL, 8th M.G. Sqdn. (Wounded, believed Killed).

11/4/17 Pte. W. H. METCALF, 8th M.G. Squadron (Killed).

9/5/17 Ptc. A. PARMENTER (Prisoner of War, Died at Darmstadt).

18/5/17 Pte. F. SEWELL, 4th Dragoon Guards (Died in Hospital at Aldershot).

16/6/17 Lieut. D. R. C. LLOYD, R.A.F. (Killed).

4/1/18 Lieut. P. D. PARKER, R.A.F. (Killed).

10/1/18 Pte. R. JOSLIN, 1/4th Suffolk Regiment (Killed).

21/3/18 Pte. H. LARKE, 2/8th Lancashire Fusiliers (Killed).

21/3/18 Lieut. F. S. OSBORNE, 2/5th Lincolnshire Regiment (Killed).

27/3/18 Sgt. R. D. TURNELL (Killed).

22/3/18 Pte. W. SCHOOLING, M.G.C. Cavalry (Missing, believed Killed).

11/5/18 Pte. J. POOLEY, 9th Essex Regiment (Killed).

/5/18 Pte. F. J. DAVIE (Died in France).

2/8/18 Lieut. SNEDDON, R.A.F. (Killed in Egypt).

8/8/18 Pte. H. E. C. USHER (Killed).

,, Pte. H. BOYDEN (Killed).

,, Pte. F. A. WILLINGALE, 7th City of London Regiment (Missing, believed Killed).

15/8/18 Pte. O S. POLL, 11th Suffolks (Killed).

23/8/18 Pte. THORN (Killed).

26/8/18 Pte. SMITH, 7th London Regiment (Died of Wounds).

2/10/18 Pte. COOK (Killed).

7/10/18 Pte. W. GODFREY (Killed).

23/10/18 Pte. L. W. TYDEMAN, 2nd Lincolnshire Regiment, Lewis Gun Section (Killed).

24/10/18 L./Cpl. W. BLAKER, 11th Suffolk Regiment (Killed).

31/10/18 Pte. L. L. LITTLE, 11th Batt. Suffolk Regiment (Died of Wounds).

,, Lieut. T. N. BROWETT, 3/5th Essex Regiment, transferred King's African Rifles (Died of Influenza at Dar-es-Salaam).

Pte. ELLIOTT (Died of Wounds in France).

DATE.

Pte. J. A. McLOUGHING (Wounded, believed Killed).

27/10/18 Pte. H. R. LINSELL, Labour Corps (Died).

11/4/17 L./Cpl. G. J. JONES, 8th M.G. Squadron (Killed).

2/9/18 Pte. A. BUNCE, 2nd Batt. Essex Regiment (Killed).

1/4/18 Sgt. SPARROW, 8th M.G. Squadron (Killed).

29/5/15 Pte. C. ABBOTT, 1st Australian Field Ambulance. (Killed at Anzac Cove.)

24/10/18 L./Cpl. T. E. HARDY, 11th Batt. Suffolk Regiment (Killed).

19/4/17 Pte. WAGSTAFF, 9th Batt. Essex Regiment (Killed).

30/4/17 Pte. J. WINTER, 9th Batt. Essex Regiment (Killed).

17/7/17 Pte. F. LAVENDER, 9th Batt. Essex Regiment (Killed).

2/10/18 Cpl. G. E. ROWELL, 15th Batt. Hampshire Regiment (Killed).

27/10/18 Pte. C. BONES, 11th Batt. Suffolk Regiment (Killed).

27/10/18 Pte. F. STOPER, 11th Batt. Suffolk Regiment (Killed).

19/5/18 Pte. J. FULLER, 11th Batt. Suffolk Regiment (Killed).

27/10/18 Pte. G. HOLMES, 11th Batt. Suffolk Regiment (Killed).

27/10/18 Pte. MORRIS, 11th Batt. Suffolk Regiment (Killed).

8/9/18 Pte. E. H. MOLES, 11th Batt. Suffolk Regiment (Killed).

27/11/18 Pte. L. H. JENKYN (Died of Influenza at Rouen).

Pte. F. C. MILLER, (Died).

Pte. B. MILLER (Died).

Pte. A. ANDREWS (Died).

2/12/18 Lieut. T. S. DRIVER, 4th Reserve Regt. Dragoons (Died of Influenza).

9/4/17 Pte. CRESSEY, 9th Batt. Essex Regiment (Killed),

9/4/17 Pte. ANDERSON, 9th Batt. Essex Regiment (Killed).

8/10/18 Lieut. BURFORD, Essex Regiment (Died of Wounds).

27/10/18 Pte. H. KNOWLES, 11th Batt. Suffolk Regiment (Died of Wounds).

30/3/18 Lieut. H. W. MANN, 178th Brigade, R.F.A. (Killed).

8/10/18 Pte. A. G. A. DAY, 1st Batt. Essex Regiment (Killed).

29/4/18 Pte. W. J. WALKER, 11th Batt. Suffolk Regiment (Killed).

Date.

8/9/18   Pte. F. C. Sutton, M.M., Tank Corps (Died of Wounds).

11/5/17   Pte. L. C. Cooper, 2nd Batt. Essex Regiment (Killed).

26/4/18   Pte. A. Medhurst, 1/4th K.O.R. Lancs. Fusiliers (Killed).

23/9/18   Pte. G. Denton, K.O.R. Lancs. Fusiliers (Died of Wounds).

15/9/16   Sgt. A. J. Baynes, Civil Service Rifles (Killed).

10/5/17   Pte. W. Pooley, 2nd Batt. Essex Regiment (Killed).

/11/18   Lieut. A. Smoothy, London Regiment (Died of Wounds).

22/4/17   Pte. F. C. Carter, 11th Batt. Essex Regiment (Killed).

23/9/18   Pte. A. Fayres, 11th Batt. Essex Regiment (Killed).

11/4/17   Pte. G. C. Foster, 8th M.G. Squadron (Killed).

9/4/17   Pte. Sulyman, 9th Batt. Essex Regiment (Killed).

2/6/18   Pte. G. Hewett, M.M., 4th Batt. Essex Regiment (Died of Wounds).

29/4/17   Pte. G. F. C. Chaplin, 9th Batt. Essex Regiment (Killed).

27/9/18   Pte. S. Francis, 1st Batt. Royal West Kent Regiment (Killed).

5/7/18   Sgt. F. H. Tyler, Australian Infantry (Killed).

21/9/18   Pte. E. R. Gater, 9th Batt. Essex Regiment (Killed).

3/8/17   Pte. S. J. Revett, 9th Batt. Essex Regiment (Killed).

17/7/17   Pte. F. L. Saville, 9th Batt. Essex Regiment (Missing, believed Killed).

30/3/17   Lieut. P. T. Wilson-Yirrell, South Midland Brigade, R.F.A. (Killed).

5/6/15   Sgt. F. W. L. Sudbury, 2/1st Essex Yeomanry (Accidentally killed at Hounslow).

5/9/18   Pte. F. J. Barkas, Essex Regiment (Killed).

4/4/18   Pte. A. J. Savage, 9th Batt. Essex Regiment (Killed).

19/10/17   Pte. C. H. Perry (Killed).

27/3/17   Pte. A. E. W. Steel, 9th Batt. Essex Regiment (Killed).

11/4/17   Pte. W. Brown (Killed).

6/10/18   Pte. W. S. Whur, Machine Gun Corps Cavalry (Killed).

21/3/18   Pte. H. C. Barrett, 11th Batt. Essex Regiment (Missing, believed Killed).

APPENDIX H *(continued)*.

DATE.

/5/17   Pte. F. H. G. CARPENTER, Canadian Infantry (Killed).

14/4/17   Pte. A. HARRINGTON, 1st Batt. Essex Regiment (Missing, believed Killed).

14/9/18   Pte. F. G. CANLER, 10th Royal Fusiliers (Killed).

4/11/18   Pte. R. B. APPLEBY, 10th Batt. Essex Regiment (Killed).

21/11/17   Pte. A. SALTMARSH, 2nd Batt. Essex Regiment (Killed).

30/11/17   L./Cpl. W. F. HOLYFIELD, 9th Batt. Essex Regiment (Killed).

2/9/18   Pte. W. A. GARNER, 2nd Batt. Essex Regiment (Killed).

11/5/18   Pte. J. POOLEY, 9th Batt. Essex Regiment (Killed).

28/2/19   Pte. S. E. NEWSON, (Died of Pneumonia).

/11/18   Pte. H. L. TATE (Died in France).

24/10/18   Pte. E. MEABY, 11th Batt. Cambridgeshire Regiment (Killed).

9/4/18   Pte. H. W. PHILLIPS, 2nd Canadian M.R. Battalion (Killed).

14/6/18   Pte. E. R. BANKS, King's Own Royal Lancaster Regiment (Died of Wounds).

26/4/18   Pte. C. H. FRENCH, King s Own Royal Lancaster Regiment (Killed).

17/5/17   2/Lieut. F. C. OSBURN, Essex Regiment (Killed).

SUMMARY.

Officers	.. ..	18
Other Ranks	.. ..	92

INDEX.

Names of those Officers and Other Ranks appearing in the Casualty Lists are not included in this Index.

318

Y

INDEX (continued).

INDEX (*continued*).

Benham and Company, Limited, Printers, 24, High Street, Colchester.

Printed in the United Kingdom
by Lightning Source UK Ltd.
124457UK00002B/57-60/A